Ned Snell

SAMS
Teach Yourself

the Internet

in 24 Hours

THIRD EDITION

SAMS

201 West 103rd St., Indianapolis, Indiana, 46290 USA

Sams Teach Yourself the Internet in 24 Hours, Third Edition

Copyright © 1999 by Sams Publishing

International Standard Book Number: 0-672-31589-0

Library of Congress Catalog Card Number: 99-61034

Printed in the United States of America

First Printing: June 1999

01   00   7 6 5

Trademarks

Warning and Disclaimer

EXECUTIVE EDITOR
Mark Taber

MANAGING EDITOR
Lisa Wilson

PROJECT EDITOR
Carol L. Bowers

COPY EDITORS
Kim Cofer
Sean Medlock

INDEXER
Eric Schroeder

PROOFREADER
Mary Ellen Stephenson

INTERIOR DESIGN
Gary Adair

COVER DESIGN
Aren Howell

LAYOUT TECHNICIANS
Ayanna Lacey
Heather Hiatt Miller
Amy Parker

Contents at a Glance

Table of Contents

About the Author

NED SNELL has been making technology make sense since 1986, when he began writing beginner's documentation for one of the world's largest software companies. After writing manuals and training materials for several major technology companies, Snell switched sides and became a computer journalist, serving as a writer and editor for two national magazines, *Edge* and *Art & Design News*.

A freelance writer since 1991, Snell has written 12 computer books and hundreds of articles, and is the courseware critic for *Inside Technology Training* magazine. Between books, Snell works as a professional actor in regional theater, commercials, and industrial films. He lives with his wife and two sons in Florida.

Dedication

For my family

Acknowledgments

I sat down and wrote a book very much like this one, but that's not the book you're holding.

The book you're holding is a better book, in which my work has been guided and shaped by the good folks at Sams Publishing, especially Mark Taber, Carol Bowers, and Kim Cofer.

If you like this book, you owe them thanks, as do I.

Tell Us What You Think!

As the reader of this book, *you* are our most important critic and commentator. We value your opinion and want to know what we're doing right, what we could do better, what areas you'd like to see us publish in, and any other words of wisdom you're willing to pass our way.

You can fax, email, or write me directly to let me know what you did or didn't like about this book—as well as what we can do to make our books stronger.

Please note that I cannot help you with technical problems related to the topic of this book, and that due to the high volume of mail I receive, I might not be able to reply to every message.

When you write, please be sure to include this book's title and author as well as your name and phone or fax number. I will carefully review your comments and share them with the author and editors who worked on the book.

Fax: 317-581-4770
Email: internet_sams@mcp.com
Mail: Mark Taber
         Associate Publisher
         Sams Publishing
         201 West 103rd Street
         Indianapolis, IN 46290 USA

Introduction

Hello? *Hellooooo?* Is anybody there? Nobody reads introductions. I don't know why I bother.

Oh well, looks like it's just you and me. So welcome to *Sams Teach Yourself the Internet in 24 Hours*, the book that gets you into and all around the Internet in a single day's worth of easy lessons. Each of the 24 chapters in this book is called an "Hour," and is designed to endow you with new Internet skills in one hour or less. (That means you and I can spend only a few minutes here in the Intro and keep on schedule.)

Before we get started, it has come to my attention that a few among the more than 100,000 readers of previous editions of this book were involved in mysterious accidents. For example, a florist in Weehauken arranged and delivered a bouquet of cellophane wrapped in roses, and a surgeon in Phoenix transplanted an appendix. An investigation revealed that these readers suffered sleep deprivation from taking the book's title too literally; they went cover-to-cover in a single, non-stop 24-hour period. Please spread your time with this book across multiple sessions *totaling* 24 hours, and keep your arms and legs inside the book at all times. Thank you.

Oops, one more thing. To save time and paper, and to help you begin learning the lingo, I may refer to the Internet here and there as "the Net," with a capital N. You'll know what I mean.

Who I Wrote This Thing For

That settled, let me tell you what you're in for. We've designed this book for people who:

- Are absolutely new to the Internet
- Want a quick, easy, common-sense way to learn how to use it
- Don't appreciate being treated like an imbecile

(By the way, being new to the Internet doesn't mean you're an idiot or dummy. You just have other priorities. Good for you.)

This book is *system neutral*, which is another way of saying you can use this book no matter what kind of computer you have. As you'll see, using the Internet is pretty much the same no matter what computer you use. Setting up each type of computer for the Internet is a little different, however, so I show you how to set up a PC or a Mac for the Internet in Hour 4, "Connecting to the Internet."

You do not need to know a thing about the Internet, computer networks, or any of that stuff to get started with this book. However, you do need to know your way around your own computer. With a basic, everyday ability to operate the type of computer from which you will use the Internet, you're ready to begin. I'll take you the rest of the way.

Don't have a computer yet? In Hour 2, "What Hardware and Software Do You Need?", I'll help you choose one that's properly equipped for the Net.

Overwhelmingly, most people on the Internet use either of two programs for most of their Internet activities: Microsoft's Internet Explorer or Netscape's Navigator (a.k.a. "Communicator").

So it's just common sense that examples in this book showing step-by-step techniques for some activities show the steps you would use in the latest versions (at this writing) of these "Big Two" programs: Internet Explorer version 5 and Netscape Communicator version 4.6.

Note, however, that there's plenty in this book for you even if you don't use one of these programs. Most of the instructions in this book are not specific to one program, but work with most Internet programs. And since both of these Big Two programs are free, you'll also learn in this book how to get one for free, if you want to switch over.

How This Book Is Organized

This book is divided into six Parts, each four "Hours" long:

- **Part I, "Getting Started,"** introduces you to the Net and the many different things you can do there, and shows how to get yourself and your computer set up for it.
- **Part II, "Making the Web Work for You,"** takes you onto the World Wide Web, the fun, graphical, incredibly useful part of the Net that everybody's talking about.
- **Part III, "Finding What You're Looking For,"** shows how to find anything and everything on the Net: People, products, news, reference information, good advice, bad advice, and so on.
- **Part IV, "Communicating with Email and Newsgroups,"** covers exchanging messages with anyone on the Internet, first through email and then through topical discussions called *newsgroups*.
- **Part V, "Beyond Browsing,"** is a grab bag of all the valuable stuff you can do on the Net that's not covered in other parts: Having a live online chat or voice/video conference, running programs on distant computers, and much more.

- **Part VI, "Getting the Most Out of the Internet,"** lets you put your accumulated skills to new and powerful tasks, such as making the Net safe for family viewing, doing business on the Net, and even creating your own Web pages that anyone on the Internet can visit.

As you can see, the Parts move logically from setting up for the Net to using it, and from easy stuff to not-so-easy stuff. So no peeking ahead to see how it ends.

After Hour 24, you'll discover an appendix, "Fun Web Sites to Visit," which offers up an easy-to-use directory of Web pages I think you might enjoy visiting.

Finally, there's a Glossary, although I must point out that I use very, very little technical terminology and I explain it very well when I do. So you'll probably never need the glossary. But just in case you want a glossary, you've got one.

Things You'd Probably Figure Out By Yourself

There's a long tradition in computer books of using the Introduction to explain the little tip boxes and other page elements that are absolutely self-explanatory to any reader over the age of six. Just call me "Keeper of the Flame."

Instructions, Tips, and Terms

Here and there, I use step-by-step instructions to show you exactly how to do something. I will always explain how to do that thing in the text that precedes the steps, so feel free to skip 'em when you want to. However, anytime you feel like you don't completely understand something, do the steps, and you'll probably get the picture before you're done. Sometimes we learn only by doing.

NEW TERM I call attention to important new terms by tagging them with a NEW TERM icon. It won't happen often, but when it does, it'll help you remember the terms that will help you learn the Internet.

You'll also see three different kinds of handy advice set off in boxes:

> A Tip box points out a faster, easier way to do something, or a cooler way. These boxes are completely optional.

A Note box pops out an important consideration or interesting tidbit related to the topic at hand. They're optional, too, but always worth reading (otherwise, I wouldn't interrupt).

A Caution box alerts you to actions and situations where something bad could happen, like accidentally deleting an important file. Since there's very little you can do on the Net that's in any way dangerous, you'll see very few Cautions. So when you see 'em, take 'em seriously.

Q&A

At the end of every hour, there's a fast, fun Q&A (Question & Answer) session that delves into a few common questions related to the Hour you've just read. Again, the Q&A is optional, but it's a great place to learn *just a little more* about the topic at hand before moving on.

One More Thing...

Actually, no more things. Start the clock, and hit Hour 1. Twenty-four working hours from now, you'll know the Net inside-out.

Thanks for spending a day with me.

PART I
Getting Started

Hour

HOUR 1

What Is the Internet and What Can You Do There?

You probably think you already know what the Internet is. And you're probably 90% right, for all practical purposes. But by developing just a little better understanding of what the Net's all about, you'll find learning to use it much easier.

Don't get me wrong: This hour is *not* about the tiny, techie details of how the Net works. You don't need to know exactly how the Net works to use it, any more than you need to know the mechanics of an engine to drive. Rather, this hour is designed to give you some helpful background—and perhaps dispel a few myths and misconceptions—so you can jump confidently into the stuff coming up in later hours.

At the end of the hour, you'll be able to answer the following questions:

- What *exactly* is the Internet?
- Where did the Internet come from, and where is it going?

- What are clients and servers, and how do they determine what you can do on the Net?
- What types of activities can you perform on the Net, given the right hardware and software?

Understanding the Net (Easy Version)

No doubt you've heard of a *computer network*, a group of computers that are wired together so that they can communicate with one another. When computers are hooked together in a network, users of those computers can send each other messages and share computer files and programs.

Computer networks today can be as small as two PCs hooked together in an office, and they can be as big as thousands of computers of all different types spread all over the world and connected to one another not just by wires, but through telephone lines and even through the air via satellite.

To build a really big network, you build lots of little networks and then hook the networks to each other, creating an *internetwork*. That's all the Internet really is: The world's largest internetwork (hence its name). In homes, businesses, schools, and government offices all over the world, millions of computers of all different types—PCs, Macintoshes, big corporate mainframes, and others—are connected together in networks, and those networks are connected to one another to form the Internet. Because everything's connected, any computer on the Internet can communicate with any other computer on the Internet (see Figure 1.1).

How It All Began

In the late '60s, the U.S. Department of Defense (DoD) recognized how dependent the U.S. government had become on its national computer network, and asked, "What would happen if an enemy knocked out our network? Could we respond without access to our computers?"

In those days, if one network in an internetwork failed, the whole internetwork collapsed. If defense computers in Washington were disabled by a bomb, power failure, disgruntled programmer, or spilled Pepsi, defense computing in far away Colorado or California could be compromised. The whole system depended on every part operating properly.

FIGURE 1.1

The Internet is a global internetwork, a huge collection of computers and networks interconnected so they can exchange information.

1

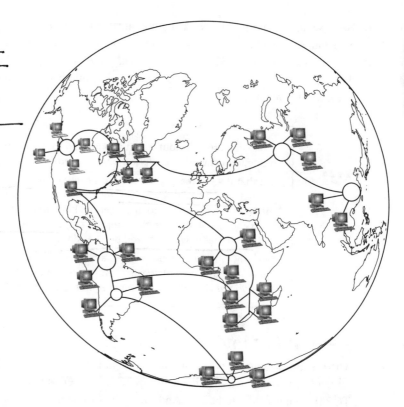

So the DoD designed a new kind of internetwork that could still function when part of the network died. The linchpin of the whole system was a set of communications rules— *protocols*—called TCP/IP. In general, any network communicating with TCP/IP can communicate with any other network communicating with TCP/IP. And if any part of a TCP/IP internetwork fails, the rest of the internetwork can keep running.

NEW TERM   **TCP/IP.** An abbreviation for the Internet's fundamental communications system. It stands for *Transmission Control Protocol/Internet Protocol*, but you don't need to know that unless you think it will impress your friends. (Pronounce it "tee see pee eye pee" and say it real fast.)

TCP/IP worked so reliably that other government (and government-related) agencies began to apply it in their own networks, even those with no defense role. By the late '70s, most large computer networks used by the government, defense contractors, large universities, and major scientific and research organizations were using TCP/IP for internetworking. (Most still use it today.)

TCP = Transmission Control protocol.

Because all of these internetworks communicated in the same way, they could communicate with one another, too. The government, defense contractors, and scientists often needed to communicate with one another and share information, so they hooked all of their computers and networks into one big TCP/IP internetwork. And that fat internetwork was the infant Internet.

When you use a computer that's connected to the Internet, you can communicate with any other computer on the Internet.

But that doesn't mean you can access *everything* that's stored on the other computers. Obviously, the government, university, and corporate entities on the Net have the ability to make certain kinds of information on their computers accessible through the Internet, and to restrict access to other information so that only authorized people can see it.

Similarly, when you're on the Net, any other computer on the Net can communicate with yours. However, that does not mean that someone can reach through the Net into your computer and steal your resume and recipes.

What It Became

The first great thing about the Internet's design is that it's open to all types of computers. Virtually any computer—from a palmtop PC to a supercomputer—can be equipped with TCP/IP so it can get on the Net. And even when a computer doesn't use TCP/IP, it can access information on the Net using other technologies, "back doors" to the Net, so to speak.

The other important thing about the Net is that it allows the use of a wide range of *communications media*—ways computers can communicate. The "wires" that interconnect the millions of computers on the Internet include the wires that hook together the small networks in offices, private data lines, local telephone lines, national telephone networks (which carry signals via wire, microwave, and satellite), and international telephone carriers.

It is this wide range of hardware and communications options, and the universal availability of TCP/IP, that has enabled the Internet to grow so large, encompassing over 65 million users on every continent (yes, including Antarctica). That's why you can get online, from your home or office, right through the same telephone line you use to call out for pizza. It's a crazy world.

> **NEW TERM**   **Online/Offline.** When your computer has a live, open connection to the Internet you could use to do something, you and your computer are said to be *online*. When the Internet connection is closed (because your computer is off or for any other reason), you're *offline*.

Making the Net Work: *Clients* and *Servers*

The key to doing anything on the Net is understanding two little words: "client" and "server." Figure 1.2 illustrates the relationship between clients and servers.

FIGURE 1.2

From your computer, you use a set of client *programs, each of which accesses a different type of* server *computer on the Net.*

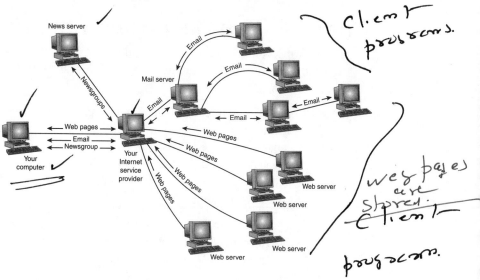

client programs.

web pages are stored. client program.

Most of the information you will access through the Internet is stored on computers called *servers*. A server can be any type of computer; what makes it a server is the role it plays. It stores information for use by clients.

A *client* is a computer—or, more accurately, a particular computer program—that knows how to communicate with a particular type of server to use the information stored on that server (or to put information there). For example, when you surf the Web, you use a client program called a Web browser to communicate with a computer where Web pages are stored—a Web server.

> **NEW TERM**   **Web browser.** A program that gives a computer the ability to communicate with Web servers and display the information stored there. You'll learn much more about Web browsers and other client programs as your 24 hours tick by.

Web is a part of the Net.

In general, each type of Internet activity involves a different type of client and server. To use the Web, you need a Web client program to communicate with Web servers; to use email, you need an email program to communicate with email servers.

This client/server business shows what the Internet really is: Just a communications medium, a virtual wire through which computers communicate. It's the different kinds of clients and servers—not the Net itself—that enable you to perform various activities. And because new kinds of clients and servers can be invented, new types of activities can be added to the Internet at any time.

What Can You Do Through the Net?

I've known people who have gone out and bought a PC, signed up for an Internet account, and then called me to say, "Okay, so I'm on the Internet. Now what am I supposed to do there?"

That's backwards. I think the marketers and the press have pushed so hard that some folks simply think they *must* be on the Net, without knowing why, sort of the way everybody thinks they need a beeper. But unless there's something on the Net you want or need to use, you don't need the Net. You shouldn't buy a rice steamer unless you like rice. You don't need a beeper if you never leave the house. Don't let Madison Avenue and Microsoft push you around.

So here's a good place to get a feel for what you can actually do on the Net. If nothing here looks like something you want to do, please give this book to a friend or to your local library. You can check out the Net again in a year or two, to see whether it offers anything new.

Browse the Web

It's very likely that your interest in the Internet was sparked by the World Wide Web, even if you don't know it. When you see news stories about the Internet showing someone looking at a cool, colorful screen full of things to see and do, that person is looking at the World Wide Web, most commonly referred to as "the Web" or occasionally as "WWW."

"The Web" is used so often by the media to describe and illustrate the Internet, many folks think the Web *is* the Internet. But it's not; it's just a part of the Net, or rather one of many Internet-based activities. The Web gets the most attention because it's the fastest growing, easiest-to-use part of the Net.

All those funky looking Internet addresses you see in ads today—`www.pepsi.com` and so forth—are the addresses you need to visit those companies on the Web. With an Internet connection and a Web browser on your computer, you can type an address to visit a particular Web site and read the Web pages stored there. (Figure 1.3 shows a Web page, viewed through a Web browser.)

NEW TERM   **Web site** and **Web page.** These terms are used flexibly, but in general, a *Web site* is a particular Web server, or a part of a Web server, where a collection of Web pages about a particular organization or subject is stored.

When you use your Web browser to contact a Web site, the information on the server is displayed on your computer screen. The particular screenful of information you view is described as one *Web page*.

FIGURE 1.3

Seen through a Web browser, a Web page is a file of information stored on a Web server.

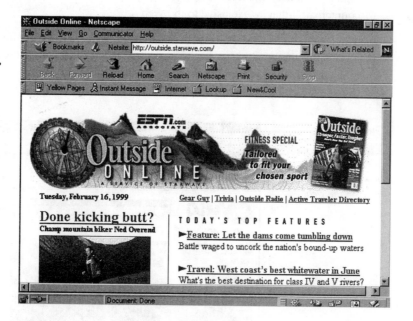

By browsing the Web, you can do a staggering number of different things, including all of the following.

Visit Companies, Governments, Museums, Schools...

Just about any large organization has it own Web site these days. Many smaller organizations have their own sites too, or are covered in pages stored on others' sites. You can visit these sites to learn more about products you want to buy, school or government policies, and much more.

For example, I belong to an HMO for medical coverage. I can visit my HMO's Web site to find and choose a new doctor, review policy restrictions, and much more. I can do this any day, any time, without waiting on hold for the "next available operator."

Just as easily, I can check out tax rules or order forms on the Internal Revenue Service Web site. Or view paintings in museums all over the world. Or find out when the next Parent's Night is at the local elementary school.

Read the News

CNN has its own Web site (see Figure 1.4), as do *The New York Times*, the *Wall Street Journal*, and dozens of other media outlets ranging from major print magazines, to fly-by-night rags spreading rumors, to small sites featuring news about any imaginable topic. You'll also find a number of great news sources that have no print or broadcast counterpart—they're exclusive to the Web.

Whatever kind of news you dig, you can find it on the Web. And often, the news online is more up-to-the-minute than any print counterpart because unlike broadcast news, you can look at it any time you find convenient. Best of all, after a news story on the Web, no one ever says, "Thanks for that report, Carla. What a terrible tragedy."

FIGURE 1.4

CNN is among the up-to-the-minute news sources available on the Web.

1

Explore Libraries

Increasingly, libraries large and small are making their catalogs available online. That means I can find out which of the dozen libraries I use has the book I need, without spending a day driving to each. Some libraries even let you borrow online; you choose a book from the catalog of a library across the state from you, and in a few days you can pick it up at a library closer to you, or right from your mailbox.

Read

Books are published right on the Web, including classics (Shakespeare, Dickens) and new works. You can read them right on your screen, or print them out to read later on the bus. (*Please* don't read while you drive. I *hate* that.) The Web has even initiated its own kind of literature, *collaborative fiction*, in which visitors to a Web site can read—and contribute to—a story in progress.

Get Software

Since computer software can travel through the Internet, you can actually get software right through the Web and use it on your PC. Some of the software is free, some isn't. But it's all there, whenever you need it—no box, no disc, no pushy guy at the electronics store saying, "Ya want a cell phone with that? Huh? C'mon!"

Shop

One of the fastest-growing, and most controversial, Web activities is shopping (see Figure 1.5). Right on the Web, you can browse an online catalog, choose merchandise, type in a credit card number and shipping address, and receive your merchandise in a few days, postage paid. Besides merchandise, you can buy just about anything else on the Web: stocks, legal services, you name it. Everything but surgery, and I'm sure that's only a matter of time. The hottest new trend in online shopping is the online auction house, a Web site where you can bid on all kinds of items, new and old, from odds and ends to *objets d'art*.

The controversy arises from the fact that sending your credit card number and other private information through the Internet exposes you to abuse of that information by anyone clever enough to cull it from the din of Web traffic. But that risk factor is rapidly shrinking as the Web develops improved security. (You'll learn about Web security in Hour 8, "Protecting Your Privacy (and Other Security Stuff).") And shopping from your PC, you can't get mugged in the mall parking lot.

FIGURE 1.5

Shopping may be the fastest-growing online activity.

Watch TV and Listen to CD-Quality Music and Radio Broadcasts

Through your Internet connection, you can actually watch live TV broadcasts and listen to radio programs (see Figure 1.6). The sound and picture quality won't be as good as you get from a real TV or radio, but the Net gives you access to programs you can't get on your own TV or radio, such as shows not offered in your area or special programs broadcast only to the Internet. With music, however, there's no compromise. Right from the Internet, you can copy CD-quality music files that you can listen to anytime, even when you're not on the Internet. You learn all about Internet-based video, radio, and music in Hour 7, "Playing Online Video, Music, and Broadcasts."

Play Games, Get a College Degree, Waste Time...

Have I left anything out? There's too much on the Web to cover succinctly. But I hope you get the idea. The Web is where it's at. In fact, there are many folks on the Internet who use the Web and nothing else. But those folks are missing out…. Read on.

FIGURE 1.6

You can watch selected TV broadcasts and listen to radio broadcasts through the Web.

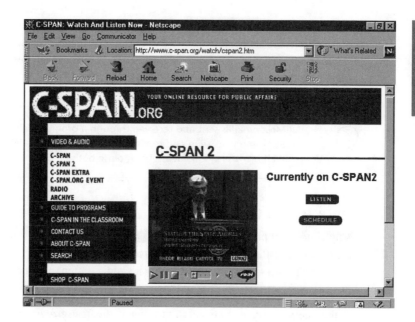

Oooops. There's one more thing you can do on the Web: *publish*. Just as you can access any Web server, you can publish your own Web pages on a Web server, so that anyone on the Internet with a Web browser can read them.

You can publish Web pages to promote your business or cause, to tell others about a project or hobby that's your passion, or just to let the world know you're you. You'll learn how in Hour 23, "Creating Web Pages and Multimedia Messages."

Exchange Messages

Email, in case you didn't know, is messages sent as electronic files from one computer to another. Using Internet email, you can type a message on your computer and send it to anyone else on the Internet.

Each user on the Internet has a unique email address; if your email address is suzyq@netknow.com, you're the only person in the world with that email address (isn't that nice?). So if anyone, anywhere in the world, sends a message to that address, it reaches you and you alone. As mentioned earlier, to use email, you need an email client program, which interacts with the email servers that store and send email around the world.

Email is great for simple messages, but these days, it can do more. You can attach computer files to email messages to send them to others, broadcast a message to two or a hundred recipients at once, and even create cool, colorful messages with graphics and sound. (You'll learn how in Hour 23.)

> Most email is sent and received through a program called an email client. But some folks send and receive email directly from a Web page, in their Web browsers. You'll learn how to use both kinds of email in this book.

Have a Discussion

Using your email program, you can join *mailing lists* related to topics that interest you. Members of a mailing list automatically receive news and other information—in the form of email messages—related to the list's topic. Often, members can send their own news and comments to the list, and those messages are passed on to all members.

But the Internet's principal discussion venue is the *newsgroup*, a sort of public bulletin board. There are thousands of newsgroups, each centering on a particular topic—everything from music to politics, from addiction recovery to TV shows.

Visitors to a newsgroup post messages that any other visitor can read. When reading a message, any visitor can quickly compose and post a reply to that message, to add information to the message, or to argue with it (usually to argue—you know how folks are). As the replies are followed by replies to the replies, a sort of free-form discussion evolves.

> You may have heard that you can pick up a lot of unreliable information on the Internet, and indeed, that's true. As when absorbing information from any communications medium—print, broadcast, Internet, water cooler, back fence—you must always consider the source, and take much of what you learn with a grain of salt.
>
> You must also trust that, just as the Internet offers a forum to nutballs with axes to grind, it also offers an incredible wealth of authoritative, accurate information that's often difficult to find elsewhere. It's just like TV: You can watch CNN, or you can watch *Hard Copy*. If you choose the latter, you can't blame the TV for misinforming you.

Chat *or* *Voice & Video Conferencing*
— live discussions:

Exchanging messages through email and newsgroups is great, but it's not very interactive. You type a message, send it, and wait hours or days for a reply. Sometimes, you want to communicate in a more immediate, interactive, "live" way. That's where *Internet Relay Chat*—a.k.a. "IRC" or just "Chat"—comes in.

Using chat client programs, folks from all over the world contact Chat servers and join one another in live discussions. Each discussion takes place in a separate chat "room" or "channel" reserved for discussion of a particular topic. The discussion is carried out through a series of typed messages; each participant types his or her contributions, and anything anyone in the room types shows up on the screen of everyone in the room.

> In addition to Chat, there are other ways to have a live conversation over the Internet. As you learn in Hour 17, "Voice and Video Conferencing," you can hold voice and video conferences through the Internet, wherein you can see and hear your partners, and they can see and hear you.

Skype: or Teams

Run Programs on Other Computers

Not everything on the Internet sits on a Web server, email server, news server, or chat server. There are other kinds of computers and servers connected to the Net—ones you can use, if you know how, through an Internet technology called Telnet. When you use a distant computer through Telnet, you can run programs on it and access its data as if you were there.

There's so much on Web and news servers these days that you may never want or need to journey beyond them. But for the adventurous, Telnet offers access to information you can't get any other way. In Hour 19, "Tools for the Serious User: FTP and Telnet," you'll discover Telnet and FTP, two powerful tools for exploiting the Net beyond the confines of the Web, email, and newsgroups.

Summary

The Internet is a huge, and growing, internetwork that nobody really planned but that happened anyway. Your job is not really to understand it, but to enjoy it and to use it in whatever way you find valuable or entertaining.

The value and entertainment are stored all over the world on a vast array of servers; to tap the benefits of the Net, you deploy a family of client programs that know how to talk

to the servers. In a way, most of this book is really about choosing and using client programs to make the most of the Internet's servers.

Q&A

Q If the Net "just happened," who's in charge? What keeps it going?

A That's one of the really neat things about the Internet: Nobody's in charge.
(Microsoft, Netscape, and America Online *want* to be in charge, but that's different.) There are volunteer committees that handle such things as making sure every
computer gets its own, unique Internet ID (which is essential to the workings of the
Net) and approving the *standards* for such things as the way Web browsers communicate with Web servers. But nobody really controls the Internet, and nobody
owns it.

It's the standards that keep the Internet going. The Internet is made up of privately
owned computers and networking equipment, whose owners have put them on the
Net for their own reasons. But because that hardware is part of the Net and obeys
its standards, you get to use it, too. It's really a big fat co-op, an amazing example
of how independent parties collaborating for their own self-interest can inadvertently create a public good.

As you'll learn in Hour 3, "Choosing an Internet Provider," you generally pay a
subscription fee to an Internet provider in order to use the Internet, but that fee
covers the provider's costs (plus profit) in maintaining its service. You're not paying "The Internet" a dime, since there's no actual organization to collect your
money. In principle (if not always in practice), the Internet is free.

Q You just mentioned America Online. Isn't that the same thing as the Internet?

A No and yes. As you'll learn in Hour 3, America Online (AOL) is a commercial
online service. It provides its subscribers with a range of information and services
that are not on the Internet, and it also provides those subscribers with access to the
Internet, just like any other Internet provider. Lots of folks use AOL, but the majority of Internet citizens use other Internet services.

Q I have this funny rash on my elbow. Is it psoriasis?

A Stick to the subject. Or, better yet, learn to search for information on the Web (as
you will in Part III, "Finding What You're Looking For"), and you can find out
everything you ever wanted to know about rashes.

In the meantime, dab on some cortisone cream, don't walk on it for a few days,
and call me if it gets worse.

Hour 2

What Hardware and Software Do You Need?

Got a computer made within the last 10 years? Then odds are you can get it onto the Internet. The power of your hardware doesn't have that much to do with whether you can get *on* the Net. But it has everything to do with what you can *do* there.

In this hour, you discover the hardware required to use the Internet, explore the available options and the pros and cons of each. Once you've settled on a computer (or the pseudo-computer alternative, a WebTV terminal), you'll need to know which client programs and other software your Net travels will demand.

At the end of the hour, you'll be able to answer the following questions:

- What kinds of computers can I use to surf the Net, and how should they be equipped?
- How fast a modem do I need?

- What's "WebTV" and how is it different from surfing the Net through a computer?
- What software do I need to get started, and where can I get it?

Modems—Wherein the *Lack* of Speed Kills

There are ways to connect to the Internet without a modem, but such options (which you'll discover at the end of this chapter) are wildly costly and complex today. Odds are that you will use an ordinary modem and telephone line for your Internet connection, so you must consider the capabilities of your modem in choosing or upgrading your computer for Internet access.

NEW TERM **Modem.** A *modem* is a device that enables two computers to communicate with one another through phone lines. Using a modem (installed inside or connected to your computer), you can communicate through your regular home or business phone lines with the modem at your Internet provider. That's how you connect to the Net.

Cab tv Connections.
ComCast

> Although "modem" most often refers to the type I just described, there are special types of modems designed not for use over phone lines, but for use over two-way cable TV connections (in areas where such lines exist, which are few), high-speed private data lines, and cellular/satellite networks.

It doesn't really matter what brand of modem you buy, or whether it's an internal modem (plugged inside your computer's case), an external one (outside the computer, connected to it by a cable), or even one on a PC card inserted in a notebook PC.

What does matter is the modem's rated speed. That speed is usually expressed in *bits per second* (bps), or rarely as a *baud rate*. Where choosing a modem is concerned, bps and baud rate are essentially the same thing. (Computer experts get their underwear all twisted up when I say that, because there is a technical difference that matters to them. But it's not a difference that matters to you. A 14,400 bps modem is the same device as a 14,400 baud modem. So there.)

The higher the number of bps, the faster the modem. And the faster your modem is, the more quickly Web pages will appear on your screen, which makes Web surfing more fun and productive. A number of other Internet activities—especially such things as watching TV broadcasts or listening to radio programs (see Hour 7, "Playing Online Video, Music, and Broadcasts")—will also run quicker and smoother over a faster modem. (Note, however, that the faster the modem, the more you'll pay for it.)

For modems rated at speeds above 9,600 bps, the term bps is usually replaced by *kilobits per second* (kbps), which is roughly 1,000 bps. That way, a modem that runs at, oh, 28,800 bps can be described as a "28.8 kbps" modem, or even just "28.8K." Using kbps instead of bps frees up space on the modem box for logos and ad copy ("New! Fast!").

2

Most modems for use with regular telephone lines are rated at one of the following speeds:

- 9,600 bps
- 14,400 bps (14.4K)
- 28,800 bps (28.8K) → minimum. Internet speed ,
- 33,600 bps (33.6K)
- 56,000 bps (56K)

The minimum modem speed for Internet cruising (including Web browsing) is 14.4K, although at that speed, you'll often face long waits for Web pages to appear. Most experts deem a 14.4K connection unacceptably slow. The minimum reasonable modem speed for using the Internet today is 28.8K.

Modems rated at 33.6K and 56K are affordable (most new PCs and Macs come pre-equipped with a 56K modem), and usually deliver performance superior to 28.8K modems, so these are the best choice. Note that, under current telecommunications law, 56K modems can only *send* information to the Internet at a full 56K; they *receive* information at a maximum rate of 53K. But that's not really a big enough difference to notice, so don't sweat it.

It's important to keep in mind that a faster modem does not always deliver vastly superior performance. A number of factors—such as the reliability and noise level in your phone line, the speed supported by your Internet provider, and the responsiveness of the servers you contact—may cause 33.6K and 56K modems to perform no better than a 28.8K modem, much of the time. In some areas, the equipment installed by the local phone company may not even support Internet connections any faster than 28K or so. Using a 33.6K modem or 56K modem through these lines won't hurt anything, but the performance you'll see will not be any better than what you'd get through a 28.8K modem. (Little by little, local phone companies are upgrading their lines to support faster access.)

Speed of the Computer to process information

Finally, although it's the most important factor, connection speed is not the only thing that governs the apparent speed with which things spring onto your screen. If it takes your computer a long time to process and display the information it receives through the Net, you'll see some delays that have nothing to do with the speed of your modem or phone lines or Internet provider. A fast computer is almost as important as a fast modem—it's a team effort.

There's a special consideration you must make when choosing a 56K modem that's not an issue with modems slower than 56K: The communications standard followed by the modem.

All new 56K modems made for PCs and Macs follow a standard called V.90. But older 56K modems may follow either of two other, older standards used before V.90: X2 and Kflex. (The box any new modem or computer comes in usually states which standards the modem supports.)

The Internet provider you select (see Hour 3, "Choosing an Internet Provider") must support the same standard as your modem; for example, if you have a V.90 modem, your Internet provider must support V.90 in order for you to get 56K access. If your modem's standard is different from your provider's, your modem will still function, but will run at a slower speed (28.8K or 33.6K).

Since V.90 has been adopted as the standard for today and tomorrow, most Internet providers who offer 56K access do so through V.90, or will soon. So when purchasing a 56K modem, make sure it's a V.90 one.

If you happen to have an X2 or Kflex modem handy, you'll probably find that many Internet providers still support those standards (in addition to V.90) for the time being. But they won't forever. Fortunately, many X2 and Kflex modems can be upgraded to V.90. Contact your modem's manufacturer to find out whether yours is upgradable.

Choosing a Computer

I've told you that almost any computer—even an older one—can be used to get on the Internet, and that's true. But to take full advantage of what the Internet offers, you need a top-of-the-line computer, or pretty close to it.

You see, some Internet tasks, such as email, demand little processing power from a computer and don't require a really fast Internet connection; they're neither *processor-intensive* nor *communications-intensive*. However, the main thing most newcomers to the Net want is the Web, and browsing the Web is just about the most processor-intensive, communications-intensive thing a computer can do.

Java is a programming language designed for
Use in the internet.

To take full advantage of the Web, a computer must be able to display and play the multimedia content—graphics, animation, video, and sound—that's increasingly built in to Web pages. Such tasks require a fast processor and plenty of memory. In fact, a Web browser capable of supporting this multimedia is about the most demanding application you can put on a PC or Mac, requiring more processing power and memory than any word processor or spreadsheet on the market.

In addition to the multimedia, more and more Web pages feature Java programs, which enable all sorts of advanced Web activities (see Figure 2.1). To run the Java programs in Web pages, your computer must use a fast 32-bit processor (such as a Pentium) and operating system (such as Windows 95 or 98), which have been available in PCs and Macs for only the last few years. As a rule, a PC that cannot run Windows 95 or higher, and a Mac that cannot run System 7.5 or higher, cannot run Java programs or the browsers that support Java.

2

NEW TERM **Java.** *Java* is a programming language specially designed for use in computer networks, such as the Internet. On the Web, programmers add Java programs to Web pages to enable the page to do stuff it couldn't do otherwise, such as collect and process order information for an online store or make images dance around the page.

Java makes the Web more powerful and interactive, but also more complex and demanding. You'll learn more about Java in Hours 7 and 8, "Protecting Your Privacy (and Other Security Stuff)."

FIGURE 2.1

To enjoy the multimedia and Java content built in to many Web pages today, you need a powerful, well-equipped computer and a fast modem.

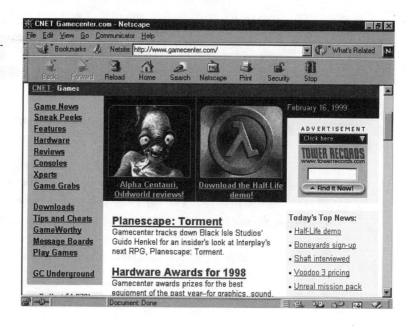

What about notebooks and other portable computers? No problem.
Notebook PCs, Mac PowerBooks, and other portables make perfectly good
Internet computers, as long as they meet the same general requirements
(processor, modem speed, and so on) that a desktop computer must meet, as
described later in this hour.

Note, however, that a portable computer always costs much more than a
desktop computer with the same specifications. Also, some portables with
otherwise acceptable specifications may have screens that are too small for
comfortable Web browsing; any screen that measures less than 12 inches
diagonally is probably too small, unless you've got really, really, really good
glasses.

Any size screen is fine, however, for email and other text-based, off-the-Web
Internet activities. That's especially handy when you use a handheld PC, or
"palmtop" computer, to use the Net on the go.

Finally, newer, more powerful computers are required to run the newest, most advanced
operating systems, such as Windows 98 on the PC or OS8 on the Macintosh. These operating systems have been designed with the Internet in mind, making setting up your computer for the Net much quicker and easier.

Again, you can get a lot out of the Internet on a less capable computer—you just won't
see or hear what your computer can't handle. But the bottom line is this: Most of the
exciting innovations on the Internet, now and in the future, are designed for use by the
newest, most powerful computers. So if you're shopping, aim high. And if you're standing pat now with an older machine, forge ahead with the understanding that your Internet
experience is not going to be all that it might be.

A PC for the Internet

To make the most of today's Internet, the minimum reasonable PC would be equipped as
follows:

- **Processor:** A Pentium processor (or a cloned Pentium equivalent, such as the
  AMD K6) is recommended for its ability to support the preferred operating systems listed next; look for a Pentium rated at 266 MHz or faster.

- **Operating System:** Windows 95, Windows 98, and Windows NT are all good
  choices. Windows 98 may be the best choice for many, since it features a built-in
  Web browser (Internet Explorer; see Hour 3) and an easy-to-use program for setting up your Internet connection.

However, Windows 98 also makes greater memory demands on your PC than Windows 95; if your PC has less than 24 MB of RAM (and you can't add more memory), you ought to stick with Windows 95. Windows NT is more costly and complex than either of its siblings, so NT should be selected only when the PC will also be used for other tasks where NT has an edge, such as company networking.

What if you have a PC that only supports Windows 3.1? How do you get online?

It can be done. First, you need to install and configure special TCP/IP communications software in Windows 3.1; a popular program called Trumpet Winsock, available from most Internet providers, works great. You also need to find client software (such as your Web browser and email program) that runs in Windows 3.1, which you may also be able to get from your Internet provider.

Note that both of the most popular Web browsers—Internet Explorer and Netscape Navigator—are available for Windows 3.1, but even in their Windows 3.1 versions those programs nevertheless require a 486 or faster processor and 16 MB of memory. Many Windows 3.1 PCs can't meet these requirements. If yours can't, you'll only be able to use older, less full-featured client programs, which will not support such recent innovations as Java.

If you really can't upgrade to a more capable computer, you might consider a shell account (see Hour 3) as a way to get an older PC online. Heck, with a shell account, you can get a decade-old DOS PC onto the Internet!

- **Display:** The ideal display for Web browsing is configured to run at 800×600 resolution and 16,000 colors (also known as "High-color" or 16-bit color). Higher-color modes, such as 24-bit color (millions of colors; often called "true color"), are fine, but little online requires those modes. A resolution of 640×480 is an acceptable alternative to 800×600, although a growing number of Web pages are designed to look their best when displayed at 800×600. Resolutions higher than 800×600 are not recommended, since they'll tend to make some items in Web pages appear too small.

- **Memory:** The bare minimum RAM for supporting Windows 95 and either of the leading Web browsers is 16 MB ,but experience teaches us that the minimum is almost always insufficient for decent performance and reliability. The reasonable minimum memory for comfortable Internet cruising on Windows 95 is 24 MB. For Windows 98 or NT, 32 MB is a reasonable minimum.

- **Hard Disk:** I can't tell you how big your hard disk should be, because I don't know how much other software you have. I can tell you that, after you've set up all of your Internet software, your hard disk should be at least 25% empty. Windows Web browsers need lots of free disk space for temporary data storage; when they don't have enough, performance and reliability suffer.

- **CD-ROM Drive:** A CD-ROM drive is not required for any Internet activity. However, you may need one to install the Internet software you need in order to get started, if you acquire that software on CD. For installing software, the speed of the CD-ROM drive is unimportant; any drive will do.

- **Other Peripherals:** There's plenty of fun sound and music online these days, and to hear it you'll need a sound card and speakers (or headphones) installed in your PC and configured in Windows. If you want to make a long-distance phone call through the Internet or have a voice conference (see Hour 17, "Voice and Video Conferencing"), connect a microphone to your sound card (or use your PC's built-in mic, if it has one), and for videoconferencing, add a PC video camera. If you plan to create your own Web pages (see Hour 23, "Creating Web Pages and Multimedia Messages"), a scanner or digital camera is a useful addition.

A Mac for the Internet

To make the most of today's Internet, the minimum reasonable Macintosh system would be equipped as follows:

- **Processor:** A 68040- or PowerPC-based Mac (such as the iMac) is recommended. A 68030-based system is a budget alternative, but cannot support the Mac OS8 operating system and may struggle with Java processing.

- **Operating System:** System 7 or OS8. If your Mac supports it, I strongly recommend OS8, which has a built-in, easy-to-use routine for setting up your Internet connection, built-in Java processing, and a complete set of Internet client programs.

- **Display:** The ideal display for Web browsing is configured to run at 800×600 resolution and 16,000 colors (also known as "High-color" or 16-bit color). Higher-color modes, such as 24-bit color (millions of colors; often called "true color"), are fine, but little online requires those modes. A resolution of 640×480 is an acceptable alternative to 800×600, although a growing number of Web pages are designed to look their best when displayed at 800×600. Resolutions higher than 800×600 are not recommended, since they'll tend to make some items in Web pages appear too small.

- **Memory:** Consider 24 MB the workable minimum for Web browsing on any Mac.

- **Hard Disk:** Large enough to leave at least 25% free space after you have installed all of your software.

- **CD-ROM Drive:** A CD-ROM drive is not required for any Internet activity. However, you may need one to install the Internet software you need in order to get started, if you acquire that software on CD. For installing software, the speed of the CD-ROM drive is unimportant; any drive will do.

- **Other Peripherals:** If you want to make a long-distance phone call through the Internet or have a voice conference (see Hour 17), you'll need a microphone hooked to your Mac, and for videoconferencing, you'll need a Mac-compatible video camera. If you plan to create your own Web pages (see Hour 23), a scanner or digital camera can be handy.

> If you're considering a Mac for the Net and have high-speed Internet service available via your cable TV supplier, I should point out that most new Macs—including that cute little day-glo iMac—come pre-equipped with the communications hardware required for using a cable modem. Most PCs do not include this hardware, which you must then purchase (or rent from the cable company).

Other Internet Options

The overwhelming majority of folks just getting online now are doing so through their own personal Mac or PC, at home or at work. That's the main scenario, and that's where much of this book's focus will rest.

However, I should point out that there are many, many folks online that are not using PCs or Macs, or are not even using their own computers or signing up with an Internet provider. Here are a few ideas for getting online without buying a computer:

- **School or Company Computer.** If the company you work for or school you attend has an Internet account, you may be permitted to use the organization's computers to explore the Net (usually within strict guidelines). Locate and speak to a person called the network administrator or system administrator; he or she holds the keys to the computer system, and is responsible for telling you whether you may use the system, and how and when you're permitted to use it.

- **Public Library.** Many public libraries have Internet terminals set up for use by patrons. You may use these terminals to do quick research on the Web or news-groups. As a rule, you cannot use them for email, since you won't have your own email address, and library machines are never equipped for chat. Even if they were, it's not polite to hog a library PC (as many evil people do) for a long, chatty Internet session.

- **Cyber Café.** In all cool cities (and also in Indianapolis), you can find *cyber cafés*, coffeehouses equipped with Internet-connected computers so patrons can hang out, eat, drink, and surf (see Figure 2.2). Some cyber cafés will let you have an email address, so you can send and receive email. Still, there may not always be a computer available when you need one, and you could probably afford your own computer with what you'll spend on Hawaiian Mocha and scones.

In general, the compromises you must make to enjoy these alternatives makes them poor long-term substitutes for having your very own computer and Internet account. However, these are great ways to get a taste of the Net, and reap some of its benefits, if you're still trying to make up your mind about the Internet or are still saving up for that new computer.

FIGURE 2.2

The Web page of a cyber café in San Francisco (where else?).

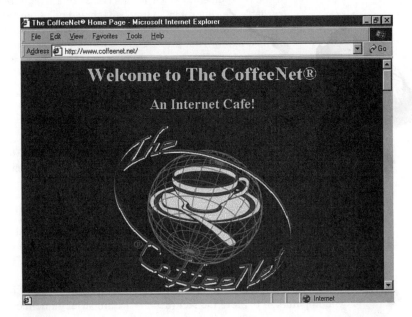

What About "WebTV"?

WebTV is based on the premise that there are people who want to use the Internet but don't want a computer. Figure 2.3 shows WebTV's promotional Web site. (WebTV is owned by Microsoft.)

Instead of buying a PC or Mac, all you need for WebTV is a WebTV terminal (a VCR-sized box) and a subscription to the WebTV Internet service. The terminal uses your TV as a display, and you navigate the Internet through the terminal's wireless remote control and/or an optional wireless keyboard. It uses your telephone line to connect to the Internet, just as a computer would.

You can find WebTV terminals at electronics and appliance stores—anywhere that sells TVs and VCRs. Models are available from Philips/Magnavox and from Sony, so shop around and compare.

Note, too, that there are two types: A WebTV "classic" terminal and a WebTV Plus terminal. The Plus version is more expensive, but it adds a number of new features. However, most of the new features work only if you use the WebTV Network as your Internet provider.

The WebTV scenario has a few advantages: First and foremost, it's cheap (less than $100 for the most basic, "classic" model; around $300 for a full-featured unit). WebTV is also comparatively easy to set up and use, if you use the WebTV Network Internet service, which is priced comparably with most other Internet providers. At last report, you can also use a WebTV terminal with almost any Internet provider; however, setup is more difficult and you lose a number of special WebTV features (unless you pay an extra $9.95 over your regular Internet charges for access to the WebTV Network *through* your other Internet provider).

WebTV enables you not only to browse the Net, but also to jump easily between TV shows and related information. While watching *The X-Files*, for example, you can display an *X-Files* Web page in a picture-in-picture window on your screen, or call up an online TV guide. You can also engage in a live chat (via typed messages) with others watching the show at the same time. By touting this capability, the WebTV people have changed their pitch lately. Instead of selling the system as an alternative to a computer, they're pitching it as a way to enhance your TV viewing. It's high-end TV, not low-end Internet.

The system also has some major drawbacks. The investment you make in a full computer buys you not only an Internet machine, but also one you can use to write letters, pay bills, do your taxes, play games, listen to CDs, teach your kids Spanish, and much more. A WebTV terminal, while technically a computer on the inside, is a single-purpose machine: You can use it for the Internet, and nothing else.

FIGURE 2.3

FIGURE 2.3

The Web site of WebTV, where the Internet meets the home video appliance.

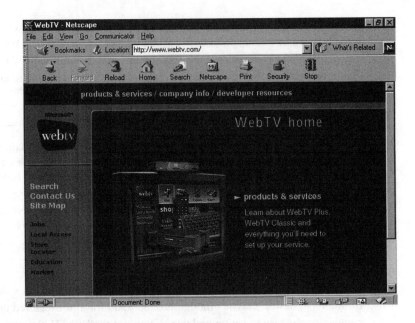

Beyond all of that is the somewhat fuzzy question of whether the Internet is easier and more fun to use from a little screen on a desktop or a big TV in the living room. Some say it's more fun in the living room; some say Web pages and email text are hard to read and navigate from a TV screen.

I guess it sounds like I'm down on WebTV, but I'm really not. I just want to make sure you understand that you get what you pay for. For a third of the cost of a decent PC, you get one-tenth the utility, and at that, you still don't get complete Internet functionality. As long as you understand that, if you think WebTV is right for you, go get it. You're the boss.

Getting Internet Software

Getting Internet software is like borrowing money: It's only difficult when you really need it. If you already have money (or Internet software), getting more is easy. So the trick is getting started.

You see, once you go online, you can search for, find, and download all the software you want, some of it for free, most at least cheap. You'll learn all about downloading software in Hour 11, "Finding Programs and Files."

NEW TERM **Download.** To *download* is to copy a file—through a network—from another computer into your own. When you get software online, you copy that software from a server somewhere, through the Internet, to your computer and store it on your hard disk.

What Do You Need?

To figure out what Internet software you need to get started, you must begin by looking at what your computer already has. Recall from Hour 1 that you need two types of software:

- Communications software, which establishes the connection between your computer and your Internet provider.

- Client programs for the activities you want to perform through the Net: A Web browser for the Web, an email program for email, a newsreader for newsgroups, and so on.

As Table 2.1 shows, Windows 98 comes with a Web browser preinstalled: Internet Explorer version 4 (IE4), at this writing. That's handy, but frankly, the newer version—Internet Explorer 5 (IE5)—is better, for a variety of reasons.

During the shelf life of this book, Microsoft may start bundling IE5 with new shipments of Windows 98, and on new PCs with Windows 98. In the meantime, though, if your PC has Windows 98 and IE4, my advice is to upgrade to IE5 at your earliest opportunity. There's nothing wrong with IE4, but IE5 is better (and free, of course) and easier to use in many ways, particularly in offline activities (see Hour 20, "Working Smarter by Working Offline").

Table 2.1 shows what each popular operating system (PC and Mac) includes.

TABLE 2.1 REQUIRED INTERNET SOFTWARE EACH SYSTEM FEATURES/ LACKS

Computer Type	Operating System	Internet Software Included	You Still Need
PC	Windows 98	Communications software, plus clients for Web browsing, email, newsgroups, and more	None

continues

TABLE 2.1 CONTINUED

Computer Type	Operating System	Internet Software Included	You Still Need
	Windows 95	Communications software. (A few clients are included, such as email, Telnet, and FTP. But these are not designed as beginners' clients, and no Web browser is included.)	Client software
	Windows 3.1	None	Communications software (such as Trumpet Winsock, supplied by most Internet providers to Win 3.1 customers) and client software
Mac	OS8	Communications software, plus clients for Web browsing, email, newsgroups, and more	None
	OS7 (System 7)	Communications software	Client software

You needn't feel that you have to get all of your client software right away. At first, all you'll really want or need is your Web browser and an email program.

You'll need no client other than your Web browser for the first half of this book—all the way through Hour 12. If you want to, you can simply set yourself up for Web browsing now, and forget about all the other software until you need it. You learn more about each of the other clients—including how to get some of the more popular options—in the hours where those clients are introduced.

Where Can You Get It?

The best place to get your start-up Internet software is from your Internet provider (which you learn to select in Hour 3).

Why? Well, again, once you're online, you can easily acquire any software you want. All you need from your startup software is a way to begin. Whatever your Internet provider offers is usually given free of charge, and may include an easy-to-use setup routine, specially designed for your Internet provider, that makes setting up your software *and* your Internet connection fast and easy.

For example, many major Internet service providers can supply a customized copy of Microsoft's Internet Explorer client software suite. If you sign up with any of these providers, you'll be provided with a copy of Internet Explorer that's preconfigured to make signing up with the provider as easy as possible.

> You'll often see "free" Internet software offered as a "bonus" by Internet providers and PC sellers, and bound into the backs of computer books (*mea culpa*). While this stuff can help you get started, and is therefore worth considering, it's a mistake to think it's as valuable as it's touted to be. Certainly, it's rarely valuable enough to be the main reason you choose a particular provider, PC, or book.
>
> Much of the software you get this way is outdated, or is "trial" software, which you may have to pay for if you use it for longer than a month or two. Often, the trial software has key features removed or disabled, to get you to pay for the full version. And even when the software truly is free, it's almost always stuff you could also download for free, for yourself, from the Web, often in a more up-to-date version.

As an alternative to using the software your provider supplies, you can walk into a software store and buy commercial Internet software right off the shelf. Most prepackaged Internet software is inexpensive ($5 to $50), and often comes with setup programs to conveniently sign you up for one or more Internet providers. Be careful, though, not to pick up a box that is designed to sign you up with one (and only one) Internet provider, unless it happens to be the one you already plan to use.

Both of the two major Internet client suites described next are available on CD-ROM at any software store.

About the Suites: Microsoft Internet Explorer and Netscape Communicator (Navigator)

In just the past few years, the two major suppliers of Web browsing software—Microsoft and Netscape—have recognized that it's confusing for Internet users to have to go out and pick separate programs for each Internet activity.

So both companies have developed "Internet suites," bundles that include a whole family of Internet programs that install together and work together well. Within each suite, you can jump from any program to any other in the suite simply by clicking a button or choosing from a menu; for example, you can conveniently jump from cruising the Web to checking your email to opening a newsgroup, all within a few clicks.

Both suites include a Web browser, email program, and newsgroup reader. Both also include a Web authoring tool for creating your own Web pages (see Hour 23). You can buy either suite on CD at any software store, or order the CD direct from the developer. You may also be able to get a copy from your Internet provider. And of course, once you're online, you can download the latest version of either program.

Netscape Communicator 4.6

The Communicator suite, sometimes called "Netscape 4.6" or "Navigator 4.6," is available for Windows 95/98/NT, Mac System 7/OS8, many UNIX versions, and Windows 3.1/Windows for Workgroups. (Note that Windows 3.1 and Windows for Workgroups versions nonetheless require a PC capable of running Windows 95, with 16MB of memory.)

Voice number for information or ordering: 650-937-3777

Suite includes

- **Navigator.** Navigator combines an easy-to-use Web browsing interface with state-of-the-art support for advanced Web features such as all multimedia types, frames, Java, enhanced security, and more. See Figure 2.4.

- **Messenger.** Many of the activities you perform in email and newsgroups are the same; in both, you compose, send, read, and organize messages. So Communicator combines email and newsreading into one program, Messenger. This is a terrific aid to learning, because you can apply most of the skills you pick up doing email to exploring newsgroups, and vice versa.

- **Composer.** A Web page editing environment that enables you to create and publish your own Web pages, almost as easily as creating a document in a word processor.

FIGURE 2.4

Netscape's home page on the Web, seen through Navigator, the Web-browsing component of Netscape Communicator.

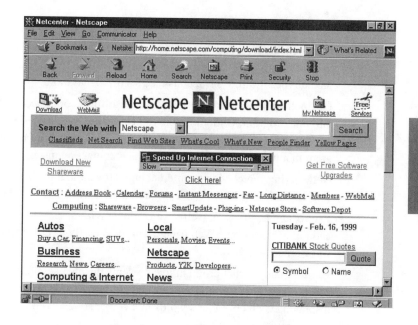

2

While the suites cover all of the bases most users want or need, it's important to understand that they do not prevent you from using other Internet software.

You can use Netscape's suite, and get a separate chat program from anywhere to fill the gap. You can install and use Microsoft's suite, but opt to use a different email program than the one Microsoft provides. You can even install more than one suite, more than one email program, more than one chat program, and so on—and on any given day use the one you feel like using. (However, you may not be permitted this flexibility if you use an online service as your Internet provider; see Hour 3.)

Microsoft Internet Explorer 5

Internet Explorer 5, sometimes called IE5, is available for Windows 95/98/NT, Mac OS7/OS8, UNIX, and Windows 3.1/Windows for Workgroups. (Note that the Windows 3.1 and Windows for Workgroups versions nonetheless require a PC capable of running Windows 95.)

Voice number for information or ordering: 800-485-2048.

Suite includes

- **Internet Explorer browser.** This browser features an easy-to-use Web browsing interface with state-of-the-art support for advanced Web features such as all multimedia types, frames, Java, enhanced security, and more. See Figure 2.5.

- **Outlook Express.** Like Netscape, Microsoft has combined email and newsreading into one program, Outlook Express. (The name is borrowed from the Outlook program in Microsoft's Office suite of programs, which is a far more powerful program that handles email, scheduling, and contact management.)

- **NetMeeting.** Voice/video conferencing software that enables you to have a live conversation with anyone else on the Internet who also uses NetMeeting.

- **FrontPage Express.** A Web page editing environment that enables you to create and publish your own Web pages, almost as easily as creating a document in a word processor.

- **Chat.** A unique chat program that presents the chat session on your screen in comic-strip form, turning each participant into a different cartoon character and displaying each character's words in a comic style "word balloon."

Some packagings of IE5 may not include the optional NetMeeting and Chat components. No biggie: They're easy to download (free) from Microsoft's Web site.

FIGURE 2.5

Microsoft's home page, seen through the Internet Explorer Web browser.

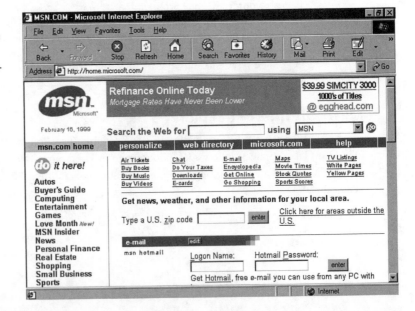

Summary

The window through which you view something frames and colors that thing, affecting your entire perception of it. Look at a yard through a big, clean window, then again through a small, dirty, distorted window, and you experience two very different yards.

A person who visits the Net through a slow, tired PC and modem or through inferior software does not perceive the same world that someone else sees through a capable PC and snappy software. When you choose your computer and software, you are defining the character of your Internet experience to come.

Q&A

Q I saw an ad for an Internet account you can get through one of those pizza-size satellite dishes. What the heck is that all about?

A The same kind of digital satellite dish used by DSS and DBS TV receivers—like those from RCA and Sony—to receive such services as DirecTV and USSB can also be used to receive high-speed Internet transmissions. But it can't *send* anything.

A company called DirecPC offers an unusual system that allows you to use the Internet, *receiving* data from the satellite dish at very high speeds and *sending* data through your phone line (at a normal modem speed). Since most of the delays on the Net are caused by receiving information rather than sending it, the system can provide dramatically faster Internet access. DirecPC costs more than a typical Internet setup (you must buy a few hundred dollars of extra equipment, and usually pay a higher monthly rate for your Internet account), but it may be a good option where poor phone lines make it impossible to get acceptable download speed. You can learn more about DirecPC from the ads you'll find in most major computer magazines.

Q Will getting Internet service from my cable TV company be a smart option soon?

A Cable companies such as Time-Warner Cable (TWC) are already offering (in limited regions) two-way, high-speed cable service that enables you not only to use the Internet at very high speed—as fast as 10 *Mbps*, over 300 times as fast as 28.8 kbps—but soon will also enable you to receive other enhanced cable services, such as video-on-demand and even local telephone service through your cable. One cool thing about cable Internet is that you don't have to connect and disconnect, as you do through phone lines; your cable Internet is live, ready for work, whenever your computer is on—24 hours a day.

Before you can take advantage of that technology, your local cable company must upgrade its hardware for two-way communication (a long and costly process) and set up its Internet service. Also, you'll need a special cable modem, which today costs at least three times as much as a regular 56K modem (although the cable company may rent one to you). Within a few years, as more cable companies get their hardware ready and cable modems get cheaper, cable Internet may be an option for you. You'll probably get it not by itself, but in a package deal that also includes your cable television service and/or local telephone service.

Before you assume that the choice will be easy, note that local telephone companies are racing to upgrade their lines to provide not only faster Internet access, but also digital TV via your phone lines. So in a few years, you may not be puzzling over where to get your Internet service. Instead, you'll be choosing which company—cable or phone—you want to use to get all of your two-way, in-home communications (TV, Internet, local phone service, and so on).

Hour 3

Choosing an Internet Provider

If you have a mailing address, you probably know about Internet providers, since they're the people who keep cramming free signup CD-ROMs and diskettes in your mailbox (creasing your *National Geographic*!) and begging you to join. Heck, you don't even need an address—you get free signup disks today in magazines, cereal boxes, and bundled along with any new computer.

The provider you pull out of your cereal box may be a perfectly good choice, but it's not the *only* choice—not by a longshot. In this hour, you'll discover the full range of different ways to get signed up for the Internet, so you can choose the provider who best matches your needs and bank account.

At the end of the hour, you'll be able to answer the following questions:

- What's an Internet provider, and why do I need one?
- What's an Internet account, and what types of accounts are there?
- How are commercial online services, like America Online, sometimes different from other Internet service providers?

- How can I find local and national providers from which to choose?
- What types of pricing plans are there, and how do I know if I'm getting a good deal?

Why Do I Need an Internet Provider?

The communications hardware and other requirements of a dedicated, full-time connection to the Internet cost thousands of dollars, and the annual leases for the data communications lines cost thousands more. The companies that offer Internet access all have their own costly, high-speed, 24-hour Internet connections. Those Internet connections have the capacity to support hundreds or thousands of individual Internet users.

Personal, day-to-day Internet users like you and me cannot afford our own full-time Internet connections; we must rent somebody else's connection. For whatever fee we pay our Internet provider, you and I buy the right to use our modems to call up the Internet provider's computers and tap into that Internet connection.

What's an Internet Account?

When you sign up with—*subscribe to*—an Internet service, you get what's call an *Internet account*.

With an Internet account, you get the right to use the provider's Internet service, your very own email address (so you can send and receive email), and all of the other information you need to set up your computer for accessing the Internet through the service. From most providers, you may also get any communications or client software you need (see Hour 2, "What Hardware and Software Do You Need?").

There are several different types of Internet accounts, described next.

Dial-Up Accounts

Most Internet accounts are called "dial-up" accounts because you use them by "dialing up" the Internet provider through your modem and telephone line. These are sometimes also described as "IP" accounts because they require your computer to communicate through TCP/IP (see Hour 1, "What Is the Internet and What Can You Do There?"). Dial-up IP accounts are the principal, general-purpose accounts offered by most Internet providers.

Dial-up accounts come in two types: PPP and SLIP. (You don't need to know what PPP and SLIP stand for; everybody always uses the abbreviations.) Using the Internet through either a PPP or SLIP account is an identical experience, since both support the same client programs, any of the popular software you've heard about: Internet Explorer, Netscape Navigator, and so on. With a PPP or SLIP account, you have access to the full range of Internet activities, and can use any client programs you want to.

> An account with an online service like AOL is also a "dial-up" account, but it's not the same thing as a regular Internet PPP or SLIP account. An online service account requires a different kind of communications software (supplied by the service) for accessing the service and its non-Internet content.
>
> When you access the Internet through an online service, the service may temporarily switch you over to a PPP account, or it may funnel you to the Internet using a different communications scenario.
>
> This is why online services often limit you to one or two different Web browsers and other clients, instead of letting you choose the one you want. Any client software used through the service must be specially configured for the service's unique communications system.

Special-Purpose Accounts

Dial-up IP accounts are the norm now, and most of this book focuses on how you can use the Internet through such an account. But there are other kinds of accounts that you may find valuable. "Shell" accounts and "email only" accounts are offered by most Internet providers (but not online services) as low-cost alternatives to their PPP or SLIP accounts.

Shell Accounts

With a shell account, your computer does not need to run TCP/IP. And although graphical Web browsing is possible through a shell account, most shell account users run special software (supplied by their Internet provider) that enables them to browse all of the text on the Web (and use email and newsgroups) but not use any of the multimedia, Java programs, or other advanced Web page stuff. Figure 3.1 shows what the Internet may look like through a typical shell account.

Those two concessions enable you to use the Internet with a far less powerful computer and much slower modem than an IP account requires—you could use the Internet with a 286 PC or ten-year-old Mac, and a 2,400 baud modem. (I once used a shell account through an IBM PCjr with 256K of memory, no hard disk, and a 300 baud modem, and lived to tell.) Shell accounts also are far cheaper than IP accounts, available for as little as $5 per month.

FIGURE 3.1

A shell account is a low-cost way to use a portion of the Internet (with compromises), or to get older, underpowered hardware online.

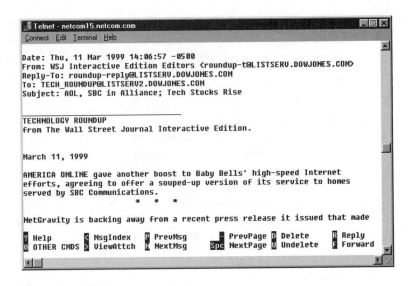

```
Telnet - netcom15.netcom.com
Connect  Edit  Terminal  Help

Date: Thu, 11 Mar 1999 14:06:57 -0500
From: WSJ Interactive Edition Editors <roundup-t@LISTSERV.DOWJONES.COM>
Reply-To: roundup-reply@LISTSERV.DOWJONES.COM
To: TECH_ROUNDUP@LISTSERV2.DOWJONES.COM
Subject: AOL, SBC in Alliance; Tech Stocks Rise
_____

TECHNOLOGY ROUNDUP
from The Wall Street Journal Interactive Edition.


March 11, 1999

AMERICA ONLINE gave another boost to Baby Bells' high-speed Internet
efforts, agreeing to offer a souped-up version of its service to homes
served by SBC Communications.
                        *   *   *

NetGravity is backing away from a recent press release it issued that made

? Help        < MsgIndex   P PrevMsg         ■ PrevPage D Delete    R Reply
O OTHER CMDS  > ViewAttch  X NextMsg     Spc NextPage U Undelete    F Forward
```

Besides those using shell accounts, there are millions of Web surfers who use computers that cannot display or play multimedia content (such as pictures, video, or sound). For this reason, Web authors used to be good about designing Web pages in such a way that nothing crucial was lost when the page was viewed through a browser that displayed only text.

But today, many Web authors have decided that they only want to reach the folks who are using multimedia-capable computers, and have stopped accommodating text-only browsers. Perhaps more importantly, many popular sites now depend upon advanced security systems, Java, and other technologies not supported in most shell accounts; for example, it's unlikely that you would be able to do much online shopping (see Hour 22, "Buying and Selling on the Net") through a shell account because of the security systems used by online stores.

For these reasons, I advocate a multimedia PC (see Hour 2) and an IP account as the only reasonable scenario for anyone who really wants to get the most out of the Internet.

Email-Only Accounts

With an email-only account, you get full access to Internet email, and nothing else—no Web, no newsgroups, no chat, no shoes, no shirt, no service. You will have access to mailing lists, however (see Hour 14, "Joining a Mailing List"), which enable you to get through email much of the same discussion content you'd see in newsgroup email.

Email accounts can be run from the lowliest of computers, and cost next to nothing. In fact, a few companies now offer you an email account free of charge, in exchange for the right to send you targeted advertisements.

What Are My Internet Provider Options?

You can get your Internet account from any of three main sources:

- A national Internet service provider (ISP).
- A local ISP, one that's headquartered in your city or town.
- A commercial online service, such as AOL or CompuServe.

Each of these options is explained next.

> Whomever you choose as your provider, make sure the company offers a dial-up telephone number for connecting to the Internet that is a local call from your PC's location. Otherwise, you'll end up paying long-distance fees to the phone company in addition to whatever your provider charges for Internet access.
>
> In most cities, finding local access numbers is no problem—any local ISP, national ISP, or online service will have a local number you can use. In some suburbs and many rural areas, finding a local number gets more difficult. Often your best bet in such circumstances is to find a local ISP (discussed later in this hour), or to see whether your local telephone company offers Internet access (many do).
>
> Some services offer a toll-free number (an 800 or 888 number) that you can use to access the service when the ISP provides no local number. But that number is rarely truly "toll-free." The ISP almost always charges a higher rate for using the service through the 800 or 888 number, kicking the toll back to you.

Commercial Online Services

You've no doubt heard of at least one of the major online services, such as America Online (AOL; see Figure 3.2) or CompuServe (CSi). These services promote themselves as Internet providers, and they are—but with a difference.

In addition to Internet access, these services also offer unique activities and content not accessible to the rest of the Internet community. These services have their own chat rooms, newsgroup-like message boards (usually called "forums"), online stores, and reference sources that only subscribers to the service can use. Setting up for an online service is usually very easy: You install the free software they provide, follow the onscreen instructions, and you're connected.

The principal drawback to online services is flexibility. You often cannot choose and use any client software you want; you must use a single client environment supplied by the service, or one program from among a limited set of options. When new, enhanced releases of client programs come out, ISP users can install and use them right away, while most online service users must wait until the online service publishes its customized version.

On the plus side, for Web browsing, most online services do supply a version of either Navigator, Internet Explorer, or both (specially customized for compatibility with the service), making the look and feel of the Web through an online service essentially identical to that of an ISP.

FIGURE 3.2

Online services such as America Online (AOL) offer Internet access and also other services available only to their own subscribers.

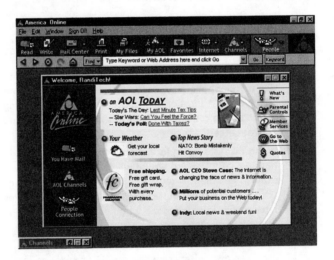

Another beef about online services is capacity. When America Online introduced more attractive pricing a few years ago, it picked up far more subscribers than it was prepared to serve. The result was that subscribers often got busy signals when they tried to connect, and could not get through to the overburdened system for hours. A few times, the system crashed altogether.

This is a legitimate complaint, as are the reports that the online services sometimes tend to supply slow, unreliable Internet access. But to be completely fair, many ISPs also get overloaded, and may be burdened by busy signals and poor performance, too.

Whomever you choose, you must be prepared for the possibility you'll get fed up and switch. You can't expect any provider to be perfect. But the possibility of losing subscribers is the only incentive for providers to continually improve.

Online services used to be dramatically more expensive than ISPs. But lately, they've adopted pricing policies that are generally competitive with the local and national ISPs, although you can still usually get a slightly better deal from a regular ISP than from any online service. For example, America Online offers a respectable flat rate of around $20 per month; if you shop around, you can get a flat rate from an ISP for as little as $15.

One final thought: In their advertising, the services often tout their ease-of-use. That claim refers exclusively to how easy it is to use the service's non-Internet content from its own client software, *not* to ease-of-use on the Internet. For all practical purposes, using the Internet is the same—no harder or easier—no matter which online service or ISP you choose.

The following online service descriptions are intended to give you a general sense of each service, not to show exact prices or features. The services are changing their features and pricing policies rapidly, so the only way to get reliable prices and other information about each is to call the 800 number shown.

3

America Online (AOL)

Voice number: 800-827-6364

America Online is the biggest of the online services (and also, therefore, the single largest Internet provider in the world), largely because of aggressive marketing and the initial convenience of setting up your account from a CD-ROM that came in your junk mail. The non-Internet content is indeed the easiest to use of all services. The Internet access, however, is notoriously slow, and busy signals continue to be a problem. AOL offers a wide range of pricing plans, including a flat rate, annual, and several different pay-as-you-go plans (see "Plans and Rates," later in this chapter).

The biggest gripe about AOL is that you can't always choose your own Web browser or other client software, or must use a special AOL version of that software or make tricky modifications to other programs in order to make them compatible with AOL. The result is that instructions for how to do things on the Net that work anywhere else often don't work on AOL. Everything on AOL works *just* a little differently.

It's worth noting that over the years AOL has incrementally smoothed out many of its wrinkles. It's very likely that within the shelf life of this book, AOL will work just like any other ISP.

CompuServe (CSi)

Voice number: 800-848-8199

CompuServe (see Figure 3.3) wasn't the first online service, but it's the oldest still in operation, and it was once the undisputed king. That legacy leaves CompuServe with an unbeatable range of local access numbers.

Functionally, CompuServe is similar to America Online in most respects, and it still offers some non-Internet content, exclusively to its own subscribers. Its reputation for providing fast and reliable Internet service is somewhat better than America Online's; its reputation for non-Internet ease-of-use, slightly worse. However, CompuServe can support almost any computer in the world, while AOL is essentially limited to popular personals: PCs and Macs.

FIGURE 3.3

The Web home page of CompuServe, an online service.

Microsoft Network (MSN)

Voice number: 800-FREE-MSN

Microsoft Network started out in 1995 as a service very much like AOL, as the first foray in Bill Gates's ongoing effort to own the Internet. (I guess for some people, having $70 billion just doesn't seem like enough power.) MSN has since evolved away from the online service model, to the point where it is now more or less a regular national (actually international) ISP, although it still supplies some content accessible only to its subscribers. MSN offers true PPP access, so you can use any browser you want to (although, not surprisingly, MSN works best through Microsoft's own browser, Internet Explorer). The service offers a variety of reasonable flat-rate and pay-as-you-go plans.

All of the online services, and most ISPs (described next), provide you with software on diskette or CD to set up your computer for using the service. This software is required for the online services, but often is optional for an ISP.

Even when it's optional, I strongly recommend getting any signup software your provider offers. The software leads you step-by-step through setting up your PC for the particular provider, and makes setting up your computer properly a no-brainer. You'll learn more about using this software—and doing without it—in Hour 4, "Connecting to the Internet."

As soon as you've selected a provider, call the provider to request the software and instructions for your computer type.

Internet Service Providers (ISPs)

Unlike an online service, an Internet service provider, or ISP, does not offer its subscribers special content that's not accessible to the rest of the Net. You get Internet access, period.

ISPs offer greater flexibility than online services, providing dial-up IP, shell, and email accounts, and enabling you (through IP accounts) to use virtually any client software you want and to add or change that software whenever you feel like it. ISPs also may offer more attractive rates and better service than the online services, though that's not always the case.

Observe in Table 3.1 that the big long-distance phone companies—AT&T, MCI, and Sprint—all offer Internet access, as well. Usually, these companies offer a discount to Internet customers who are also long-distance customers.

All offer package deals wherein you buy your Internet service, long-distance phone service, paging and cell-phone service all from the same company, and get a discount on the bundle—plus the convenience of a single bill for all your communications.

Similarly, many local telephone companies also offer Internet service, though not necessarily to every customer and neighborhood where they supply phone service.

There are many large, national ISPs that provide local access numbers all over the U.S. (and often across North America). Table 3.1 lists a few of the major national ISPs and their voice telephone numbers, so you can call to learn more about the service and also find out whether the service offers a local access number in your area. Just in case you have access to the Net through a computer at school, work, or the local library, the table also shows the address of a Web page where you can learn more about each service.

TABLE 3.1 A MORE-OR-LESS RANDOM SELECTION OF NATIONAL ISPs

Company	Voice Number	Web Page Address
Earthlink	800-395-8425	www.earthlink.net
MindSpring	800-719-4664	www.mindspring.com
Netcom	800-638-2661	www.netcom.com
Sprint	800-747-9428	www.sprint.com
MCI Internet	800-550-0927	www.mci.com
AT&T WorldNet	800-967-5363	www.att.com/worldnet
PSINet	800-827-7482	www.psi.net
US Internet	888-277-6422	www.usinternet.com
Voyager Online	800-864-0442	www.vol.com

What About All Those Signup Icons on My New Computer?

All of the online services and a few of the biggest national ISPs pay computer manufacturers to bundle their signup software on their products. When you buy almost any brand of new computer, you'll find on it a conspicuous collection of icons for signing up with various services. To start the signup process, you make sure your new computer's modem is connected to a telephone line, then you click or double-click the icon for the service you want to sign up for. (See Hour 4 to learn more about using signup programs.)

There's no reason not to use one of these icons, if the service matches your needs. But it's important to keep in mind that nearly any other provider will mail you a CD (or diskettes) of signup software that's just as easy to use. In fact, using such a CD may get you set up even more quickly. Usually, the CD contains all the software you need, which is quickly copied from the CD to your computer. But using an icon that came on your computer may require the computer to download much of the provider's software from the Internet during the setup process, which can take much longer.

My advice? (Gee, thanks for asking!) Forget about the icons for now, and continue with this hour to learn how to choose a provider. Once you've chosen one, if there's already an icon for that provider on your computer, go ahead and use it. If not, call your chosen provider (or stop by the provider's office, if it's local to you) to get the signup CD.

> If you're about to buy a new, low-cost computer for the Net, be sure to read the fine print. Many of the best-looking deals look good in part because of a rebate you get *only* if you happen to sign up for a particular Internet provider (often a service run by the computer manufacturer itself).
>
> Nothing prevents you from using a different provider through the same computer, but then you don't get a rebate. So before buying that computer, check out whether the service is right for you. If it isn't, reconsider buying the computer based on what it will cost *without* the rebate.

3

Finding a Local ISP

Besides the national ISPs, there are thousands of local ISPs in cities and towns all over the U.S. and Canada. Typically, a local ISP cannot offer access numbers beyond a small, local service area of a few cities, towns, or counties. But it can provide reliable Internet access, personal service, and often the best rates you can get. If you're having a problem, it can be a terrific help to be able to stop by your Internet provider's office and chat face-to-face. Local providers also play a vital role in keeping the big national providers honest; the continual reduction of rates by the big providers was spurred in large part by competition from even lower-priced local ISPs.

Unlike online services and national ISPs, local ISPs don't have the marketing muscle to advertise heavily or send out free disks. That's what makes them harder to find, but it's also why they're often cheaper. Finding a local ISP is getting easier all the time. Friends, co-workers, and local computer newsletters are all good sources for finding a local ISP. You can also check the Yellow Pages for ISPs: Look first under *Internet*, then try *Computers—Internet Services*. The folks at your nearest computer store may also know of a good local ISP or two.

> If you have access to the Internet (through a friend's computer, your job, a local library, or cyber café), you can search online for an ISP. A Web site called the List (see Figure 3.4) at `thelist.internet.com` is one of several that lists hundreds of ISPs in the U.S. and in many other countries.

FIGURE 3.4

Using somebody else's Internet account or an Internet terminal at your local library, you can visit the List to find a local ISP.

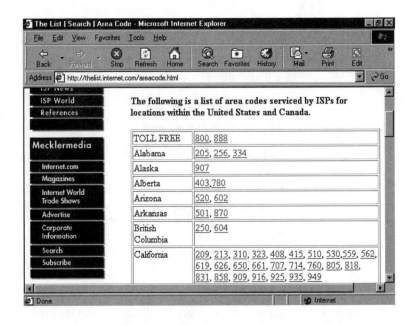

Don't forget that, depending on where you live, your local cable TV company may also offer Internet access. It'll cost more, for a number of reasons (see Hour 2), but it'll be much faster than any online service or ISP. If you're not sure whether your cable company offers Internet service, call the company's customer service department.

How Do I Choose?

Now that you know how to find the online services and ISPs, how do you pick one?

Beats me. If there were one reliable way to choose the best Internet provider, we'd all be using the same one. But different people have different priorities: For some it's price, for others it's range of access numbers, for others it's speed. Some people have a particular need to use content that's available only through a particular online service; most people don't. You have to check out how each of your available ISP options addresses your own priorities.

Obviously, if you have friends who use the Internet, find out which services they use, and ask whether they're happy. It's always a good idea to use a friend's Internet account to test the service the friend uses, and to explore your other options. Magazine reviews can help, but they rarely cover more than the online services and the largest national ISPs. To judge a local ISP, you need to listen to the word of mouth.

For what it's worth, the next few pages describe various criteria you may want to consider when evaluating your options.

> Stressed out over making a choice? Relax, and remember that—unless you agree to a long-term deal—you can always quit and try another service if your first choice disappoints you.
>
> The only caveat to switching services is that your email address changes any time you switch. But many services will forward your email to your new service for a few months after you quit, and you can always get in touch with all your email partners and let them know your new address.
>
> Of course, switching services also provides an excellent opportunity to *not* tell some folks your new email address, if those folks have been getting on your e-nerves.

Plans and Rates

Most providers offer a range of different pricing plans (see Figure 3.5), just to confuse you. (It's like choosing a long distance phone plan—do you go with the plan that's a dime at night and a quarter during the day, or the one that's 15 cents all the time, or the one that's 20% off after $20 and free on Tuesdays? Cripes.)

The kinds of plans you'll see most often, however, are unlimited access (or "flat rate") and pay-as-you-go, both described next.

FIGURE 3.5

Most Internet providers offer a choice of different pricing plans.

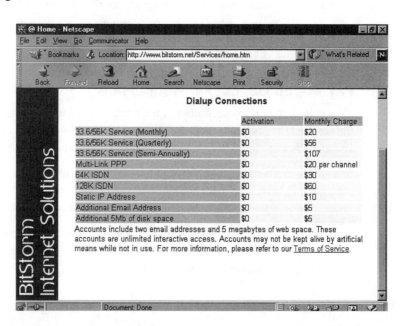

Dialup Connections

	Activation	Monthly Charge
33.6/56K Service (Monthly)	$0	$20
33.6/56K Service (Quarterly)	$0	$56
33.6/56K Service (Semi-Annually)	$0	$107
Multi-Link PPP	$0	$20 per channel
64K ISDN	$0	$30
128K ISDN	$0	$60
Static IP Address	$0	$10
Additional Email Address	$0	$5
Additional 5Mb of disk space	$0	$5

Accounts include two email addresses and 5 megabytes of web space. These accounts are unlimited interactive access. Accounts may not be kept alive by artificial means while not in use. For more information, please refer to our Terms of Service.

Unlimited Access, or "Flat Rate" Plans

With a flat rate plan, for a monthly fee of between $15 and $25, you can use the Internet all you want. In the last few years, such accounts have become the norm, and are available from virtually all online services and ISPs.

Except for folks who expect to use the Internet only sparingly, flat rate plans make the most sense. While exploring the Net, you don't want to feel like you must keep one eye on the clock. "Unlimited" does not mean you can stay online all day. To keep users from abusing their unlimited accounts, most providers automatically disconnect you from the service if you're "idle"—not actively using any Internet feature—for 10 or 15 minutes. This is not a big inconvenience; if you get disconnected while making a sandwich, you can just re-connect. But the practice does protect you from accidentally leaving your Internet connection open all day and hogging system resources that other, busy subscribers to the service may need.

Finally, some providers may attach strings to their best unlimited access rates. For example, a provider may offer unlimited access for $15 a month if you pay a full year up front, or $20 if you pay month to month. Always read the fine print.

Some providers charge a "startup fee" of some sort, often as much as $30–$50, you pay once on top of your first month's charges when you sign up. This trick is used most often by providers who advertise rates that look too good to be true; an $18 monthly rate plus a $30 one-time signup fee works out to $20.50 per month, for the first year.

Better providers have long since done away with startup fees. When offered a deal that includes one, my advice is to move on.

Pay-as-You-Go, or "Per Hour" Plans

These plans charge you according to the number of minutes per month you actually use the service. They typically start out with a monthly minimum charge (around $5–$10) and a number of "free" hours you can use the service (usually from 5 to 20 hours).

In any month where you don't exceed the number of "free" hours, you pay only the monthly minimum. But in any month where you exceed the free hours, you pay the minimum plus an extra $1, $2, or more per hour for each hour over the limit.

To decide whether you should go with such a plan, you must guess the number of hours you expect to use the Internet each month, calculate the cost under pay-as-you-go, and compare that to the provider's flat rate plan.

Bear in mind that most newcomers to the Internet spend many more hours online than they think they will. There's also a tendency among newcomers to spend lots of time online for the first few months, then to spend less time as the novelty wears off and they learn to work more efficiently.

Because of these patterns, I generally recommend that new users first choose a flat rate plan with no long-term commitment, and then keep track of their monthly hours for six months or so. If you do that, you'll know whether you're getting your money's worth at the flat rate or should switch to a per-hour plan.

> In Hour 20, "Working Smarter by Working Offline," you'll discover ways to cut your online time by applying smart tips for doing more of your Internet work *offline*. These tips are useful under any pricing plan (for one thing, they free up your telephone line), but obviously, they can also save you big bucks if you choose a pay-as-you-go plan.

3

Billing Options

Most providers will bill your monthly charges automatically to any major credit card. Some local ISPs can bill you by mail, and some others can actually add your monthly Internet charges to your regular monthly telephone bill (itemized separately from your calls to Grandma, of course). All other things being equal, you may lean toward the provider who will bill you in the way that's most convenient for you.

Access Numbers

Obviously, you want a provider that offers a local access number in the area where your computer resides. But what if you will need to use your account from both home and work, using two different computers or bringing a portable back and forth? Does the provider offer local access numbers that work from both locations?

What if you want to be able to use the Internet when you travel? Does the provider offer local access everywhere you and your computer might go? If you really want access from everywhere, you're probably going to wind up with one of the online services or larger national ISPs, who offer the greatest number and range of local access numbers.

Most folks know this already, but just case, note that just because a number is in your area code doesn't make it a local call. Most folks have local, free access to only certain nearby exchanges within their area code. (The exchange is the middle part of the number; in the number 555-777-8888, the exchange is 777.)

In most cases, if you tell an Internet provider the area code and exchange from which your computer will dial the Internet, the provider can tell you whether he has any dial-in numbers that are local to you. If in doubt, get the dial-in numbers from the provider, then call your phone company and double-check that the numbers are local from your exchange.

Supported Modem Speeds

Make sure the provider you select supports the maximum speed of your modem. If you use a 33.6K modem now, look for a provider that supports both 33.6K and 56K access now, so you can be sure to have a way to move up if you choose to.

Many providers support 56K modems. If you want 56K access, be sure to find a provider that supports it, and ask whether a higher price is charged for that access. Keep in mind that 56K access demands a very clean, clear phone connection. Even if your provider offers 56K access and you use a 56K modem, you may notice that your Internet connection usually runs at a slower speed to compensate for line noise.

Finally, recall from Hour 2 that there are three types of 56K modems: X2, Kflex, and V.90. Ideally, you should have a V.90 modem (or an X2 or Kflex modem that has been upgraded to V.90), and should use an Internet provider that supports V.90 on all of its 56K lines. If you happen to have an old X2 or Kflex modem that can't be upgraded to V.90, in order to get 56K Internet access you'll have to use a provider who still supports the same standard as your modem.

If you'll need to use more than one access number, note that providers do not always offer their highest speed through all numbers. For example, you may find that the provider offers a 56K connection from your office, but only 33.6K from your home. Look for a provider that gives you the speed you want on every access number you're likely to use.

Software Supplied

The online services require that you use a software package they supply for setting up your connection, using their non-Internet content, and often for using the Internet, too. That software may be included on the signup CD (the one you get in your cereal box or if you call the service to order it), or some of it might be transferred to your computer automatically from the service during signup.

Most ISPs can also supply you with any communications or client software you require, although using the ISP's software package is optional. If you need software to get started, you may want to consider what each ISP offers as a software bundle. (More about that in Hour 4.)

Web Server Space

If you think you might want to publish your own Web pages (see Hour 23, "Creating Web Pages and Multimedia Messages"), you'll need space on a Web server to do so. Many ISPs and most online services offer an amount of Web server space free to all customers; others charge an additional monthly fee.

Newsgroup Access

You'll learn all about newsgroups in Hour 15, "Reading and Posting to Newsgroups." For now, just be aware that there are tens of thousands of newsgroups, and that not all providers give you access to all of them.

Some providers—including, to varying extents, the online services—take it upon themselves to censor newsgroups, preventing their subscribers from accessing any that might contain strong sexual or other controversial content. If that censorship appeals to you, keep in mind that the approach generally blocks access not only to genuinely racy groups, but also to many perfectly benign, G-rated groups that get lumped together with the racy ones.

Some other providers don't bother carrying all newsgroups. Instead, they carry only the newsgroups their subscribers have specifically requested. If you want to access a newsgroup that's not already carried by a provider like this, you must send in a request by email and wait a day or two to get access. That scenario prevents you from quickly, easily finding information you need, which is what the Net is supposed to provide.

If you want easy, universal access to all newsgroups, be sure to choose an ISP that supplies it.

Summary

Well, I'd say you've had just about enough prelude and general fooling around by now. In these first three hours, you've learned what the Internet is, what hardware and software you need to get on the Internet, and how to find and choose your Internet provider.

That's all the preparation you need—it's time to set up your computer and get on the Net. You'll do that in Hour 4, "Connecting to the Internet."

Q&A

Q **If I choose WebTV instead of a computer, which online service or ISP should I use?**

A When WebTV (see Hour 2) debuted, buyers were required to use the WebTV Network as their ISP. Today, WebTV terminals can support a variety of ISPs (but not all), with one catch.

One of the main benefits of WebTV is the way it offers program directories and other services that enhance TV viewing. You can get these services only as a WebTV Network subscriber. If you use another ISP, you can still access WebTV Network services through your ISP, by paying WebTV Network a $9.95 per month fee in addition to what you already pay the ISP.

HOUR 4

Connecting to the Internet

You've got your hardware and software, and you've selected a provider. It's time to get your computer onto the Internet.

To connect to the Internet, the communications software on your computer has to be supplied with certain information about your Internet provider. You can give it this information simply by running the signup program that you received from your Internet provider, or by configuring your communications software on your own. In this hour, you'll learn to do both.

At the end of the hour, you'll be able to answer the following questions:

- What are my Internet username and password, and why do I need them?
- What are the advantages of using a signup program?
- If my provider doesn't offer a signup program, how do I set up my computer by myself?
- How can installing Internet Explorer or Mac OS8 make setting up easier?
- After setting up, how do I get online?

Keys to Your Account: Username and Password

No matter how you set up your account and computer, you'll wind up with three pieces of information that are essential to getting online:

- **Local access number.** The telephone number your modem dials to connect to your Internet provider.

- **Username.** To prevent just anybody from using its service, your Internet provider requires each subscriber to use a unique name, called a username (or sometimes user name, user ID, or userID), to connect.

- **Password.** To prevent an unauthorized user from using another's username to sneak into the system, each subscriber must also have his or her own secret password.

Entering your username and password to go online is called "logging on" (or sometimes "logging in" or "signing in") and the name used to describe that activity is "logon" (or "login," or "sign-in"). If you use a signup program to set up your Internet account and computer as described next, you'll choose your username and password while running the program. If you set up your computer without a signup disk (as described later in this hour), you'll choose a username and password while on the phone with your provider to open your account.

Every user of a particular Internet provider must have a different username. If you choose a large provider, there's a good chance that your first choice of username is already taken by another subscriber. In such cases, your provider will instruct you to choose another username, or to append a number to the name to make it unique. For example, if the provider already has a user named CarmenDiaz, you can be CarmenDiaz2.

There are rules regarding what you can and cannot use for your username and password.

The rules vary by provider, but in general, your username and password must each be a single word (no spaces or punctuation) of five or more letters and/or numerals. Nonsense words, like FunnyDad or MonkeyMary, are fine as usernames. For a password, avoid using easy-to-guess items such as your birthday or kids' names. *Total* nonsense—like xkah667a—makes the most effective password, as long as you can remember it.

Your username often doubles as the first part of your email address; if your username is Stinky, your email address might be something like Stinky@serveco.com. Before choosing a username, consider whether you also like it as an email address, which your friends and associates will see and use.

Some systems are *case-sensitive*; that is, they pay attention to the pattern of upper- and lowercase letters. On a case-sensitive system, if your username is SallyBu, you must type SallyBu to log on—sallybu, SALLYBU, or sallyBU won't work.

Using a Signup Program

As I pointed out in Hour 3, "Choosing an Internet Provider," a special signup program is required for each online service provider, and many ISPs can also supply you with a signup program for your computer. I *highly* recommend using signup programs whenever they're available, even when they're optional.

You can get free signup disks by mail from the providers, just by calling them on the telephone (see Hour 3). Also, signup programs often come preinstalled on new computers, and in computer magazines and junk mail. If you choose to go with a local ISP, you can usually pick up a signup CD or diskettes just by stopping by the provider's office.

Why Use a Signup Program?

Why? Well, first, the signup programs kill two birds at once: They sign you up with a provider *and* configure your computer to access that provider (see Figure 4.1). The program automatically takes care of all the communications configuration required in your computer, some of which can be tricky for inexperienced computer users.

Depending upon the provider you select, the signup program may or may not set up all your client software.

After completing any signup program, you'll be able to connect to the Internet and to use your Web browser to explore the Web. However, in some cases, your email, news, and other programs may require a little further setup before you can use them. You'll learn about configuring each type of client software in the hour that covers it.

4

FIGURE 4.1

All online services and many ISPs supply programs that lead you step-by-step through signing up and configuring your computer.

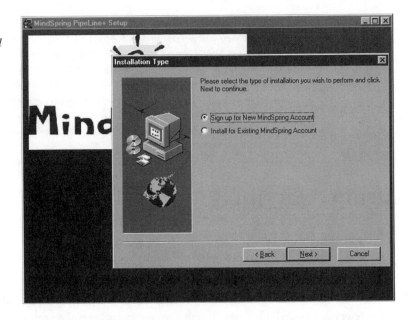

Running a Typical Signup Program

Before running a signup program, make sure your modem is connected to a telephone line, because the signup software usually dials the provider at least once during the signup process. Also, make sure you have a major credit card handy; you'll need to enter its number and expiration date to set up payment.

Signup programs are almost always designed to set up credit card payments for your Internet service. If you do not want to pay by credit card, you may not be able to use the signup program. (Actually, you may not even be able to use a particular provider; some accept payment solely by credit card.)

Call your selected provider to ask about payment terms. If the provider accepts other payment methods, but its signup program handles only credit cards, you can establish your account over the telephone, then set up your computer without a signup disk, as described later in this hour.

You'll find instructions for starting the program on a page or card that accompanies it, or printed right on the CD or diskette.

Once you start the program, just follow its lead. The program will prompt you to type in your name, address, phone number, and credit card information, and to choose a logon username and password, email address, and email password. The program may also present you with a list of payment plans from which to choose (see Figure 4.2).

When you choose each of the following during signup, be sure to jot it down for later reference:

- You logon username and password.
- Your email address.
- Your email password (sometimes different from your logon password; used to retrieve email others have sent to you).
- The telephone number of your provider's customer service and/or technical support departments.

Once or twice during the signup process, the program uses your modem to contact the provider. It does this to verify your payment information, find the best local access number for you, check that your selected username is not already taken, and ultimately to send all of the information it collected to the provider to open your account.

When the program closes, your computer and account are ready to go online and explore.

4

FIGURE 4.2

A typical signup program prompts you for all the info required for setting up your account, such as choosing a payment method.

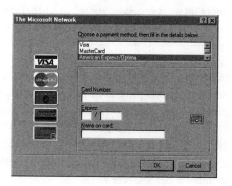

Setting Up Without a Signup Program

Setting up your computer without a signup program is a little more difficult, but well within anybody's capabilities.

The instructions in this section are for setting up dial-up IP accounts, the most popular type. If you intend to use another type of account, such as shell or email (see Hour 3), you must obtain specific instructions and software from your Internet provider for setup.

When you don't use a signup disk, you must set up your account with your selected Internet provider over the telephone first, then configure your computer. While setting up your account, your provider will tell you all of the communications settings required for the service, and will work with you to select your local access number, username, and password.

It's important that you make careful notes of everything your provider tells you. You'll use all of that information when setting up. In addition to your access number and logon username and password, you'll probably come out of the conversation with the following information:

- Whether the account is the PPP or SLIP type (see Hour 3).
- One or more *IP addresses* required for communicating with the provider (see the following section, "About IP Addresses").

More and more Internet providers are set up so that they automatically assign you an IP address whenever you connect to the Internet.

- The addresses of the provider's email and news servers. (You'll need these addresses to configure your email program and newsreader; see Hours 13, "Sending and Receiving Email" and 15, "Reading and Posting to Newsgroups.") Email server addresses may be described as "SMTP" and "POP3" servers, and news servers may be described as "NNTP" servers. (You don't need to know what the abbreviations mean; just know that if your provider mentions an "NNTP server," he's talking about a news server.)
- Your own email address, the one others can use to send email to you.
- Your email username and password, required for retrieving email people have sent to you. (These may be different from your logon username and password.)
- The telephone number and hours of the provider's customer service or technical support departments.
- Any other special communications steps or settings the particular provider requires.

No matter how you go about it, setting up your computer for the Internet is a simple matter of entering this information in your communications software. Once that's done, you can go online.

> If you use Windows 3.1 and do not use a signup disk, you can manually configure your Internet account, just as you can for the Mac or Windows 95/98. But you need some special software first. See the Q&A at the end of this hour.

About IP Addresses

Sigh. Once upon a time, understanding the Internet's IP addressing system was essential to getting online, a required topic in the Internet 101 curriculum. Today, you often need not ever deal with, or even know about, IP addresses. They're an issue *only* when you set up your computer to use a particular provider; once you're set up, you can forget about 'em. And if you use a signup program as described earlier, the program takes care of the IP addresses—you won't even see 'em.

However, if you set up your computer without a signup program, you'll need to configure your communications software with one or more IP addresses that enable your computer to communicate with your provider's.

So here it is: The very least you need to know about IP addresses, if you need to know it at all. Every computer on the Internet has its own, unique address; that's why one computer on the Internet can find and communicate with any other. This address can be expressed in either of two ways: as an IP address or as a domain name.

An IP address is a set of four numbers, separated by periods, that expresses the Internet address of a particular computer, for example,

`195.25.100.14`

To make getting around the Internet easier, most activities support *domain names* rather than IP addresses. A domain name is a word-based equivalent of an IP address, for example,

`news.netco.com`

When a domain name is used, a computer called a *domain name server* (DNS) is used to automatically convert it to an IP address, behind the scenes, to locate the computer to which it refers. For most Internet activities—including the Web and email—you will deal exclusively with domain addresses. You'll learn more about these addresses as you go along.

4

When setting up your account, your provider may supply you with any or all of the following addresses for configuring your computer (not all may be required for a given setup):

- Your own Internet IP address. (Some providers do not require this; their computer automatically assigns you an IP address each time you log on.)
- The IP address of one or more DNS servers. When your provider gives you more than one DNS server address, one address is called the "primary" DNS server, and any others are called "secondary" or "alternate" DNS servers.
- The IP address of a *gateway*, a device some providers use to manage Internet traffic on their service.
- The IP address of a *subnet mask* (or *netmask*), an address that identifies your computer to the ISP's local network.
- Email and news server addresses. (These may be expressed as IP addresses, but are more often expressed as domain names.)

Setting Up Windows 95 or 98 for an ISP

Short of a using a signup program, the next easiest way to set up an ISP account on a PC running Windows 95 or 98 is to set up Internet Explorer and run its Connection Wizard. Internet Explorer is included in every copy of Windows 98, and often included with Windows 95. (See Hour 2, "What Hardware and Software Do You Need?".)

At this writing, the version of Internet Explorer you're most likely to find on your PC is Internet Explorer 4 (IE4). However, the very latest version is Internet Explorer 5 (IE5). Both versions include the Connection Wizard program for setting up an Internet account.

If you already have IE4, you may find it easiest to use IE4's Connection Wizard to set up your Internet connection first. Later, you can install IE5 (or any other browser you may want to use, such as Netscape). The new browser will automatically use the Internet connection set up by IE4; you will not be required to set it up all over again.

The Connection Wizard leads you through each step of the process, prompting you for all of the required information, such as IP addresses. That's almost as easy as using a signup disk, except that the Connection Wizard doesn't sign you up with your ISP—you must take care of that first—and it prompts you for your IP address and other setup information, which a signup program can supply for itself.

The following To Do shows how to use the Connection Wizard built in to IE5 to configure a PPP connection in Windows 95. Note that the steps for using the Connection Wizard in IE4 (and IE3, for that matter) are very similar. Just have handy your notes of any addresses, phone numbers, or other info your ISP gave you, and do what the wizard tells you to do.

To Do: Run Internet Explorer 5's Connection Wizard

Before running the Connection Wizard, first install the IE5 software. Doing so takes just a few minutes, and requires choosing from among options on a short series of dialogs.

When you finish installing the software, the Connection Wizard may open automatically to set up your Internet connection. If it doesn't, start it by opening your Windows Start menu and choosing Programs, Accessories, Internet Tools, Connection Wizard. (If using IE4 instead of IE5, you would choose Programs, Internet Explorer, Connection Wizard.)

From the Welcome dialog that appears, follow these steps:

> If at any point in using the wizard you change your mind about any choices you made in earlier steps, click the Back button to go back to any earlier step and change your choices. Nothing becomes permanent until you click the Finish button in step 7.

4

1. Choose one of the following options and then click Next (see Figure 4.3):

   - If you want Microsoft's help choosing an ISP from a limited selection Microsoft offers, select I Want to Sign Up for a New Internet Account and then follow any instructions that appear.

   - If you have already signed up with an ISP and are now setting up your account on your PC, choose I Want to Set Up My Internet Connection Manually, then click Next and proceed to step 2.

The middle option, I Want to Transfer My Existing Internet Account to This Computer, is for people who already have an Internet account and are switching PCs.

▼

FIGURE 4.3

Step 1: Choose whether you want to set up a new Internet account or transfer an existing account.

2. Choose I Connected Through a Phone Line and a Modem, then click Next (Figure 4.4). If you're setting up an Internet connection at work through a local area network (LAN), you should probably get help from your system administrator or Help Desk.

FIGURE 4.4

Step 2: Choose whether you want to connect through a phone line or through a LAN.

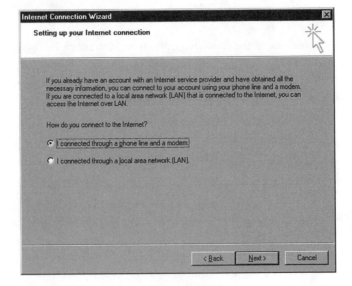

▼

▼   3. Complete the area code and phone number used to connect to your ISP, then click
          Next (Figure 4.5).

If your ISP is a local call (and it should be!), then clear the check box next to
Dial Using the Area Code....

FIGURE 4.5

Step 3: Type in the
phone number for your
Internet service
provider.

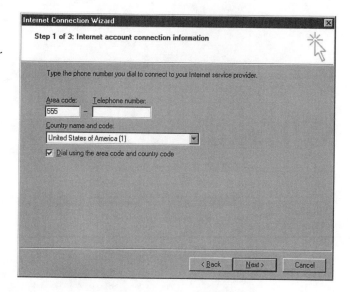

      4. Enter your Internet username and password. (When you type the password, aster-
          isks appear onscreen instead of the password; that's so no one can steal your pass-
          word by peering over your shoulder while you type it (Figure 4.6).) Then...

          If you are setting up a PPP account, and if your ISP told you that IP addresses and
          DNS server addresses are assigned automatically, click Next and proceed to step 5.

          If you are setting up a SLIP account or your ISP gave you IP addresses you must
          enter, click the Advanced button to display a dialog on which you can type your IP
          addresses. After completing that dialog, move on to step 5.

      5. Type a name (anything you want) to identify your Internet account (Figure 4.7). If
          you don't type anything, the wizard names the connection "Connection to" plus the
▼   telephone number, which is fine. Click Next.

FIGURE 4.6

Step 4: *Enter your username and password.*

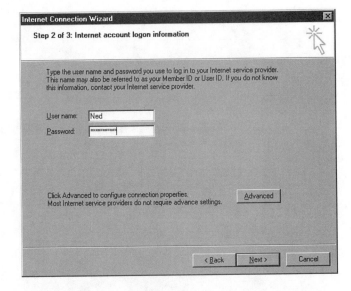

FIGURE 4.7

Step 5: *Type in a name for your Internet account.*

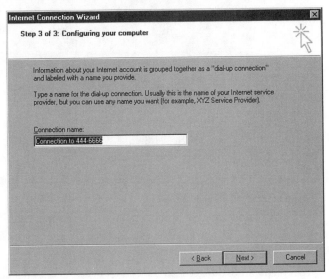

6. Choose Yes (to set up IE5's email program) or No (to leave that for later), then click Next (Figure 4.8).

   If you choose Yes, you'll be led through a short series of dialogs in which you'll be asked to supply your email address, server addresses, and other such information, after which you may go on to step 7.

▼   If you choose No, you go straight ahead to step 7.

FIGURE 4.8

Step 6: Decide whether to set up an email account or not.

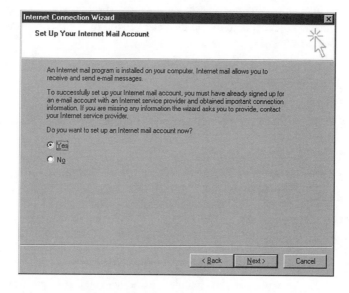

7. Click Finish to complete the setup (Figure 4.9).

FIGURE 4.9

Step 7: Click Finish.

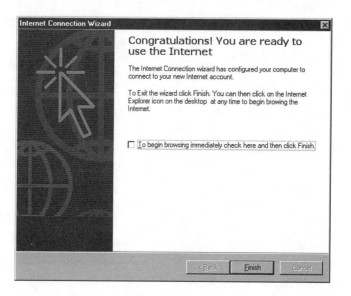

▲

Setting Up a Mac for an ISP

Just as in Windows 95 and 98, the easiest way to set up your Mac connection (short of an ISP signup program) is to install the Mac version of Internet Explorer and use its Connection Wizard.

> The Mac's current operating system includes signup software for America Online. If you use a Mac and have selected AOL as your Internet provider, open the AOL signup icon to sign up with AOL and configure your Mac for Internet/AOL access.

Getting Online

Once your account, connection, and software are all set up on your computer, you can connect to the Internet at will by opening your connection program or your browser.

> It generally doesn't matter whether you first connect to the Internet, then open the Internet program you want to use, or open your program first, then connect to the Internet.

Exactly how you open your connection program differs, depending upon your computer, the software you select, and whether you chose an ISP or an online service:

- Online services generally deposit an icon that looks like their logo right on your Windows or Mac desktop. To go online, choose that icon. Often, the online services deposit a new menu item in your Programs or Apple menu, too.

- If you used an ISP signup program, you will probably also see a new icon or easily identifiable menu item for opening the connection.

- If you will use Internet Explorer 4 or 5, or Netscape Navigator 4.6, you can open your connection by opening the browser. Doing so usually opens automatically the Internet connection software as well as the browser.

  To open Internet Explorer 5 in Windows, click the icon in the Windows taskbar (see Figure 4.10), or open the Windows Start menu and choose Launch Internet Explorer Browser from near the top of the menu.

To open Netscape Navigator 4.6 in Windows, click the icon in the Windows taskbar (see Figure 4.10), or open the Windows Start menu and choose Programs, Netscape Communicator, Netscape Navigator.

FIGURE 4.10

Internet Explorer 4 and 5, and Netscape Navigator 4.6, deposit icons in the Windows taskbar that open the browser and your Internet connection.

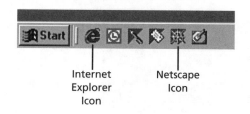

Internet Explorer Icon

Netscape Icon

Once the connection program opens, you're usually presented with a dialog in which to type your Internet username and password (see Figure 4.11). To connect, type your user-name and password. (When you type your password, it usually appears on screen as a series of asterisks, so no one can learn it by peering over your shoulder.) Then click the button on the dialog labeled "OK," "Connect," or "Open."

4

Most connection dialogs, like the one in Figure 4.11, let you choose an option that enables the dialog to "save" or "remember" your username and password, so you needn't type them each time you go online.

This is a handy feature (I use it), with two drawbacks you must consider. If you allow your connection software to remember your password:

- Anyone who has access to your computer—kids, co-workers, very smart dogs—can access the Internet using your account.

- Since you never type your password, and it does not appear on the dialog (asterisks take its place), you may forget your password. If you switch computers or install different connection software, you'll need to call your provider and request a new password.

Your connection program instructs your modem to dial your Internet provider, and sends your username and password to log you on.

If all goes well, you'll see a dialog or message indicating that you are connected. That dialog usually also is used for disconnecting when you're finished using the Net. Choose Close or Disconnect on the dialog, or just close the dialog, to go offline.

FIGURE **4.11**

After opening your connection program, you supply your user-name and password to log on to the Internet.

From time to time, you will not be able to connect to your ISP or online service. You may get a busy signal if your ISP is temporarily overcrowded, or temporary glitches in the ISP's system may prevent you from logging on successfully.

If your connection software can't get you online, it hangs up and tells you so. You can try again in a few minutes. (Some communications programs automatically re-try for you every few minutes until they succeed, or until you close them.) You can have a cookie while you wait.

If this happens only occasionally, it's normal, and not a sign that you set up your PC wrong, bought a bad modem, or chose a bad provider. If it happens often, you'll start running out of cookies, so you better shop for a more reliable Internet provider.

Summary

Getting set up for the Internet isn't all that tricky—especially if you use a signup program. And you know what? That's the hardest part of the whole Internet—from here, it's a ride downhill!

Q&A

Q Can I set up Windows 3.1 for the Internet?

A Some ISPs and online services still supply signup disks for Windows 3.1. As always, a signup program is your best option. In fact, if an online service doesn't supply a Windows 3.1 signup disk, you probably can't use that particular service.

To set up Win 3.1 for an ISP that doesn't have a signup disk, you must ask the ISP for a copy of Trumpet Winsock, a Windows 3.1–based TCP/IP communications program that enables Win 3.1 to use a PPP account. Better ISPs send out a copy of Trumpet Winsock that's preconfigured with an IP address, local access number, and all of the other information you need to connect. Following instructions from the provider, all you need to do is install Trumpet Winsock, choose a few options, install the browser and other software the ISP provides, and you're ready to go.

Q Is configuring for the Internet getting any easier?

A Oh, my yes. Signup disks from ISPs are becoming far more common, and the slow death of SLIP and shell accounts has reduced the number of options, setting the stage for easy-to-use PPP setup programs. All new operating systems—such as Windows 98 and Mac OS8—have easy Internet setup routines built in to them. And more and more ISPs are supporting automatic IP address assignment and other techniques that make setting up on the user's end simpler.

Setup is simplifying itself so rapidly that, if you'd just waited another year or two, this hour of the book would have been only six minutes long. I could grant you a 54-minute nap and still stay on schedule.

4

PART II
Making the Web Work for You

Hour

HOUR 5

Browsing the Web

Here it is, the $64,000 hour. The Web is the main reason interest in the Internet has exploded in the last five years, and the main thing that draws newcomers to it. In this one hour, you'll pick up the basics of getting all around the Web.

In fact, many Web surfers never apply any skills beyond those you'll pick up in this hour. But in Hours 6 through 12, you'll build upon what you learn here so that you can not only travel the Web, but also make the most of it.

At the end of the hour, you'll be able to answer the following questions:

- What's that Web page that always appears as soon as I open my browser?
- What do all those Web addresses mean, and how do I visit a Web page address?
- How can I use *links* to jump from place to place on the Web?
- How do toolbar buttons like Back and Home make navigating the Web easier?
- What are *frames*, and how do they make getting around a Web page different?

About Your "Home Page"

Most Web browsers are configured to go automatically to a particular Web page as soon as you open them and connect to the Internet. This page is generally referred to as the browser's "home page."

NEW TERM **Home page**. A Web page a browser is configured to go to automatically when you open it, to provide a starting point for your Web travels. It's also sometimes called the "startup page." But remembering that the page is "home" is important, as you'll learn later in this hour.

Note that "home page" has two meanings in Web parlance: It also describes a Web page that serves as the main information resource for a particular person or organization. For example, www.toyota.com may be described as Toyota's "home page."

For example, if you get Internet Explorer directly from Microsoft, it opens at a special "Start" page on Microsoft's Web server. If you get Netscape Navigator directly from Netscape, it opens automatically to a similar startup page at Netscape. (Incidentally, these Microsoft and Netscape home pages were both shown in Hour 2, "What Hardware and Software Do You Need?", in Figures 2.4 and 2.5.)

However, if you get your software from your Internet provider, your browser may have been reconfigured with a new home page, one that's set up by your provider as a starting point for its subscribers (see Figure 5.1). This home page also serves as a source of news and information about the provider and its services.

FIGURE 5.1

Your browser goes automatically to its "home page." The home page may have been selected by the browser maker or by your Internet provider.

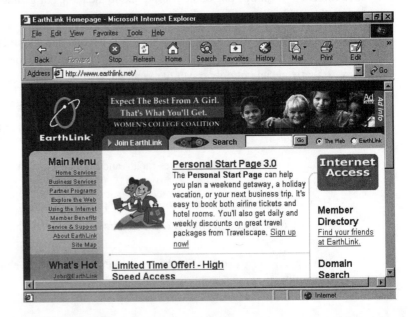

A few specific Web sites are used as home pages by a very high proportion of Web users because these pages offer a convenient set of links to the things many folks like to do as soon as they go online: Search for something, check out the latest news, weather, or sports scores, or other common activities.

Some folks call these sites *Web portals* because they function as an everyday point of entry to the Web. Popular portals include such search pages as Yahoo!, Excite, and Snap, and other sites such as Netscape's Netcenter.

In Hour 6, "Revisiting Places You Like," you'll learn more about choosing and using a Web portal. In Part III, "Finding What You're Looking For," you'll learn all about using search pages.

You don't have to do anything with your home page. You can just ignore it, and jump from it to anywhere on the Web you want. But some home pages provide valuable resources, especially for newcomers.

Often, you'll find a great selection of *links* on your home page to other fun or useful pages. If your home page happens to be one set up by your local ISP, the page may even contain local news, weather, and links to other pages with information about your community. Now and then, before striking out onto the Web, be sure to give your home page a glance to check out what it has to offer.

NEW TERM **Link.** A *link* is an object in a Web page that you can activate to jump to another page, or another part of the page you're on. Links can appear onscreen as a block of text or as a picture. In most browsers, you go where the link leads simply by pointing to it with your mouse and clicking it. See "Basic Jumping Around," later in this hour.

Don't like your home page, and wish you had a different one? That's okay with me—in Hour 6, you'll learn how to change your home page.

Understanding Web Page Addresses

Using the Web is easy—that's why it's so popular. But if there's one thing about Web surfing that trips up newcomers, it's using Web page addresses effectively. So here and now, I'll set you straight on Web page addresses so that you can leap online with confidence.

For the most part, you'll deal with only two kinds of addresses for most Internet activities (although there are other types, most of which you'll discover in Part IV, "Communicating with Email and Newsgroups," and Part V, "Beyond Browsing"):

- **Email addresses**, which are easy to spot because they always contain an "at" symbol (@). You'll learn all about email addresses in Hour 13, "Sending and Receiving Email."

5

- **Web page addresses**, which never contain an @ symbol. Web page addresses are expressed as series of letters separated by periods (.) and sometimes forward slashes (/), for example, `www.microsoft.com/index/contents.htm`. A Web page address is sometimes referred to as a *URL*.

NEW TERM **URL.** A *URL* (Uniform Resource Locator) is the official name for the address format you use when telling a Web browser where to take you. (You can pronounce it "you-are-el" or "earl.")

Although most URLs are Web page addresses, other types of URLs may be used in a Web browser for accessing other types of Internet resources. You'll learn about Web page URLs in this hour, and about other types later in this book.

If you keep your eyes open, you'll see Web page addresses everywhere these days. By typing an address in your Web browser (as you learn to do shortly), you can go straight to that page, the page the address "points to." Just to give you a taste of the possibilities, and to get you accustomed to the look and feel of a Web site address, Table 5.1 shows the addresses of some fun and/or interesting Web sites.

 As Table 5.1 shows, many addresses begin with the letters "www". But not all do, so don't assume.

TABLE 5.1 A FEW OUT OF THE MILLIONS OF FUN AND INTERESTING WEB SITES

Address	Description
`www.cnn.com`	Cable News Network (CNN)
`www.ebay.com`	eBay, an online auction house
`www.epicurious.com`	A trove of recipes
`www.scifi.com`	The SciFi Channel
`www.carprices.com`	A site where you can learn all about buying a new or used auto
`www.uncf.org`	The United Negro College Fund
`www.rockhall.com`	Cleveland's Rock & Roll Hall of Fame Museum
`www.un.org`	The United Nations
`www.nyse.com`	The New York Stock Exchange
`college-solutions.com`	A guide to choosing a college
`www.sleepnet.com`	Help for insomniacs
`www.nasa.gov`	The space agency's site

Address	Description
www.adn.com	The Anchorage, Alaska Daily News
www.mommytimes.com	Parenting advice
us.imdb.com	The Internet Movie Database, everything about every film ever made
www.amazon.com	Amazon.com, a popular online bookshop
www.nhl.com	The National Hockey League

Appendix A, "Fun Web Sites to Visit," contains a directory of many more fun Web sites you may want to visit.

Anatomy of a Web Address

The address of a Web site (sometimes called a URL, but more about that later) is made up of several different parts. Each part is separated from those that follow it by a single, forward slash (/).

The first part of the address—everything up to the first single slash—is the Internet address of a Web server. Everything following that first slash is a directory path and/or filename of a particular page on the server. For example, consider the following fictitious URL:

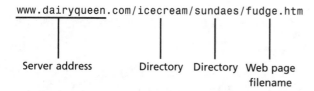

The filename of the actual Web page is `fudge.htm`. (Web page files generally use a filename extension of `.htm` or `.html`.) That file is stored in a directory or folder called `sundaes`, which is itself stored in the `icecream` directory. These directories are stored on a Web server whose Internet address is `www.dairyqueen.com`.

Sometimes, an address will show just a server address, and no Web page filename. That's okay—many Web servers are set up to show a particular file to anyone who accesses the server (or a particular server directory) without specifying a Web page filename.

For example, if you go to the address of Microsoft's Web server, `www.microsoft.com`, the server automatically shows you an all-purpose Web page you can use for finding and jumping to other Microsoft pages. Such pages are often referred to as "top" or "index" pages, and often even use "index.htm" as their filename.

5

Technically, every Web page address begins with "http://" or "https://",
particularly when described as a *URL* (Uniform Resource Locator), the technical designation for the address format you use when working in a Web
browser.

But the latest releases of Netscape Navigator and Internet Explorer no
longer require you to type that first part. For example, using either of those
browsers, you can surf to the URL http://www.mcp.com just by typing

www.mcp.com

(In fact, you don't even need to type the "www" part—if it's required, these
browsers will fill it in for you.) Because of this change, Web page addresses
often appear in advertising, books, and magazines with the "http://" part
left off.

If you use a browser other than the Big Two, or older versions of the Big
Two, however, you probably have to include the http:// part when typing
URLs in your browser. For example, to go to www.pepsi.com, you must type

http://www.pepsi.com

You'll learn more about URLs later in this book.

To Do: Find the Address of Your Home Page

1. Connect to the Internet and open your Web browser. After a few moments, your
   home page (whatever it may be) appears (Figure 5.2).

FIGURE 5.2

*Step 1: Open your
browser to your home
page.*

My Home Page

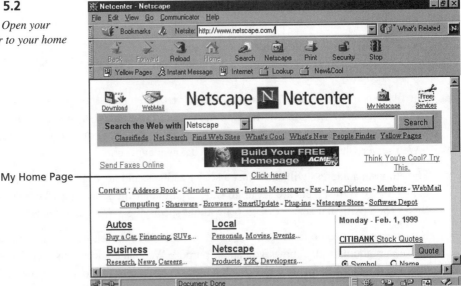

▼ 2. Examine your browser's toolbar area. The address you see there is the address of your home page (Figure 5.3).

Address of home page

FIGURE 5.3

Step 2: Find the address of your home page.

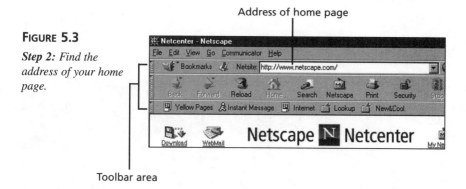

Toolbar area

3. Make a mental note of the spot where you saw the home page address (Figure 5.4). That's where you'll always see the address of whatever page you're currently viewing. That's usually also the place where you'll type addresses to navigate the Web, as described next.

FIGURE 5.4

Step 3: Remember where the address appears.

Going Straight to Any Web Address

Before you can jump to a page by entering its address, you must find the place in your browser provided for typing addresses. The term used to describe this area varies browser to browser, but to keep things simple, I'll just call it the "address box." Figure 5.5 shows the toolbar area of Internet Explorer, with the address box containing an address.

In both Internet Explorer and Netscape Navigator, you'll see the address box as a long text box somewhere in the toolbar area, showing the address of the page you're currently viewing. If you don't see it, the toolbar that contains the address box might be switched off.

To switch on the toolbar that contains the address box:

• In Internet Explorer, choose View, Toolbars, and make sure a check mark appears next to Address Bar in the menu that appears. If not, click Address Bar. If you still don't see an address box, try dragging each toolbar to the bottom of the stack, so that all toolbars are visible and none overlap.

• In Netscape Navigator, choose View, Show, Location Toolbar. If you still don't see it, it's there, but collapsed so it's not visible. Click at the far-left end of each line in the toolbar area, and it should appear.

Address Box,
showing URL of
current page

FIGURE 5.5

In most graphical browsers, you'll see an address box in the toolbar area where you type an address to go to a particular Web page or site.

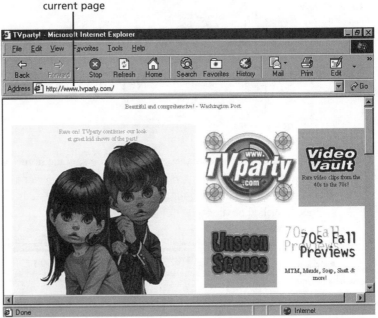

 If you use a browser other one of the Big Two (Internet Explorer or Netscape), you may see an address box in the toolbar area, or at the bottom of the browser window. In some browsers, you may have to choose a menu item to display a dialog that contains the address box. Look for a menu item with a name like "Enter URL" or "Jump to New Location."

Entering and Editing URLs

Once you've found the address box, you can go to a particular address by typing the address you want to visit in the box and pressing Enter. When the address box is in a toolbar, you usually must click in it first, then type the address and press Enter.

Before you type an address in the address box, the address of the current page already appears there. In most Windows and Mac browsers, if you click once in the address box, the whole address there is highlighted, meaning that whatever you type next will replace that address.

If you click twice in the address box, the edit cursor appears there so that you can edit the address. That's a handy feature when you discover that you made a typo when first entering the address.

Note that, when you type an address to go somewhere, your starting point doesn't matter—you can be at your home page or on any other page.

When typing the address, be careful about the following:

- Spell and punctuate the address exactly as shown, and do not use any spaces.

- Match the exact pattern of upper- and lowercase letters you see. Some Web servers are case sensitive, and will not show you the page if you don't get the capitalization in the address just right.

- Some addresses end in a final slash (/), and some don't. But servers can be quirky about slashes, and many print sources where you see addresses listed mistakenly omit a required final slash, or add one that doesn't belong. Always type the address exactly as shown. But if that doesn't work, and the address appears not to end in a filename, try adding or removing the final slash.

- If you do not use a recent version of Internet Explorer or Netscape Navigator, you may be required to include the "http://" prefix at the beginning of the URL. For example, when you see an address listed as www.discover.com, you must enter it in your address box as

```
http://www.discover.com
```

5

What happens if you type an address wrong? Nothing bad—you just don't go where you want to go. Usually, your browser displays an error message, reporting that the browser could not find the address you requested. Check that you spelled, punctuated, and capitalized the address correctly. If you discover a mistake, edit (or retype) the address and press Enter to try again.

Note that Web servers and their pages are not permanent. From time to time, an address will fail not because you made a mistake, but just because the page or server to which it points is no longer online, either temporarily (because of a system glitch) or permanently.

To Do: Go to Macmillan Computer Publishing's Web Site

Honest, I'm not shilling for Macmillan Computer Publishing (MCP) here, even though MCP published this book. It's just that Web pages come and go. Most Web site URLs for large organizations work fine for years. But addresses can change, and Web pages and sites do disappear from time to time.

I want to give you a reliable set of steps, and I know that the MCP Web site will still be around when you read this.

1. Connect to the Internet and open your Web browser (Figure 5.6).

FIGURE 5.6

Step 1: Open your Web browser.

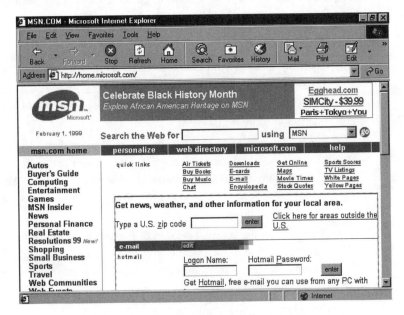

2. Find your address box, and click in it once (Figure 5.7).
3. Type the URL (Figure 5.8):

   `http://www.mcp.com`

   (That URL will work in any browser, but if you use Internet Explorer version 3.02 or higher, or Netscape Navigator 4 or higher, you may omit the `http://` prefix.)
4. Press Enter. Macmillan's Web site appears (Figure 5.9).

Address box

▼

FIGURE 5.7

*Step 2: Click in your
address box.*

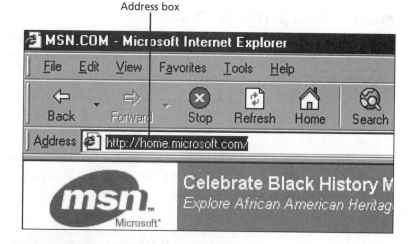

FIGURE 5.8

Step 3: Type in the URL
`http://www.mcp.com`.

FIGURE 5.9

Step 4: Press Enter.

5

▲

Basic Jumping Around

I've shown you first how to move about the Web by entering an address, in part so you could discover along the way a number of important concepts that will help you navigate successfully.

Now I must show you that many—even most—of the times you jump from page to page, you won't type an address. All you'll do is click a link or button.

Sorry to show the hard way before the easy ones, but you must understand that you're not always going to find a link that takes you exactly where you want to go. URLs are like cars—they take you directly to a particular place. Links are like the bus: They often take you just to the right neighborhood.

> Here is as good a place as any to point out that some Web pages take a long time to appear, even if you have a fast modem and Internet connection. If some pages do seem terribly slow, don't worry that there's something wrong with your computer, modem, or connection. The problem is probably that the page you're accessing is very complex.
>
> You see, each time you display a particular Web page, the whole page must travel through the Internet to your computer to appear on your screen. A page that's mostly text appears quickly, because text pages contain little data, and thus travel quickly through the Net. Pictures, multimedia, and Java programs balloon the number and size of the files that make up the Web page, and thus take much longer to appear.

Finding and Using Links

Activating a link in most browsers is simple: Point to the link, click it, and your browser takes you wherever the link leads.

Most links lead to another Web page, or to another part of a long Web page you're viewing. However, links can do much more. For example, some links, when activated, may start the download of a software file (see Hour 11, "Finding Programs and Files") or play a multimedia file (see Hour 7, "Playing Online Video, Music, and Broadcasts").

It's not using links that can be tricky, but finding them in Web pages that aren't designed well enough to make the links obvious. Links appear in a Web page in any of three ways:

As text. You'll notice text in Web pages that appears to be formatted differently from the rest. The formatting differs depending upon your browser, but text that serves as a link is usually underlined (see Figure 5.10) and displayed in a different color than any other text in the page.

As pictures. Any picture you see in a Web page may be a link. For example, a company logo may be a link leading to a page containing information about that company.

As imagemaps. An imagemap is a single picture that contains not just one link, but several (see Figure 5.11). Clicking on different parts of the picture activates different links.

Text links are usually easy to spot because of their color and underlining. Picture and imagemap links can be harder to spot at a glance.

But most browsers provide a simple way to determine what is and is not a link. Whenever the mouse pointer is on a link, it changes from the regular pointer to a special pointer that always indicates links (usually a hand with a pointing finger; see Figures 5.10 and 5.11).

FIGURE 5.10

In most browsers, when you point to a link, your pointer changes to indicate the link.

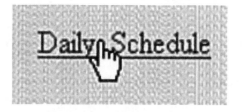

FIGURE 5.11

Each part of this imagemap is a different link. You click different areas of the picture to do different things.

5

Using Navigation Buttons: Back, Forward, Home, Stop

In most browsers for Windows and the Mac, you'll see a whole raft of toolbar buttons, many of which you'll discover as this book progresses. But by far, the most important are the Big Four: Back, Forward, Home, and Stop (see Figure 5.12). These buttons help you move easily back and forth among any pages you've already visited in the current online session, and to conveniently deal with the unexpected.

For example, when exploring a particular Web site, you often begin at a sort of "top" page that branches out to others. After branching out a few steps from the top to explore particular pages, you'll often want to work your way back to the top again, to start off in a new direction. The Big Four buttons make that kind of Web navigation simple, and typing-free.

FIGURE 5.12

The main toolbars in Netscape Navigator (shown here) and Internet Explorer prominently feature the invaluable Back, Forward, Stop, and Home buttons.

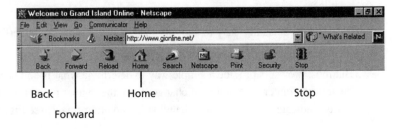

Here's how you can use each of the Big Four buttons:

Back retraces your steps, taking you one step backward in your browsing each time you click it. For example, if you move from Page A to Page B, clicking the Back button takes you back to A. If you go from A to B to C, pressing Back twice returns you to A. When you reach the first page you visited in the current online session, the Back button is disabled; there's nowhere left to go back to.

Forward reverses the action of Back. If you've used Back to go backward from Page B to A, Forward takes you forward to B. If you click Back three times—going from D to C to B to A—clicking Forward three times takes you all the way ahead to D. When you reach the page on which Back was first clicked, the Forward button is disabled because you can only move Forward to pages you've come "Back" from.

Home takes you from anywhere on the Web directly to the page configured in your browser as "home," described at the start of this hour. Going Home is a great way to re-orient yourself if you lose your way and need to get back to a reliable starting point.

Stop immediately stops whatever the browser is doing. If you click Stop while a page is materializing on your screen, the browser stops getting the page from the server, leaves the half-finished page on your screen, and awaits your next instruction.

Back, Forward, and Home do not care how you got where you are. In other words, no matter what techniques you've used to browse through a series of pages—entering URLs, clicking links, using buttons, or any combination of these—Back takes you back through them, Forward undoes Back, and Home takes you home.

Back and Stop are particularly useful for undoing mistakes. For example, if you click on a link that downloads a file, and while the file is downloading you decide you don't want it, you can click Stop to halt the download but stay on the current page, or click Back to halt the download and return to the preceding page.

To Do: Practice Using Links and Buttons

1. Go to the MCP Web site at www.mcp.com, find any interesting-looking link, and click it (Figure 5.13).

FIGURE 5.13

Step 1: Go to www.mcp.com *and click on a link.*

Link

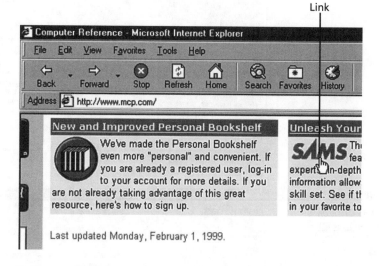

2. A new page opens, the one the link you clicked points to. Click Back to return to the top MCP page (Figure 5.14).

3. Click another link on the top MCP page (Figure 5.15). On the page that appears, find and click yet another link (Figure 5.16). (If you see no links, click Back to return to the top MCP page, and try another route.)

4. Click Back twice to return to the top MCP page (Figure 5.17).

5. Click Forward twice. You go ahead to where you just came back from (Figure 5.18).

6. Try a new URL: Enter www.akc.org, the American Kennel Club (Figure 5.19).

7. From the AKC page, click Back once. You return to a page at MCP (Figure 5.20).

8. Click home. Welcome Home (Figure 5.21).

5

Back
button

▼

FIGURE **5.14**

Step 2: Click the Back button.

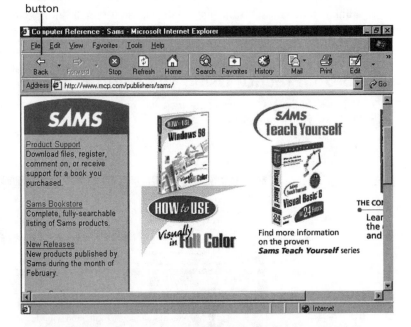

FIGURE **5.15**

Step 3: Click on another link.

Another
link

FIGURE **5.16**

Step 3: Click on yet another link.

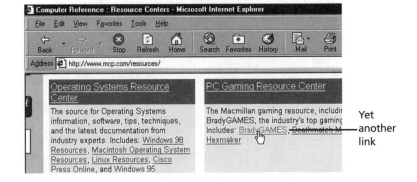

Yet
another
link

▼

Back
button

FIGURE 5.17

Step 4: Click Back twice.

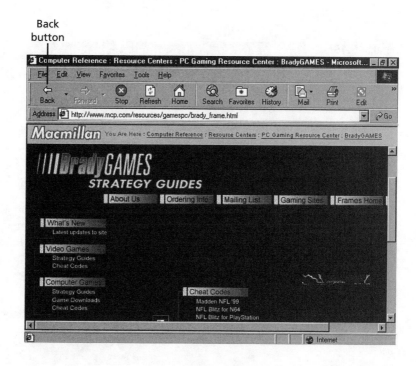

Forward button

FIGURE 5.18

Step 5: Click Forward twice.

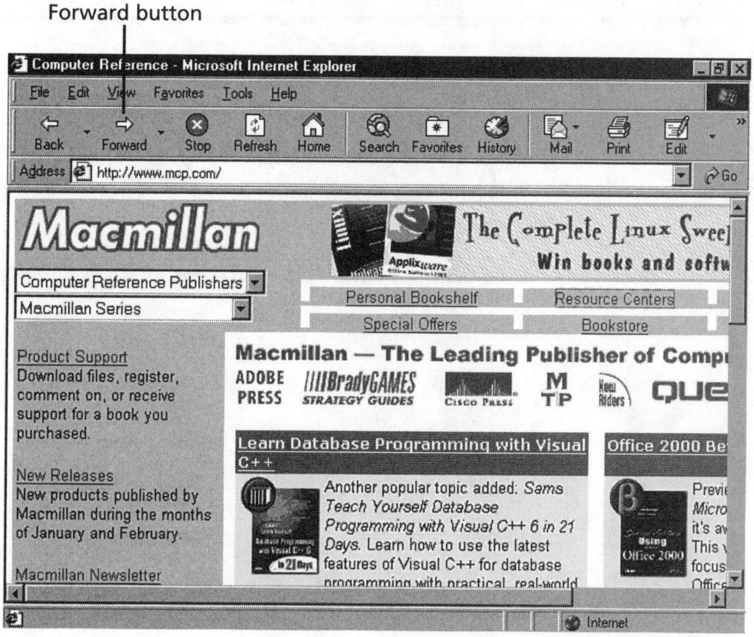

5

FIGURE 5.19

Step 6: Enter a new URL.

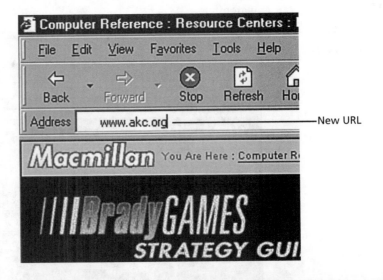

New URL

FIGURE 5.20

Step 7: Click Back once.

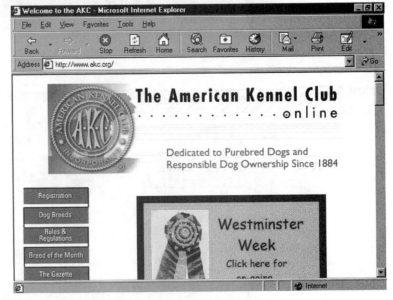

FIGURE 5.21

Step 8: Click home.

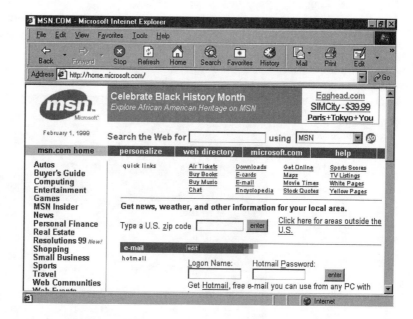

Fussing with Frames

Some pages you'll find are split into *frames*, two or more separate panes (see Figure 5.22).

In effect, each pane in a frames page contains its own, separate little Web page. That enables each pane to operate independently of the others; for example, clicking a link in one pane can change the contents of another.

Some folks get all boxed up by frames, but using a frames-based page doesn't have to be tricky. Just remember the following tips:

- To use the links or other stuff in a particular pane, click anywhere within the pane first to select that pane as the "active" pane. Then do what you want there. Anytime you move to another pane, click there before doing anything.

- Some panes have their own scrollbars. When you see scrollbars on a pane, use them to scroll more of the pane's contents into view.

- While you're on a frames page, the Back and Forward buttons take you back and forth among the panes you've used in the current frames page, *not* among pages. Sometimes, it can be tough to use Back to "back out" of a frames page to the page you saw before it; at such times, it's often easier to enter a new URL or click Home to break free of the frames, then go from there.

5

- Some pages use "borderless" frames, and so do not appear at first glance to be frames pages. But after a little experience, you'll quickly learn to identify any frames page when it appears, even when the frames are implemented subtly.

Pane

FIGURE 5.22

Frames pages show two or more separate documents at once, each in its own pane.

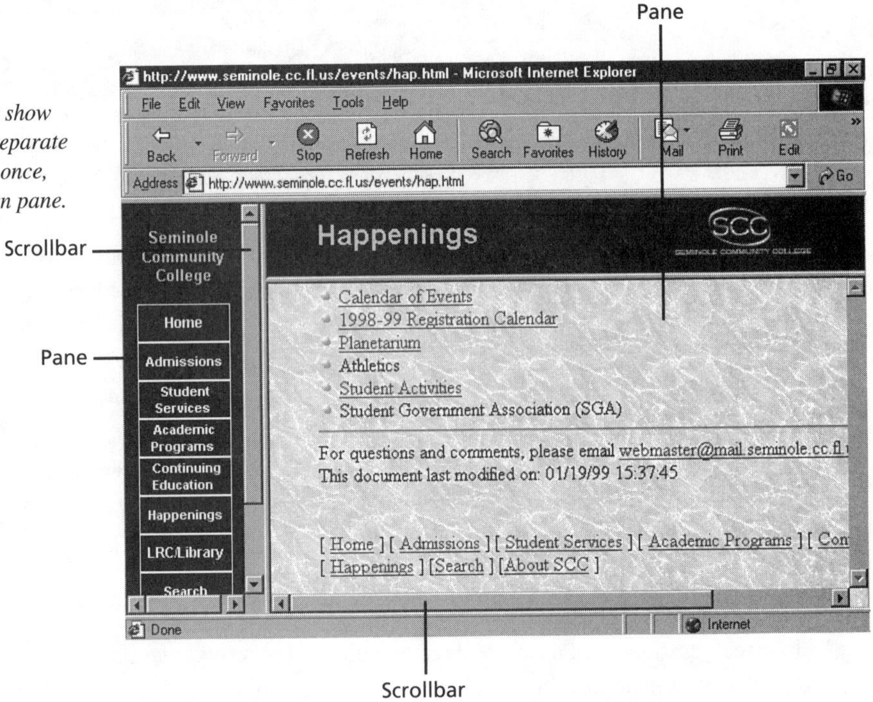

Scrollbar

Pane

Scrollbar

Internet Explorer, Netscape Navigator, and a few other major browsers support frames, but some others do not.

For this reason, many frames pages are preceded by a non-frames page that provides two links: One for displaying the frames page, and another for displaying the same content in a no-frames version.

If your browser can't handle frames—or if your browser can handle them but you can't—just choose the no-frames version. Life's too short.

Summary

That's all there is to basic browsing. Just by entering URLs, clicking links, and using buttons like Back and Home, you can explore near and far. Little bumps like frames add a little complexity to the mix, but nothing you can't handle.

Q&A

Q I've already started doing a little Web browsing on my own, and from time to time I hit a page that says I need a "plug-in" to continue. What's that all about?

A People are always inventing new kinds of content to put on the Web, such as faster, better forms of online video or interactive gaming. When something new goes online, all the browsers out there don't know how to play that new content yet.

A plug-in is a program that adds a new capability to your browser so it can do something new, like play a new kind of multimedia. Because most of the plug-ins you're likely to need will be plug-ins for playing new forms of online multimedia, you'll learn about finding and using plug-ins in Hour 7.

Q I was on a page, and suddenly a box popped up reporting some gobbledygook about "Java." What did I do wrong?

A Nothing at all. (Stop blaming yourself!) Another way Web programmers teach a browser new tricks is by running any of several different kinds of program code in it. The two main kinds are called Java and JavaScript. You don't have to know how to do anything to take advantage of Java and JavaScript programs; they run automatically.

However, sometimes the program code contains mistakes, or you are using a browser that has little glitches in its compatibility with the program code. That's when you see these error messages.

The best way to prevent the messages is to try to always use the most recent version of Internet Explorer or Netscape Navigator (see Hour 2). If you do, you'll see such messages rarely. When you do see the messages, just ignore 'em.

You'll learn a little more about dealing with program code in Hour 8, "Protecting Your Privacy (and Other Security Stuff)."

5

Q **You said that the http:// prefix indicates that a URL is a Web page. If URLs are used only in Web browsers, why would a URL need to point to anything *other* than a Web page?**

A Web browsers are the Swiss Army Knives of the Internet. Many Web browsers are designed to serve as a client for several different types of servers.

Of course, their main gig is showing Web pages on Web servers. But many Web browsers can also show newsgroup messages on news servers, and interact with other server types you'll learn about in Hour 19, "Tools for the Serious User: FTP and Telnet." Finally, a Web browser can be used to view various types of files that are stored not on the Internet, but right on your local computer or network.

For each of the different types of resources a Web browser can access, a different URL prefix is needed. For example, the URL for a resource on an FTP server begins not with http://, but with ftp://.

In upcoming hours, you'll learn more about accessing non-Web stuff through a Web browser. You'll also learn that it's often better to use a specific client for these activities, rather than your Web browser. A real corkscrew or screwdriver usually works better than the one in your Swiss Army Knife.

HOUR **6**

Revisiting Places You Like

There are millions of Web pages, and only one of you. Yes, that's part of what makes you oh-so-special. But even though you're special, if you're at least a little bit like most people, your Web surfing will eventually settle into a pattern wherein you revisit certain favorite pages often. And if you revisit certain pages often, you need a more convenient way of getting there than having to type URLs all the time.

In this hour, you discover the various ways you can easily revisit places you've been, even when you don't remember the address. You'll also learn about saving and printing what you see online, so that you can revisit that information *offline*, any time.

At the end of the hour, you'll be able to answer the following questions:

- How can I change my home page so that I automatically visit my very most favorite page every time I go online?
- What's a Web portal, and how can I use one?
- How can I create a way to go straight to a page I like without having to type its URL?
- How can I find and revisit a page I visited an hour, day, or week ago if I can't remember its URL?
- How can I save information I find on the Web?

Changing Your Home Page

On your Web travels, you'll discover many different pages you'll want to revisit. But you may also discover one page you like or need so much that you want to visit it first, every time you go online.

If you find such a page, why not make it your browser's home page, so that your browser automatically goes straight to it every time you go online, and every time you click the Home button? Most browsers that use a home page—including Netscape Navigator and Internet Explorer—also enable you to choose that page.

Since the home page you use now was probably pre-configured in your browser either by the company that made the browser or by your Internet Provider (if that's where you got your browser program), you may soon find you'd like to personalize your Internet experience by picking a new home page.

Of course, no law says you *must* change your home page. You may find the preconfigured home page meets your needs just fine. The standard home pages for Internet Explorer and Netscape each offer built-in search tools (which you learn to use in Part III, "Finding What You're Looking For") and links to news, weather, and other handy resources.

If your home page is one set up by your Internet provider, leaving it in place can help you keep up with useful news from your provider; for example, new pricing plans or the introduction of new services.

And note that you can skip over your home page when you want to go straight to another page without stopping off at home on the way. You learn how later in this hour.

Pick Your Portal

A number of pages online are designed as all-purpose Web entry points, places that put an array of the most-used Web resources within easy reach. Some folks call these Web sites *portals*.

NEW TERM **Web portal.** A Web site that offers news, search tools, and other handy links, designed as an all-purpose point-of-entry for the Web. Web portals typically display lots of ads, which pay for the services they provide.

The main feature of most portals is one or more tools for searching the Net (you learn how to use these in Part III). In fact, most portals started out as search pages before the whole portal idea came into vogue. The most widely used portal, Yahoo! (see Figure 6.1), is also the most widely used search tool on the Internet, and has been for years.

FIGURE 6.1

Web portals, such as Yahoo!, provide a great Web starting point (or home page) by combining search tools, links to news and weather, and other popular services all from one place.

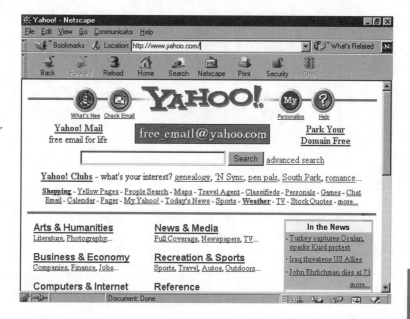

Table 6.1 lists some of the most popular Web portals. One of these may fit your home page needs nicely, so explore each one.

TABLE 6.1. A FEW POPULAR WEB PORTALS

Portal Name	Address
Excite	www.excite.com
Yahoo!	www.yahoo.com
Snap	www.snap.com
Netcenter	home.netscape.com
MSN.COM	home.microsoft.com

Some portals are customizable—you can actually change the way the portal page appears to you, so that it shows you the tools and links you want, or always shows you particular items of interest right away—local news and weather, sports scores, your local TV schedule, and so on.

For example, you can click the Personalize link on the MSN.COM portal (see Table 6.1) to customize it, or click the My Yahoo! link in Yahoo! to customize it.

Since you're new to the Net, it's best not to customize your portals until you've gained some more experience. Leave the portals alone for awhile so they can do their job: showing you the range of resources available to you online.

Making the Switch

To make any page your home page, all you have to do is go to that page, then find your browser's dialog where the Web address of the home page is shown. You replace that address with the address of the page you want to use as your new home page, as shown in the following To Dos.

After you make the change, the home page you selected will appear first whenever you go online, and will also appear anytime you click the Home button.

To Do: Change the Home Page in Internet Explorer 5

1. Surf to the page you want to use as a home page (Figure 6.2).

2. While viewing that page, choose Tools, Internet Options from the menu bar (Figure 6.3).

3. On the General tab of the Internet Options dialog , in the Home page section click the Use Current button. The address in the Address box will change to the address of the page you're currently viewing (Figure 6.4). Click OK.

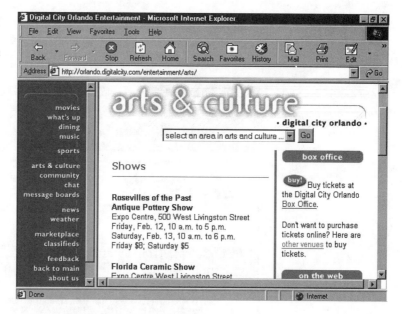

FIGURE 6.2

Step 1: Open your would-be home page in Internet Explorer.

FIGURE 6.3

Step 2: Choose Tools, Internet Options.

FIGURE 6.4

Step 3: Click the Use Current button in the Home page section of the General tab.

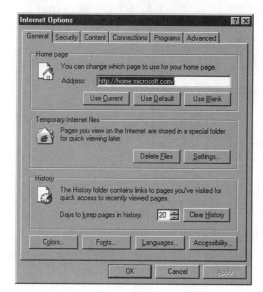

6

To Do: Change the Home Page in Netscape Navigator 4.6

1. Surf to the page you want to use as a home page (Figure 6.5).

FIGURE 6.5

Step 1: Open the page in Netscape.

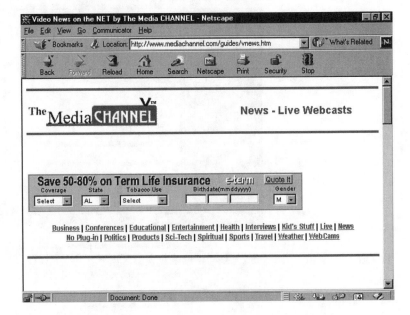

2. While viewing that page, choose Edit, Preferences from the menu bar (Figure 6.6).

FIGURE 6.6

Step 2: Choose Edit, Preferences.

3. Make sure Home Page is the selected option in the box labeled Navigator Starts With (Figure 6.7).

4. Click the Use Current Page button, then click OK.

FIGURE 6.7

Steps 3 and 4: Select Navigator Starts with Home Page, then click Use Current Page.

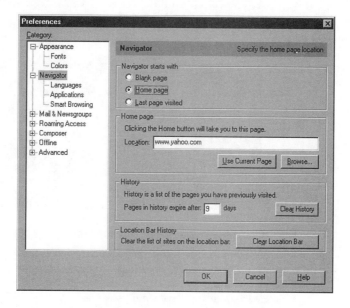

Creating Shortcuts to Pages You Like

Most browsers let you build and maintain a list of shortcuts to pages you plan to revisit often.

While viewing a page you know you'll want to revisit one day, you can create a shortcut to it so that anytime you want to visit that page, you needn't type (or even remember!) its URL—all you do is choose the page's name from a menu, and your browser takes you there.

NEW TERM **Bookmarks** and **Favorites**. The term used to describe the shortcuts you create for easily revisiting Web pages differs by browser. The shortcuts are called *bookmarks* in Netscape Navigator, and they're called *favorites* in Internet Explorer. I don't know why, so don't ask.

Figure 6.8 shows a menu of these shortcuts, created in Internet Explorer. I can click on any item in this menu to go directly to the page it describes. Observe that some items in the list are folders. As the figure shows, clicking a folder opens a submenu from which you can select a shortcut or another folder.

6

FIGURE 6.8

By creating bookmarks or favorites (like those shown in this Internet Explorer list) you give yourself an easy way to return to pages you like.

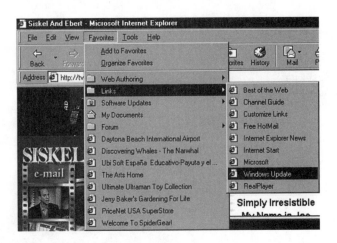

If you open the list of shortcuts in your own browser (see "Going Where a Bookmark or Favorite Leads," later in this hour), you'll see a long list of shortcuts you didn't create. These are shortcuts your browser maker has added to your list to help you get started.

Feel free to explore the shortcuts you see. But note that you can delete any or all of these shortcuts whenever you want to, to make room for you own shortcuts (see "Managing Your List of Shortcuts," later in this hour).

Adding a New Bookmark or Favorite

Before creating a new bookmark or favorite, you go to the particular page you want to make a bookmark or favorite for. Once there, you choose a quick button or menu item to create the shortcut. When creating the shortcut, you'll have a chance to type a new name for it. You don't have to—in your list, the name of the bookmark or favorite will be the title of the Web page it points to, which usually serves just dandy as a name. If later on you decide that the title is not sufficiently descriptive, you can edit the bookmark as described later in this hour to give it a new name.

To Do: Create a Bookmark in Netscape Navigator

▲ To Do

1. Go to the page you want to create a bookmark for, then click the Bookmarks button on the toolbar (Figure 6.9), or choose Communicator, Bookmarks from the menu bar.

Bookmarks button

FIGURE 6.9

Step 1: Click the Bookmarks button.

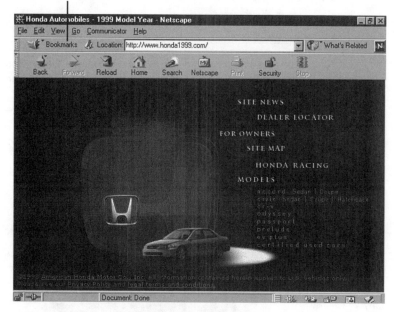

2. In the menu, click Add Bookmark (Figure 6.10).

FIGURE 6.10

Step 2: Click Add Bookmark.

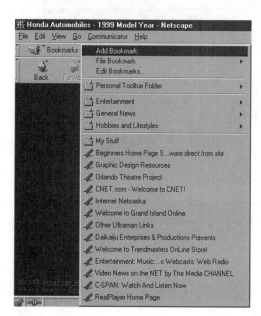

6

To learn how to use your new bookmark, see "Going Where a Bookmark or Favorite Leads," later in this hour.

> Observe in both To Dos that you can click a folder to store the new shortcut in a particular group of shortcuts. This is valuable when you have lots of shortcuts—and soon, you will.
>
> But you needn't fuss with folders right when you create the shortcut. Instead, you can quickly create the shortcut as shown in the To Do so you can get right back to surfing. Later (even offline) you can organize your shortcuts into folders, as described later in this hour.

To Do: Create a Favorite in Internet Explorer

1. Go to the page you want to create a favorite for, then choose Favorites, Add to Favorites from the menu bar (Figure 6.11).

FIGURE 6.11

Step 1: Choose Favorites, Add to Favorites in Internet Explorer.

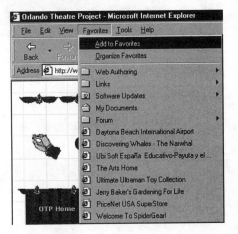

2. Click OK (Figure 6.12).

To learn how to use your new favorite, see "Going Where a Bookmark or Favorite Leads," later in this hour.

FIGURE 6.12

Step 2: Click OK.

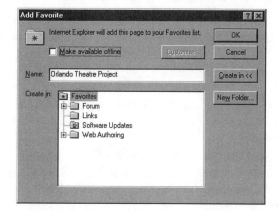

The Make Available Offline check box you see in step 2 of the preceding To Do is used to designate certain pages for offline browsing. Internet Explorer can automatically store and update the content of such pages on your PC so you can view them anytime, whether you're online or off. You learn more about this option and other offline techniques in Hour 20, "Working Smarter by Working Offline."

Going Where a Bookmark or Favorite Leads

From the moment you create a new favorite or bookmark, it appears as an item in the Bookmarks or Favorites menu. To use bookmarks and favorites, you simply open the menu and choose an item from the list.

- To display Netscape Navigator's Bookmarks list, click the Bookmarks button on the toolbar, or choose Communicator, Bookmarks from the menu bar.
- To display Internet Explorer's favorites list, choose Favorites from the menu bar.

In Internet Explorer 4 and 5, as an alternative to opening the Favorites menu as described earlier, you can click the Favorites button in the toolbar. Doing so displays your favorites list in the Explorer bar, a panel in the left side of the window.

The Explorer bar can display not only your Favorites, but also a few other kinds of lists. You'll learn more about the Explorer bar in Hour 9, "Getting Started with Searching." In the meantime, note that it's usually easier to use the Favorites menu (as described earlier) than to use the Explorer bar.

6

Choosing a Favorite *Before* You Open Your Browser

The Favorites list you create in Internet Explorer in Windows is accessible not only
from within the Internet Explorer program, but also from the Windows Start menu (see
Figure 6.13).

> If you use Windows 98, your Internet Explorer Favorites will appear auto-
> matically in your Start menu. If you use Windows 95, the Favorites appear in
> the Start menu only if:
>
> You install Internet Explorer version 4 or higher, *and*
>
> During installation of IE, when asked if you want to include the Windows
> Desktop Update feature, you choose Yes. If you choose not to install the
> Windows Desktop Update in Windows 95, the Favorites menu is not added
> to the Start menu.

FIGURE 6.13

*Internet Explorer's
Favorites list shows up
in your Windows Start
menu, so you can jump
straight from Windows
to a favorite site.*

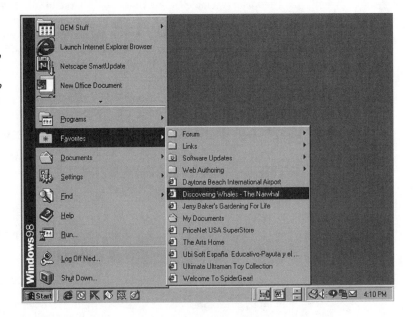

Using this menu, you can initiate an Internet session straight from the Start menu, without opening your browser or Internet connection first. Just click Start, choose Favorites,
and choose the Favorite you want to go to. Windows will open Internet Explorer, connect
to the Internet (pausing, if necessary, so you can enter your username and password), and
go straight to the page you selected—*bypassing* your home page.

Although this technique makes the most sense when Internet Explorer is closed, note that you can use this menu anytime you want to—it works whether IE is open or closed, and whether you're online or off.

Managing Your List of Shortcuts

Over time, your list of shortcuts can become too long and unwieldy. To make it more manageable, you can delete bookmarks and favorites you no longer use, or you can organize them into folders. You manage your shortcuts in a simple dialog (see Figure 6.14) that lets you delete, move, or rename bookmarks and favorites much as you would do with any group of file icons in a Windows or Mac folder.

To open the dialog for managing shortcuts:

- In Internet Explorer 4, choose Favorites, Organize Favorites from the menu bar.
- In Netscape Navigator 4, click the Bookmarks button in the toolbar (or choose Communicator, Bookmarks), then choose Edit Bookmarks.

FIGURE 6.14

Internet Explorer and Netscape Navigator both include easy-to-use dialogs in which you can delete old shortcuts or organize them in folders, to keep your list tidy.

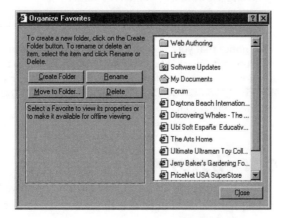

Putting a Shortcut on a Toolbar Button

6

If you know of a few pages that you want *really* fast access to, you can easily create toolbar buttons to those pages. When you want to visit one of those pages, you needn't open your Favorites or Bookmarks list—all you have to do is click a button on a toolbar in your browser.

In Internet Explorer, the buttons you create appear on a toolbar called Links. In Netscape Navigator, the buttons appear on a toolbar called the Personal toolbar (see Figure 6.15).

FIGURE 6.15

By storing a few short-cuts in a particular folder, you can create toolbar buttons that take you straight to favorite sites.

Personal toolbar

In both Internet Explorer and Netscape Navigator, you add a toolbar button by creating a shortcut and storing that shortcut in a particular folder:

- In Internet Explorer, any Favorite you store in the Links folder becomes a button on the Links toolbar. (If you don't see a Links toolbar, display it by choosing View, Toolbars, Links.)

- In Netscape Navigator, any bookmark you store in the Personal Toolbar folder becomes a button on the Personal toolbar. (If you don't see a Personal toolbar, display it by choosing View, Show, Personal Toolbar.)

You'll notice that your Links toolbar or Personal toolbar already has some shortcuts in it—places Microsoft or Netscape want you to visit. Using the techniques described earlier in this hour (see "Managing Your List of Shortcuts"), you can delete (or move) these shortcuts from the Links or Personal toolbar to make room for your own buttons.

Reliving Your *History*

Bookmarks and favorites are the best way to go back where you've been. But suppose you want to revisit a page you didn't create a shortcut to, and you can't remember the address. How can you find it?

Of course, getting back to any page you've visited in the current session is never a problem; you can use the Back button (see Hour 5, "Browsing the Web"). In addition to the Back button, most browsers can display a menu of sites you've visited in the current session. You'll find that list at the bottom of the Go menu in Netscape, and on the File menu in Internet Explorer.

From the Back button in both of the Big Two browsers, you can drop down a menu of places you can go Back to, places you've visited in the current session. You can click any item on the list to go back there.

To display the list in Internet Explorer, carefully click on the tiny arrow on the right side of the Back button.

To display the list in Netscape Navigator, point to the Back button, then click and hold.

But what about pages you visited yesterday, or last week? To help you get back to those, browsers keep a record of where you've been: your *history file* (see Figure 6.16). To revisit any page you've visited lately, you open your browser's history file, locate an entry describing the page, and choose that entry.

To find a particular page in the history file, it helps to understand that the file lists its entries from those you've visited most recently to those you visited longer ago. In other words, the farther you scroll down in the list, the older the entries are.

Note that the history file keeps track of where you've been, no matter how you got there. Every time you go to a page—whether you get there by URL, link, bookmark, or favorite—the visit is recorded in your history file.

To open the history file:

- In Internet Explorer 5, click the History button, or choose View, Explorer Bar, History. The list opens in the Explorer bar, a panel on the left side of the window. (You learn more about using the Explorer bar in Hour 9.)

- In Netscape Navigator, choose Communicator, Tools, History.

FIGURE 6.16

From this history file in Netscape Navigator, you can return to any page you've visited recently by finding it in the list and double-clicking it.

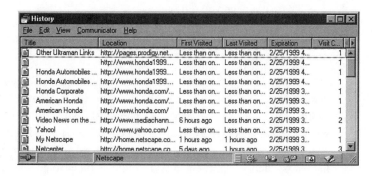

6

Recalling Addresses You've Typed

Your history file keeps every page you've visited, no matter how you go there. But in addition to the history file, browsers keep a separate list of every address you've typed in the address box. This list makes retrieving and reusing an address you've typed much easier.

In either Netscape Navigator or Internet Explorer, you can take advantage of this list in either of two ways: the drop-down list or AutoComplete.

Drop-Down List

At the far-right end of the address box in either browser, you'll see an arrow. Click the arrow, and a list of URLs you've typed drops down (see Figure 6.17). To visit any of the addresses listed, click it in the list.

FIGURE 6.17

The addresses you've typed are stored in a list that drops down from the address box, for easy recall.

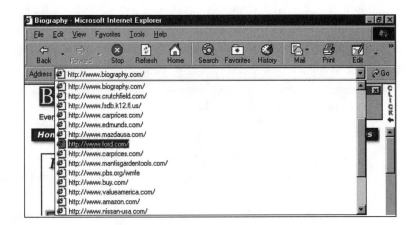

AutoComplete

To use the AutoComplete features of IE and Netscape, begin typing the address in the address box. What happens next depends on the browser you're using:

- In Netscape Navigator, once you've typed enough of the address for the browser to guess which URL you're typing, the browser fills in the rest of the address in the address box. For example, if you've previously typed www.monkeys.com, and that URL is the only one in the list that begins "www.mo," you need type only that much of the address in the address box—the rest suddenly appears, and you can press Enter to go where it leads.

- In Internet Explorer 5, once you've typed enough of the address for the browser to come up with a short list of guesses as to which URL you may be typing, it displays that list underneath the address box (see Figure 6.18). You can click on the address you want in the list, or press your down-arrow key until the address you want is highlighted, then press Enter.

FIGURE 6.18

As you type an address in the address box, the browser anticipates what you're typing.

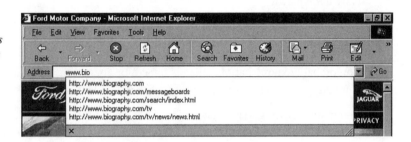

Printing and Saving Pages

Finally, there's the amazingly low-tech way of returning to a Web page: Don't.

You revisit a Web page because you expect its content to have changed, because you want news. But for information that doesn't change, there's no reason to keep going back to the Web page. Instead, save that information in a form you can consult offline, anytime.

The easiest way to do that is to print Web pages. In most browsers, that's as easy as clicking a Print button on the toolbar, or choosing Print from a menu (usually a File menu). Note that the browser prints all of the page you're currently viewing, not just the screenful you see. If a page can be scrolled through multiple screenfuls of information, the whole thing is printed out, usually across multiple paper pages.

Alternatively, you can save Web pages on your hard disk. On the File menu of most browsers, you'll find a Save As item. Choose that, and you can save the current Web page as a file on your hard disk. You can then open and view the page in your browser anytime, offline. (You'll learn much more about working offline in Hour 20.)

When you save pages in some browsers, only the text of the page is saved, not its images. If the images are an important part of the information the page contains, you may want to print the page rather than saving it.

6

In most browsers, the dialog for opening saved Web pages appears if you choose File, Open. However, if you simply open the folder in which you saved the page and then open the file icon for the Web page, it will probably open in your browser automatically. When you install them, Windows and Mac browsers usually configure the operating system so that anytime you open a saved Web page file icon, the browser opens automatically to display it.

Summary

You probably know that Magellan is famed for attempting to circumnavigate the globe. But you may not know that he didn't make it—he kicked the bucket along the way.

The moral? Getting to new places, as you learned to do in Hour 5, is only half of navigating. The other half is getting *back* to places you've been. If poor Magellan had had bookmarks (or favorites), a history file, or even a lowly Home button, he'd have made it full-circle.

Don't even get me *started* on Columbus.

Q&A

Q You said in Hour 5 that because Web pages may go away or change their addresses, links and URLs can fall out of date and not work anymore. Will that happen to my bookmarks or favorites?

A Sure, eventually any bookmark or favorite can go bad, if the page to which it points moves or is deleted. One hedge against that is to point them to a site address or a "top" page from which you can then use a link or two to get to a particular page. Specific pages on a server come and go often, but that top page generally stays put.

Netscape Navigator versions 4 and higher can check your bookmarks and optionally fix any that have fallen out of date. In the dialog used for editing bookmarks (Communicator, Bookmarks, Edit Bookmarks), choose View, Update Bookmarks.

HOUR 7

Playing Online Video, Music, and Broadcasts

Your PC is not really your TV yet. But it's getting there. Already, you can watch live or recorded video through the Internet, and listen to live radio broadcasts and CD-quality recorded music, too.

Your ability to do that depends upon your browser. Good, up-to-date browsers come pre-equipped to play most of the multimedia content on the Web (sometimes with a little help from programs built in to the Windows or Mac operating systems). Good browsers are also *extensible*; that is, they can be refitted to deal with new file types and Internet services as they come along. New stuff always does come along, all because petulant teenage geniuses keep inventing new multimedia formats (like CD-quality music files) and putting 'em online.

Taking advantage of today's hottest multimedia—and tomorrow's—requires an understanding of the accessory programs—often called *plug-ins*, *players*, or *helper programs*—that endow your browser with new powers. In this hour, you discover not only how to fit your browser to play the coolest online multimedia, but also how to make your browser play anything even newer and cooler that may come along.

At the end of the hour, you'll be able to answer the following questions:

- How does the Web teach my browser new tricks?
- What are *plug-ins*, *players,* and *helper programs* and how do I use them to help my browser do new things?
- How do I play audio and video files I've downloaded from the Internet?
- How do I watch live video and hear live radio broadcasts on the Internet?
- How do I use new audio/video tools in Internet Explorer 5?
- How can I get CD-quality music from the Internet and listen to it offline, anytime?

You'll hear a lot about "downloading" files in this hour. If you're not already familiar with downloading files, fear not: You'll learn all about it in Hour 11, "Finding Programs and Files."

In the meantime, you may find that you can figure it out on your own. Simply put, to download a file, you click a link (you already know how to do that!), then do whatever your browser tells you to do.

Understanding Plug-Ins, ActiveX, and Java

Up-to-date versions of Internet Explorer and Netscape Navigator come pre-equipped to play most (but not all) of the stuff you'll encounter online. So the most important step in preparing to play multimedia is making sure you have the latest version of your browser.

When a browser has the built-in ability to play a particular kind of file, the browser is said to include *native* support for that file type.

Anything the browser can do without help from another program is native; any capability in which the browser must call on another program (such as those that follow) is *non-native*.

As part of being extensible, Netscape Navigator and Internet Explorer can, in effect, be reprogrammed through the Web to acquire new capabilities. This happens chiefly through four types of program files:

- **Plug-ins:** A plug-in is a program that implants itself in the browser to add a new capability. Usually, after you install a plug-in, that new capability appears to be a native, built-in part of the browser, as if it had always been there.

- **Helper programs:** A helper program is a separate program that the browser opens automatically to deal with a particular type of file. For example, when you play a video file from within Internet Explorer 5 in Windows, IE5 typically opens up the Windows Media Player—a separate program—to show you the file.

In practice, there's often not a whole lot of difference between a helper and a plug-in. In fact, the terms are often used interchangeably (and therefore incorrectly).

The main difference is that a plug-in is generally more tightly integrated with the browser, and usually can't play if the browser is closed. A true helper is self-contained—it can be opened as needed by the browser, but can also be used when the browser is closed.

- **Applets and scripts** (Java, JavaScript)**:** Both Big Two browsers can run program code delivered to them from servers—in effect, little programs that run once and then go away. This code—sometimes described as a script (when in JavaScript) or an applet (Java)—is used increasingly to enable advanced multimedia and other cool, interactive stuff on Web pages.

- **ActiveX controls:** An ActiveX-control is a file of program code that teaches the browser how to do new things.

In general, you don't have to do anything special to take advantage of scripts, applets, or ActiveX; they're delivered to the browser automatically by Web sites. You just have to make sure that you use the most up-to-date version of Internet Explorer or Netscape Navigator, and you'll be all set.

Internet Explorer has built-in support for ActiveX controls. Netscape Navigator requires an ActiveX plug-in to handle ActiveX. You can get the ActiveX plug-in for Netscape Navigator from a company called NCompass Labs at

www.ncompasslabs.com

7

Most other capabilities are delivered today through plug-ins (or plug-in–like helpers). Although plug-ins are occasionally delivered automatically, more often than not you must deliberately download and install a particular plug-in to enjoy whatever it does.

Finding Plug-Ins and Helpers

Usually, when you come across a Web site or a file that requires a particular plug-in or other program, it's accompanied by a link for downloading the plug-in.

In fact, when you first enter the site, a message may appear on your screen, informing you that a particular program is required and giving you a link for downloading it. On some sites requiring a specific program you do not have, your browser may show you a message telling you about the program. Often, that message includes a button you can click to get the program right away (see Figure 7.1).

FIGURE 7.1

Sometimes, when you enter a site that requires a particular plug-in or other program, you'll see a message that provides a handy way to go get the program you need.

Occasionally, though, the site doesn't help you get the right program, and you have to go hunting for it.

Fortunately, several excellent indexes are devoted to these programs. The logical first stop is Netscape, where a full directory of plug-ins is maintained, along with links to the latest, coolest ones to come out (see Figure 7.2). You can reach Netscape's Plug-Ins index at

```
home.netscape.com/plugins/
```

The simplest way to find out what file types your computer is already equipped to play is to simply try files as you find them. If, when attempting to play a particular file type, you see a message telling you that your computer or browser doesn't know what to do with that file, you need to find and install a player program for that file type.

Again, the most sensible way to ensure that your computer is equipped for most file types is to use the latest operating system and browser. Failing that, you can use the techniques described in Hour 11 to find and install the programs for the file types you want to play.

FIGURE 7.2

Netscape offers a terrific directory of plug-ins.

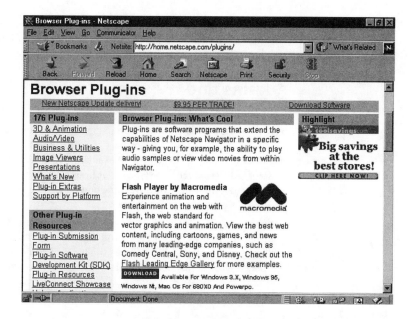

Installing and Using Plug-Ins and Helpers

Because these programs can come from any software publisher, no single method exists for installing them. Typically, though, you have to run some sort of installation program, and then specify the directory in which your Web browser is installed.

So when you come across a link to a plug-in or helper program a site requires, carefully read any instructions you see, click the link, and follow any prompts that appear.

When you click a link to get a required program, you'll actually be *downloading* the program file—copying it from the Web server to your computer. If you're unfamiliar with downloading, don't worry—just click the link and do whatever your computer tells you to do, and you'll probably do fine.

But if you really want to learn more about downloading before you start getting programs to enhance your browser, just wait until you reach Hour 11. (That's only four hours from now. You can wait for four hours, can't you?)

After you install the program, you really needn't think about it any more. Anytime you initiate an action in your browser that requires the plug-in or other program, it springs into action automatically. For example, if you've installed a plug-in that plays a particular kind of audio file, anytime you click a link for that type of file, the plug-in kicks in to play it.

7

If you keep up with the latest release of your browser, you may not come across many occasions when you need to add anything to it, and you can deal with the rare situations one by one, as they arise.

Still, there are a few enhancements you're likely to need fairly soon. One is RealPlayer, described later in this hour. Two more are the programs for playing two types of advanced media online: Flash (which enables you to see certain kinds of animation in Web pages) and Shockwave (which enables you to use certain advanced interactive features in some Web pages). Players for both Flash and Shockwave are available for download free from Macromedia (www.macromedia.com), although sites containing Flash and Shockwave content nearly always include an easy-to-find link for downloading the necessary programs.

Internet Explorer 5 comes with a built-in Flash player, so if you have IE5 you may not need a plug-in for Flash. And, Netscape Communicator 4.6 comes with a Shockwave plug-in. However, the types of content these kinds of plug-ins play are constantly being updated, necessitating upgraded players.

Playing Audio and Video

Audio and video come in many different file types online. But all of the audio and video can be divided into two basic types:

- **Download and play:** These audio and video file types—including sounds in .WAV, .AU, .MID, and MP3 formats and video clips in .AVI, .MOV, and .MPG formats— are generally downloaded to your computer, then played. Once downloaded, these files play anytime, whether you're online or off.

- **Streaming:** *Streaming* audio and video begin to play a few moments after the audio or video data begins arriving at your computer; in other words, while you're watching or listening to a few seconds of audio or video, the next few seconds are being transmitted to your computer. Streaming is essential for live broadcasts, but is also used to give you faster gratification with some non-live audio and video.

In the next two sections, you'll learn about playing each type.

Besides the aforementioned Windows Media Player and the about-to-be-mentioned RealPlayer, another important program for playing video clips is the QuickTime player. Available both as a Netscape plug-in and as a separate helper program, it equips a computer to play video clips stored in .MOV format, of which there are many online.

This free player is not quite as critical as the two I just mentioned, though. All Macs include native support for QuickTime files (they can play them without a separate player program), and most Windows systems already have a QuickTime player installed that browsers will automatically use as a helper. (Recent versions of Windows Media Player play QuickTime, and on older systems, a QuickTime player has usually been installed at some time or other by a multimedia CD-ROM program that featured QuickTime video.) If you have a Mac, or if your PC already has a player, Internet Explorer or Netscape Navigator will probably use the existing player to play .MOV files.

If you have trouble playing .MOV video, however, get the player at `www.apple.com/quicktime/`.

Playing Downloaded Audio or Video Files

If you have a computer equipped with the latest operating system (Windows 98 on a PC or OS8 on a Mac) and an up-to-date version of Internet Explorer or Netscape Navigator, you will find that you already have everything you need to play all of the common video and audio file types (non-streaming) you can download from the Web.

When you click a link that downloads an audio or video file, a dialog generally appears (see Figure 7.3), asking whether you want to save the file on disk or open it as soon as it finishes downloading.

FIGURE 7.3

When downloading a media file, you can choose to save it (for later play) or to open it (play it as soon as it finishes downloading).

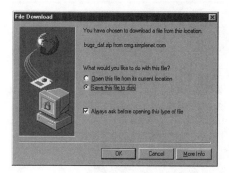

- Choose Save This File to Disk, so you can play it later (online or offline). A regular save dialog opens, just as it does when you download any file. On that dialog, you choose a location where the file will be stored. After downloading, you can play the file at any time by going to the folder or directory you chose to store the file in, and double-clicking the file's icon.

- Choose Open This File from Its Current Location to play the file as soon as it finishes downloading, so you can watch it right away and you don't have to fiddle with choosing where the file will be stored.

7

If you choose to open the file (instead of saving it), does that mean you can't play it again later, offline? Well, that depends on the type of system you have, but usually you can play the file later, offline—all you have to do is find its icon on your computer, and double-click the icon.

The icon will appear in whatever directory or folder is designated on your system as the "temporary" location for storing files from the Internet. On most Windows systems (95, 98 and NT), that folder is C:/Windows/Temp.

Note that this applies only to downloadable file types, like .AVI or .MOV. Streaming audio and video (described next) must be played online.

When you play a file (whether online or off), your computer automatically uses whatever program it has that's registered (assigned) to play that type of file. For example, in Windows, nearly all audio and video file types play in the Windows Media Player program (see Figure 7.4).

Observe that Windows Media Player has buttons that look like the buttons on a VCR or tape recorder. You use these buttons the same way you would on those devices: The Play button plays the file, Stop stops play, Fast-Forward skips ahead, and so on.

FIGURE 7.4

Programs that play audio and video files typically show buttons that mimic the functions of similar buttons on a VCR or tape recorder (Play, Stop, etc.).

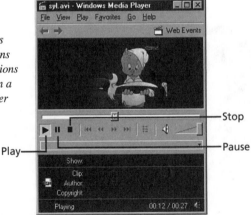

Early shipments of Windows 98 did not include the latest version of the Windows Media Player. On top of that, the Media Player is updated and improved from time to time.

The best way to ensure that you always have the latest player is to use Windows 98's Update feature. Just click the Start button and then choose Windows Update; Windows 98 contacts Microsoft through your Internet connection to see whether there are any updates available for your version (including Media Player upgrades and other enhancements).

If updates are available, you will be presented with the option to easily download and install them (free), right then and there.

Playing Streaming Audio/Video Broadcasts

Streaming audio and video is the fastest-growing type of multimedia content on the Internet. It enables you not only to enjoy various multimedia programs designed for delivery through the Internet, but also to experience broadcast TV and radio programs from all over the world—programs you could not otherwise see or hear without first jumping on a plane to the places that these programs are actually broadcast to.

NEW TERM **Streaming audio or video.** Audio or video (or both together) that begins to play on your computer before it has been completely downloaded. The main use of streaming audio and video is to present live Web broadcasts of audio or video content, or to reduce your wait when playing a very large audio or video file.

Windows Media Player plays most popular streaming audio and video types currently in use, so if you have Windows 98, you may not need another program for streaming audio/video.

But if you have another type of system, you'll need a player program to play streaming audio and video. And even if you do have Windows Media Player, it never hurts to pick up another streaming audio/video player (as long as it's free). In either case, the best choice is RealPlayer, at www.real.com.

RealPlayer enables you to play streaming video and audio feeds, from television and radio broadcasts to news updates to live music. The RealPlayer home page (see Figure 7.5) also provides links to fun places where you can try out RealPlayer.

7

FIGURE 7.5

Download RealPlayer to play streaming audio and video from the Web.

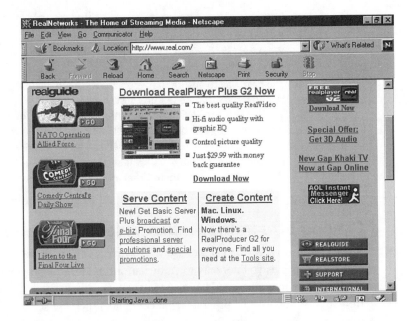

Once you download a non-streaming multimedia file type—such as an AVI video clip—that file is stored on your computer, and you can play it anytime you want to (even offline), until you choose to delete the file.

Streaming audio and video, on the other hand, just pass through your computer. You can only play streaming audio and video while online.

Once you have a streaming audio/video player properly installed, it opens automatically anytime you click a link in a Web page that opens one of the streaming audio or video file types the player is built for (see Figure 7.6). Like regular audio/video play programs, streaming audio/video players feature the familiar VCR buttons (Play, Fast Forward, and so on) for controlling playback.

When you go to download RealPlayer, you'll be offered two versions: A free one, and an enhanced version that costs a few bucks. Up to you. The free version usually does everything you need; the enhanced version does that and more, and doesn't cost much.

Pause

Play | Stop

FIGURE 7.6

Like Windows Media Player, RealPlayer plays streaming audio/video.

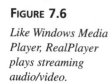

Taking Advantage of Special Audio/Video Toolbars in Internet Explorer 5

Internet Explorer 5 has a new toolbar—a Radio toolbar, which puts buttons for playing radio broadcasts and controlling the volume within easy reach, in the toolbar area (see Figure 7.7). Note that broadcasts you open and control through the toolbar are ones you could also play from RealPlayer in Netscape or IE5—it doesn't give you access to anything special, but rather makes accessing the regular stuff easier.

To open or close IE5's Radio toolbar, choose View, Toolbars, Radio.

The new toolbar also features a Radio Stations button that opens a menu of favorite stations; you create the menu by going to your favorite stations, clicking the Radio Stations button and choosing Add Station to Favorites. At the bottom of the Radio Stations menu, there's a link to the Radio Station Guide (also shown in Figure 7.7), a Microsoft Web page offering easy access to popular Web broadcast stations.

In another handy IE5-only enhancement, the current free version of RealPlayer—RealPlayer G2—adds to IE4 the RealGuide Explorer bar, a frame at the bottom of the IE5 window that keeps the RealGuide—a Web page of links to popular streaming sites—in view at all times.

To use the RealGuide Explorer bar, install RealPlayer, close IE5, then open IE5 and choose View, Explorer Bar, RealGuide.

7

FIGURE 7.7

IE5's new Radio toolbar can make accessing and controlling live Web radio broadcasts more convenient.

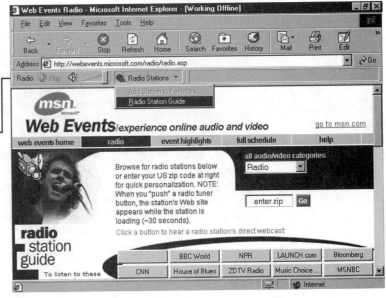

Radio toolbar⎯

Where Can I Get Streaming Audio/Video?

You'll come across it all over the Web, in sites devoted to other subjects. But here are a few good starting points for getting to some of the good stuff:

- RealGuide (`www.realguide.com`)—One-stop access to lots of great sites with streaming content
- Film.com (`www.film.com`; see Figure 7.8)—Film clips and movie trailers
- Broadcast.com (`www.broadcast.com`)—One-stop shopping for live audio/video broadcasts
- Cspan (`www.cspan.com`)—Live Congressional action!
- Emusic (`www.emusic.com`)—Live (and not) streaming music programming

Downloading and Playing CD-Quality Music (MP3 Files)

Although most audio and video you can get online is pretty small and scratchy, one file format online supplies top-quality sound: MP3. MP3 files—which have the filename extension .MP3—are downloadable files containing CD-quality music or other high-quality audio.

FIGURE 7.8

Film.com offers streaming film clips.

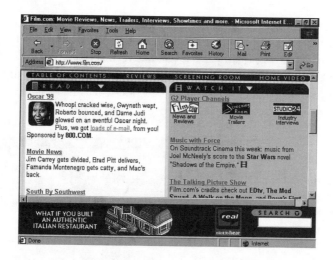

There are lots of sites with MP3 files and players. But the best place to start with MP3 is (you guessed it):

www.mp3.com

Getting MP3 Files

Downloading MP3 files is like downloading any other type of file; you typically click a link in a Web page, then wait for the file to download to your computer. Once the file is on your computer, you can play it anytime, even offline. A typical MP3 file containing one pop song is between 3 MB and 4 MB; over a 56K connection, it typically takes no more than about 15 minutes to get the file.

Many MP3 files are stored on a kind of Internet server called an *FTP server*. Even if you find these files through the Web (and you probably will), you may find that downloading them is easier if you do so through a program called an FTP client, not your browser. To learn more about FTP, see Hour 19, "Tools for the Serious User: FTP and Telnet."

7

Of course, the trick with MP3 files isn't downloading them—it's finding the exact song you want to hear from among the thousands available online. To help with that, there are MP3 search pages, which you use just like regular search pages (see Part III, "Finding What You're Looking For"), but which are specifically designed to find MP3 files online when you supply all or part of the song's title or the artist's name. Check out `mp3.lycos.com` (see Figure 7.9).

FIGURE 7.9

There are MP3 search engines that help you find exactly the song you want to hear.

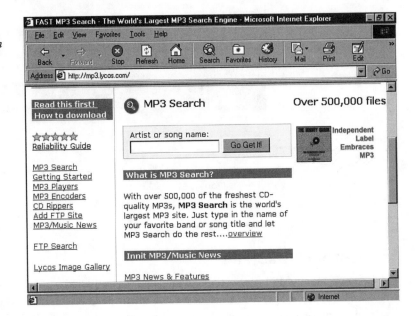

Playing MP3 Files

If you use Windows and have a recent version of Windows Media Player, you'll find that it plays MP3 files you've downloaded from the Web. Otherwise, you'll need to pick up an MP3 player to hear MP3 files. Good shareware and freeware players are available all over the Web; here are a few sites to check out for good players:

- Sonique (see Figure 7.10), at `www.sonique.com`
- Win Amp, at `www.winamp.com`
- Mac Amp (for Mac), at `www.macamp.com`

Most MP3 players not only play MP3 files, but also serve as all-purpose sound players, playing other sound file formats and also audio CDs in your CD-ROM drive.

FIGURE 7.10

Sonique is one of many great freeware and shareware MP3 players available online.

Besides playing them on your computer, you can also play MP3 files offline, *off-computer*, on portable devices (several are available). For example, Rio (from Diamond Multimedia, www.diamondmm.com) is a small, battery-operated player that looks sort of like a small portable radio (see Figure 7.11) and holds up to an hour of MP3 songs you copy onto it from your computer through a supplied cable.

The music industry's frustration with MP3 (see the Q&A at the end of this hour) spiked when Rio was announced. Obviously, the ability to, in effect, build your own little program of MP3 files in a Rio and take it with you may undercut CD sales.

At this writing, the Record Industry Association of America has sued to stop Rio, so far unsuccessfully. But by the time you read this, there may or may not be a Rio, or something else like it.

7

FIGURE 7.11

Rio lets you take MP3 files with you, to play anywhere, anytime, without your computer.

Summary

If you have the latest version of Netscape Navigator or Internet Explorer, your browser comes equipped to do so much that you'll rarely come across a situation in which it needs enhancement. Still, no matter how fast developers enhance their browsers, the new file types and programs stay one step ahead. Knowing how to deal with plug-ins and helper programs ensures that you don't get left behind when something new and wonderful hits the Web.

Q&A

Q **Should I go out and get as many plug-ins as I can find, so I'm ready for anything?**

A Nah. For the most part, outside of streaming audio/video and Shockwave, plug-ins are rarely necessary. Smart Web developers want to reach as many people as possible, and they know that forcing people to get a plug-in may scare some folks off. Also, plug-ins are known to drag your browser's performance; there's no sense bogging down your browser (and filling up your hard disk) with plug-ins you may not use. Besides, not all plug-ins are free.

When you come across something you really want to see or do, and it requires a plug-in, make your move. Otherwise, don't worry about it.

Q **I read in the paper something about MP3 and piracy. Am I breaking the law when I listen to an MP3 file?**

A Yes and no… (Why do you ask these difficult questions? What do you *want* from me? I just write computer books. That alone should tell you how little I know about ethics.)

Early in the MP3 boom, a large number of copyrighted songs began circulating the Net in MP3 files. The music publishers—rightly feeling that they were losing a royalty on all these free files—caught wise and started to crack down on sites that distribute these files. But many MP3 files are still available online, and new ones are put online every day in spite of the record companies' efforts. When you download one of these "bootleg" MP3 files, you're aiding and abetting a violation of copyright law.

The legal issues are still being worked out, so don't hold me to this, but it appears a model is evolving wherein record companies would permit (even encourage) the distribution of MP3 files of a very few, select songs from a CD as samples, with the hope that these would encourage listeners to buy the whole CD. This is especially the case, obviously, with groups that aren't well known and want people to listen to their songs.

To support this concept (and keep the sharks at bay), a growing number of MP3 sites are featuring links to online CD stores, such as CDNow (www.CDnow.com) and CD Universe (www.cduniverse.com), so visitors can jump straight from the site where they heard the song to a place where they can buy the CD.

7

HOUR 8

Protecting Your Privacy (and Other Security Stuff)

You may hear a lot on the news about what a dangerous place the Internet can be. Since you're reading this, you're brave enough to go online anyhow, even if you're a little concerned. (I like that about you.)

Although there are a few online pitfalls to watch out for, most of the stuff you hear about danger online is hype, and the few real risks are easily avoidable.

In this hour, you learn the basics of keeping your computer out of trouble on the Web. At the end of the hour, you'll be able to answer the following questions:

- How do I fill in online *forms*, and why must I be careful when doing so?

- What are *certificates*, and how do I use 'em?

- How does my browser protect my computer's security online, and how can I customize my security settings?

- What are *cookies*, and how can I control 'em?

In addition to the security tips you'll pick up in this hour, you'll learn other ways to protect yourself in hours to come:

- In Hour 11, "Finding Programs and Files", you'll learn about protecting yourself from computer viruses in files you download from the Web.

- In Hour 16, "Emailing Through the Web, Stopping Junk Mail, and Other Tips," you'll learn about protecting yourself from viruses in email messages you receive.

- In Hour 18, "Chatting Live!," you'll learn about protecting your anonymity in a chat room.

- In Hour 21, "Enjoying Safe Family Fun and Games," you'll learn how to self-censor the Web to prevent the appearance of material you deem unsuitable for your kids or yourself.

Smart Surfing

There's one important browsing technique I haven't shared with you yet; it's filling in online *forms* (see Figure 8.1). I had a reason to stall: Forms are the one part of Web browsing where you really need to be careful about your privacy.

 Form. A *form* is an area in a Web page where you can supply information that will be sent back to the Web server.

You'll practice filling in a form later in this section, after I've explained the security issues you must consider before using a form. But for now, I'll tell you that filling in an online form is pretty much like filling in any form in Windows or on a Mac. You'll see many of the same methods used for making selections or typing entries, such as:

- **Text boxes.** An empty box where you can type something. You just click on the box and type.

- **Lists.** A list of choices, in which you click an item to select it. Some lists work like Windows pull-down lists; you have to click an arrow on the list box to display the choices.

FIGURE 8.1

An online form, including text boxes, radio buttons, and check boxes.

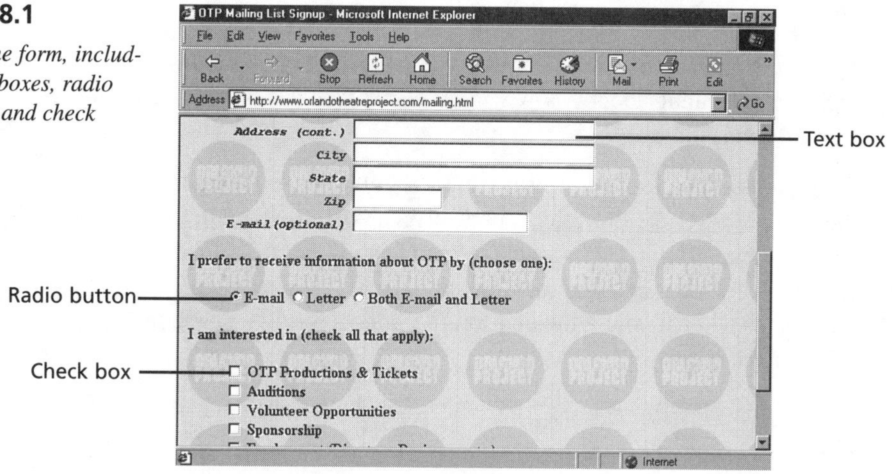

8

—— Text box

Radio button ——

Check box ——

- **Check boxes.** A small, empty square in a form is a check box. Click it to put a check mark in it, which selects or enables the item next to it. To remove the check mark, click the check box again.

- **Radio buttons** (sometimes also called option buttons). A small, empty circle in a form is a radio button. Click it to fill it in (make it a black circle), which selects or enables the item next to it. To deselect a radio button, click it again.

When you finish making all of your entries and selections in a form, you send it to the server. A button always appears near the form, usually labeled "Submit," "Send," or "Done." (I'll just call it the submit button from here on, as long as you remember that it's not always labeled that way.) When you click the submit button, your form entries are sent to the server.

Nothing you do in a form goes to the server until you click the submit button. You can fill in all or part of a form, and as long as you don't click that button, you can jump to another page or go offline, and you will not have sent a word to the server.

Before you click the submit button, you can also go back and change any entries you made in the form.

Why Are Forms Risky Sometimes?

In general, when you visit a Web site, you retrieve information from the server, but you don't *send* anything about yourself to the server. You can browse all you like, and you're basically anonymous.

When you fill in a form, however, you send to the server the information you supplied in the form. Most of the time, that's perfectly safe because the information you're sending isn't anything private. For example, as you learn in Part III, "Finding What You're Looking For," you perform most Internet searches by typing a *search term*, a word or two related to what you're looking for, in a simple form. A search term really doesn't reveal much about you.

However, some forms want more from you, including such potentially sensitive information as:

- Your name
- Your email address
- Your mailing address or telephone number
- Your credit card number
- Your Social Security number

Most often, a form collects this information when you're making a purchase. (You'll learn much more about online shopping in Hour 22, "Buying and Selling on the Net.") If you join some sort of online organization or club, you may also be prompted to supply detailed information about yourself.

And a growing number of sites prompt you to "join" the site in order to use it; to join, you must supply a little information about yourself, which the owner of the site typically uses for market research purposes or sells to other companies.

Important Safety Questions

To make the most of the Web, you can't remain totally private; sooner or later, you're probably going to fill in a form with information about yourself. But before filling in any form, ask yourself four very important questions:

- **Is the information requested by the form really necessary?** Some forms collect more information from you than is really required. Don't feel like you must fill in every blank. Include only as much information as you're comfortable sharing. If you find that the form requires you to fill in blanks you don't want to, consider whether the benefits of the form are worth the risks.

> On many online forms, each required field is marked with an asterisk (*), meaning you can skip the rest. My advice? Never fill in any unrequired field (why reveal more than you have to?), and again, if there's anything in the *required* fields that you'd rather not reveal, skip the form altogether. Nothing offered through that form is worth exposing yourself in any way you're not fully comfortable with.

8

- **Do I trust the owners of this site with the information I'm providing?** Is the site operated by a known company, one you trust, or is it a company you've never heard of? Just as you would over the telephone, think twice about who you're dealing with before revealing anything about yourself. Of course, the more sensitive the information you're sending, the more you must trust the site. You can be much more casual about sharing your email address than about revealing your credit card number.

- **Is the site *secure*?** Sending information to a secure site does nothing to protect you if the site owner is unscrupulous. But it does protect you against someone other than the site owner seeing the information you send.

NEW TERM **Secure site.** Some Web sites that collect information through forms (especially sites that sell online) employ a security system in which information you send is scrambled when travelling between you and the server. The scrambling prevents anyone other than you and the server owner from seeing the information.

Sites that do not use a security system are called **unsecure sites**.

- **What is the site's privacy policy?** Many sites provide a link that leads to a page outlining the site's *privacy policy*—the particular set of rules that site promises to follow regarding what it can and cannot do with information you enter on forms there (see Figure 8.2). Checking out the privacy policy may help you decide whether to send information—just remember that there's really no way to know whether a site honestly follows the policy it promises.

Identifying Secure Sites

To use the security systems built in to secure sites, your browser must be compatible with the security systems used; both Internet Explorer and Netscape Navigator are compatible with the systems used by secure sites today.

FIGURE 8.2

Look for a site's "pri-vacy policy" to learn what the site promises to do (and not to do) with information you send to it.

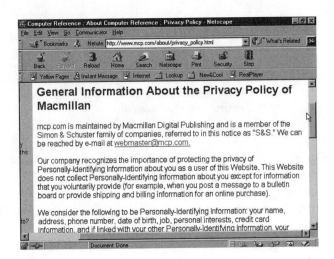

When you send information to an unsecure site, it's possible (although difficult) for a criminal to "harvest" that information on its way. For example, if you send your name and credit card info, a crook could intercept that information en route between you and the server, and later use it to make a purchase or perpetrate some other kind of fraud.

Using a security-compatible browser to send information to a secure Web site makes harvesting impossible; the information you send will be seen only by the owner of the site to which you send it. Of course, if the site owner is a crook, you still have a problem— he or she can use your information, so you still need to be careful. But secure sites do protect you from intrusion by a third party.

Most browsers show you whether a page you're viewing is on a secure site or not:

- Internet Explorer versions 4 and higher display a locked yellow padlock at the bottom of the window (near the center) when you're communicating with a secure site. The lock does not appear at all when you're on an unsecure site.
- In Netscape Navigator (versions 4 and higher), a tiny padlock appears in the lower-left corner of the browser window (see Figure 8.3). When the padlock appears to be unlocked, as in the figure, you are not connected to a secure site. When the padlock is locked and yellow, the site is secure.

In security dialogs and warnings in Netscape Navigator, secure sites are often described as *encrypted sites*. The meaning is the same.

FIGURE 8.3

Netscape Navigator shows an unlocked padlock when the page you're viewing is not secure.

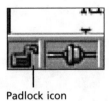

Padlock icon

8

In addition to little locks and keys, most browsers also have a failsafe: They display a warning message (see Figure 8.4) to you before you send information to an unsecure site, so you have a chance to cancel (if you want) before actually sending anything. When you are about to exit a secure site, another warning appears to tell you that, so you can resume exercising the caution you apply when you're on unsecure sites.

Depending upon how they're configured, Internet Explorer and Netscape Navigator display such a warning before you send anything to any site, secure *or* unsecure. The dialog always informs you whether you're sending to a secure or unsecure site, and gives you a chance to cancel. You can click Yes to go ahead and send the information, or No to abort the transmission.

FIGURE 8.4

Most browsers warn you before sending any information to an unsecure site, giving you a chance to cancel.

To Do: Filling In a Form

Now that you know what to watch out for, you can safely complete an online form. Try filling in this form to order a clothing catalog from Lands' End. (I'm not hawking for Lands' End here; it's just that I needed an all-purpose example, and everybody wears clothes.)

You do not actually have to order the catalog—this is just for practice. In the steps that follow, I'll show you how to cancel the form after filling it in, so you don't order a thing.

▼

▼ 1. Go to the Lands' End page at `www.landsend.com`, and click the link labeled Catalog Requests (Figure 8.5).

FIGURE 8.5

Step 1: Click on the *Catalog Requests link.*

Catalog Requests link ——

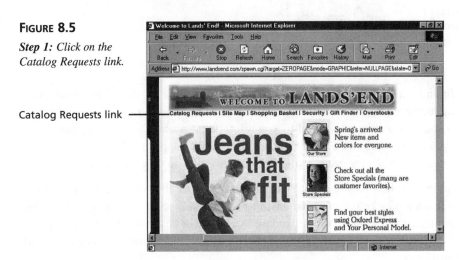

2. Scroll down to where you see a row of catalog pictures, and choose one or more catalogs by clicking the check boxes above the ones you want (Figure 8.6).

FIGURE 8.6

Step 2: Choose a catalog or two by checking boxes.

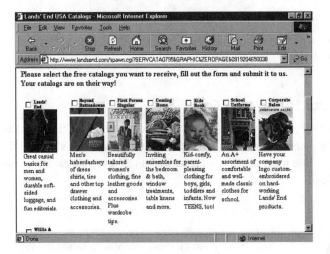

▼ 3. Scroll farther down, to the form for filling in your name and address (Figure 8.7).

FIGURE 8.7

Step 3: Scroll down to the form.

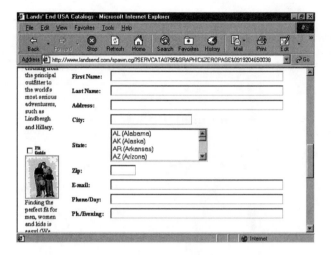

4. Point to the text box next to First Name, click, and type your first name there. Click in the text box next to Last Name, and type your last name (Figure 8.8).

> In many online forms, you can jump from one box in the form to the next by pressing your Tab key, which makes filling in a long form easier.
>
> Depending on the form itself, your computer system, and other factors, you may find that you have to point to each part of the form and click before you can use that part. Try it both ways, and see which one works for you.

FIGURE 8.8

Step 4: Type in your first and last name.

5. Complete the form, then scroll down to where you see the Submit button (Figure 8.9).

6. If you *don't want* the catalogs, click Back, or jump to any other page. You have not ordered anything, and Lands' End knows nothing about you they didn't already know before you arrived at their Web page.

▼   If you *do* want the catalogs, click the Submit button.

▼

FIGURE 8.9

Step 5: Complete the form to the end.

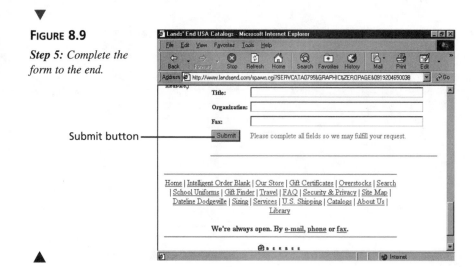

Submit button ————

▲

If you click the Submit button, your browser may warn you that you're sending over an unsecure site. The forms at Lands' End that collect credit card numbers for purchases are secure, but catalog ordering is not. That's pretty much the rule among online shops.

Knowing Who You're Dealing With: *Certificates*

If you use Netscape Navigator or Internet Explorer, now and then you'll come across a certificate on the Web (see Figure 8.10). When you first see one, it seems like a big deal, but it's not. You won't see certificates often, and when you do, you can deal with them in just a click or two.

NEW TERM **Certificate.** A *certificate* is a dialog that appears when you enter some Web sites to certify the identity of the site and its owner. They provide assurance that you're actually communicating with the company you think you're communicating with. They appear most often when a site is sending some sort of program code, such as Java or a plug-in (see Hour 7, "Playing Online Video, Music, and Broadcasts"), to your browser; the certificate identifies the company so you can decide whether you trust that company enough to let it run a program in your browser.

Because a certificate positively identifies the company you're communicating with, you can better decide whether to accept program code, send your credit card or other info, or do anything else that might expose you to risk.

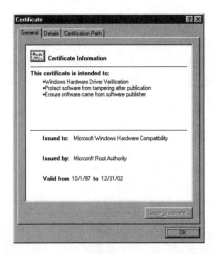

FIGURE 8.10

A certificate, which identifies the site you're connected to.

8

When a certificate appears, your browser usually presents you with a few options for dealing with it: You can accept the certificate (to interact with the site) or reject it. The exact options differ depending on the certificate.

Sometimes, when dealing with the certificate, you'll be prompted to choose whether to accept Java or other *script* code from the site. If you don't trust the site, that gives you the option to reject the certificate to prevent it from sending program code to your computer.

Protecting Yourself with Browser Security

Most browsers let you customize the way they handle security. You can often choose the circumstances under which a browser displays security warnings, choose which sites can run Java or other program code on your computer, and more.

I want to put you in the driver's seat, to give you as much Internet education as is possible in 400 or so pages, so that's why I'm describing the ways you can customize your browser's security settings.

I *strongly* caution you, however, to leave your security settings alone until and unless you begin to feel that your browser is applying security that's too lenient or too strict for your particular needs.

The default security settings built in to most browsers strike just the right balance between safety and convenience. So unless you have reason to think they're broke, don't fix 'em.

Customizing Security in Netscape Navigator

To open Netscape Navigator's security dialog (see Figure 8.11), click the Security button on the toolbar or choose Communicator, Tools, Security Info from the menu bar. When the dialog opens, it shows any security information pertinent to the site you're currently viewing, such as whether the site is secure and any certificates in force.

On the left side of the dialog, a list of items for which you can customize security appears. In the list, click Navigator.

Use the check boxes and lists in the Navigator security dialog to choose when warnings should appear. (For maximum security, make sure all check boxes on this dialog are checked.) To learn more about what each setting means, click the dialog's Help button.

FIGURE 8.11

Customizing security settings in Netscape Navigator.

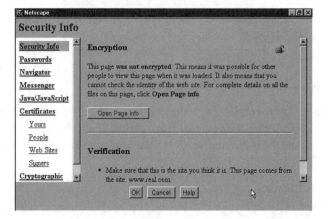

 To control whether servers can run Java or JavaScript code on your computer, open Navigator's preferences dialog (Edit, Preferences) and click Advanced in the list on the left side of the dialog. A dialog opens on which you can check or uncheck check boxes to enable or disable Java and JavaScript.

Increasingly, sites assume that your browser can run Java and/or JavaScript, and are not built to deliver their information effectively to any browser that can't. So in general, it's best to leave these items enabled. However, if you frequently visit particular sites with poor Java or JavaScript programming on them (resulting in a flood of annoying error messages to you) or if a particular activity requires that you shut off Java or JavaScript processing (as some online training sites do), it's handy to know where the "off button" for Java and JavaScript is located.

Customizing Security in Internet Explorer 5

To open Internet Explorer's security settings dialog (see Figure 8.12), choose Tools, Internet Options to open the Internet Options dialog, then click the Security tab.

FIGURE 8.12

The Internet Options dialog's Security tab, where you customize security in Internet Explorer.

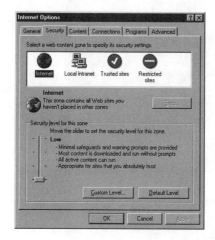

Internet Explorer's security system divides all sites into four different security *zones*:

- **Internet zone:** All Internet Web sites that you have not included in your trusted sites zone or your restricted sites zone.
- **Local intranet zone:** Includes all pages on your local intranet, if you have one.

NEW TERM **Intranet.** An *intranet* is an internal, private network, usually a company network, that looks and acts like the Internet but isn't open to the outside world. If your computer is not part of a company network, you can ignore the local intranet zone.

- **Trusted sites zone:** Includes Web sites you have selected as trusted sites, those for which you may want less strict security than others.
- **Restricted sites zone:** Sites you don't particularly trust, generally ones for which you'll want higher security than for other zones.

Using the Security tab, you can add sites to your trusted sites and restricted sites zones, and choose security settings for each of the four zones.

To Do: Add a Site to a Zone

1. Open the Security tab—choose Tools, Internet Options, Security (Figure 8.13).
2. Select the zone to which you want to add sites, then click the Sites button.

FIGURE 8.13

Step 1: Open the Security tab in Internet Options.

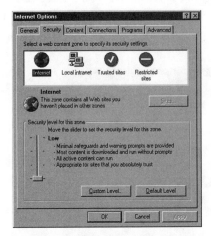

FIGURE 8.14

Step 2: Select a zone and then click Sites.

Zones

Sites button

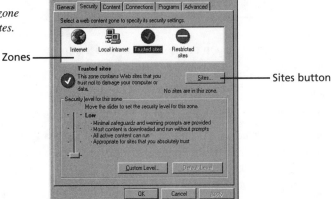

3. Type the URL of a site you want to add to the zone, then click Add to add it to the list (Figure 8.15).

4. When done adding sites to this zone, click OK to close the dialog.

In step 3 of the preceding To Do, if the check box for Require Server Verification is checked, IE5 will accept in the zone *only* sites whose URL begins with https:// (secure sites). To add sites that are not secure sites, clear this check box.

FIGURE 8.15

Step 3: Type in the URL and click Add.

Understanding Zone Security Settings

The security settings for a zone determine how aggressive the security system in Internet Explorer will be when communicating with Web sites in that zone. There are four standard security levels: Low, Medium-Low, Medium, and High. For example, you can always view pages on any site, regardless of security settings. (To completely block access to particular sites, use Internet Explorer's Content Advisor, as described in Hour 21.) But within a zone for which high security is in effect, if a server attempts to send a script or other program code that could give your computer a virus or other problem, Internet Explorer prevents the code from reaching your computer.

By default, each of the four zones has a reasonable security setting: high for Restricted Sites, medium for the Intranet and Internet zones, and low for Trusted Sites.

But if you tire of being prompted every time an Internet page sends some Java to your computer, you might want to change the security level for the Internet zone to low. Conversely, if you've experienced lots of problems with downloaded scripts, you might want to apply high security to the whole Internet zone. And if you trust your co-workers, you might want to change your Intranet zone to low security.

To Do: Choosing Security Settings for Zones

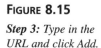

To change the security level for a zone:

1. Open the Security tab—choose Tools, Internet Options, Security (Figure 8.16).
2. Click the icon for the zone for which you want to change security (Figure 8.17).
3. Drag the slider control to each of the four levels, and read the description that appears to learn how content is restricted at that level (Figure 8.18).

FIGURE 8.16

Step 1: Open the Security tab in Internet Explorer's Internet Options.

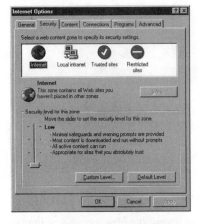

FIGURE 8.17

Step 2: Choose a zone.

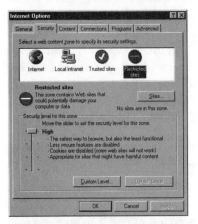

FIGURE 8.18

Step 3: Move the security level slider.

Slider ——

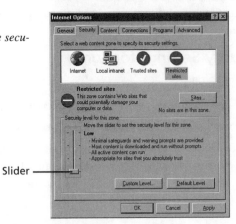

▼   4. Leave the slider positioned on the level you want to use for this zone, and click OK
       (Figure 8.19).

FIGURE 8.19

*Step 4: Leave the
slider where you want
and click OK.*

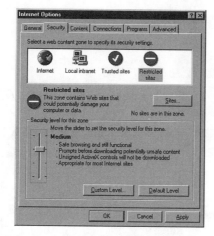

▲

I Want a Cookie! I *Don't* Want a Cookie!

Besides scripts, servers can put another thing on your computer you may not know
about: *cookies*.

NEW TERM   **Cookie.** A *cookie* is a small amount of information a server stores on your computer, for later reference. Typically, a server stores an identifying code of some
sort on your computer so that it can automatically identify you any time you visit.

Cookies are usually harmless, and often useful. For example, an online store from which
you've purchased once may put on your computer a cookie that identifies you. Anytime
you return to that site to shop, the server automatically knows who you are, and you
needn't bother filling in a form to identify yourself.

But your computer is your domain, and you get to decide what someone else can put
there. You can customize either of the Big Two browsers to accept or reject cookies.

To Do: Control Cookies in Netscape Navigator

1. Choose Edit, Preferences (Figure 8.20).

FIGURE 8.20

Step 1: Choose Edit, Preferences in Netscape Navigator.

2. In the list along the left side of the dialog, click Advanced (Figure 8.21).

FIGURE 8.21

Step 2: Click Advanced in the Preferences dialog.

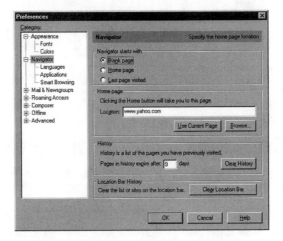

3. Choose how you want cookies handled (Figure 8.22):

- Choose Accept All Cookies to automatically accept any cookie.
- Choose Accept Only Cookies That Get Sent Back to the Originating Server to accept most cookies, but to reject any that might be readable by servers other than the one who sent you the cookies. This prevents cookies on your computer from being read by any server other than the cookie's creators.
- Choose Disable Cookies to reject all cookies.
- Check the check box next to Warn Me Before Accepting a Cookie if you want Netscape Navigator to display a dialog before accepting a cookie, and to offer you buttons for optionally accepting or rejecting the cookie.

FIGURE 8.22

Step 3: Choose how you want cookies handled.

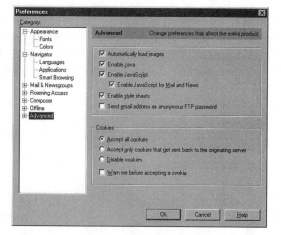

To Do: Control Cookies in Internet Explorer 5

1. Open the Internet Options dialog (choose Tools, Internet Options) and click the Security tab (Figure 8.23).

FIGURE 8.23

Steps 1 and 2: Click the Security tab in Internet Options, click Internet, and then Custom Level.

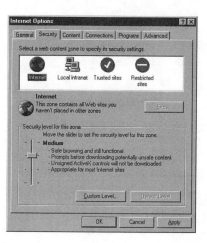

2. Click the icon for Internet zone, then click the Custom Level button (Figure 8.23).

3. Scroll to the bottom of the list in the Security Settings dialog (Figure 8.24).

4. Use the radio buttons to select the way you want cookies handled (Figure 8.25).

Internet Explorer's Security Settings dialog is a valuable but tricky place. After you gain experience, you can use it to customize the browser to a high degree. But before you have experience, making random changes here is likely to change your online life in ways you won't enjoy.

If you inadvertently change something in the dialog and don't know how to fix it, click the Reset button.

FIGURE 8.24

Step 3: Scroll to the bottom of the dialog.

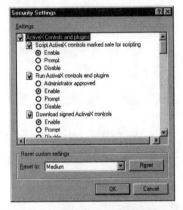

FIGURE 8.25

Step 4: Select the way you want cookies handled.

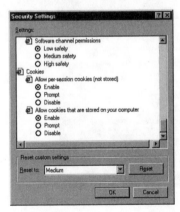

Summary

Leading browsers have become very secure. By understanding what a server might do to your computer, and by deploying your browser's security force field smartly, you'll protect yourself pretty well.

But no browser can protect you from saying too much about yourself. You are responsible for preserving your privacy. Be careful what you say in a form and to whom you send that form, and avoid saying anything at all in a form that will be sent to an unsecure site.

Q&A

Q **Is it really safe to give my email address to anyone?**

A Well, it's safer than some other kinds of information you can send, such as your real name. And there are many good reasons to reveal your email address, such as signing up for a mailing list.

Still, if your email address falls into the wrong hands, you can be flooded with annoying junk email (called *spam*), or you might get weird or annoying messages from some online stranger. So the same watchwords apply: Never tell more about yourself than you have to, and be sure who you're dealing with.

You'll learn more about email privacy in Part IV, "Communicating with Email and Newsgroups."

8

PART III

Finding What You're Looking For

Hour

HOUR 9

Getting Started with Searching

There's just too much on the Web. It's like having a TV set with a billion channels; you could click the remote until your thumb fell off and still never find the *Law & Order* reruns.

Fortunately, a number of search sites on the Web help you find exactly what you're looking for, anywhere on the Web, and even *beyond* the Web in other Internet arenas. In this hour, you'll discover what searching the Web is all about, and discover a simple but effective searching method: cruising categories. In the remaining three hours of Part III, you'll discover even more powerful, targeted search methods.

At the end of this hour, you'll be able to answer the following questions:

- What are *search sites*, and where can I find them?
- How do I use features in my browser that can make searching more convenient?

- How does Netscape Navigator's What's Related button help me find stuff?
- How can I conduct a simple search by clicking through a series of links?

What's a Search Site?

Put simply, a search site—which you may also see variously described as a search page, search tool, or search service— is a Web page where you can conduct a search of the Web. Such pages have been set up by a variety of companies, who offer you free Web searching and support the service, at least in part, through the advertising you'll see prominently displayed on most search sites. Figure 9.1 shows a popular search site, Excite.

The term *search engine* is sometimes used to describe a search site. But this term more accurately describes the program a search site uses, behind the scenes, to perform searches. When you hear someone refer casually to a "search engine," just remember that they probably mean "search site."

FIGURE 9.1

Excite, a popular search site.

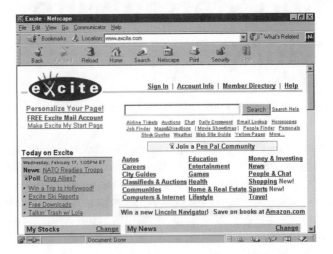

No matter which search site you use, and no matter how you use it, what you get from a search site is a page of links, each pointing to a page the search site thinks may be a match for what you're looking for. Your job when using a search site is to provide that tool with enough information about what you're searching for, so that this "hit list" contains lots of good matches for you to explore. See Figure 9.2.

FIGURE 9.2

Search sites show you list of links—a "hit list"—of Web pages and other resources that match what you told the search site you were looking for.

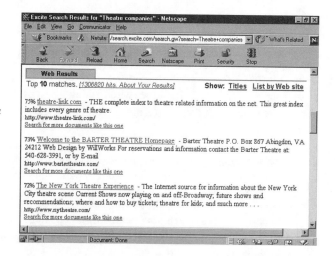

9

Can I Really Search the Whole Web?

Well, yes and no…. (Don't you *hate* that answer?)

Although using the various search sites is similar, each has its own, unique search methods. But more important, each has its own, unique set of files—a *database*—upon which all searches are based.

You see, no search site actually goes out and searches the entire Web when you ask it to. A search site searches its own index of information about the Web—its database. The more complete and accurate that database is, the more successful your searches are likely to be.

The database for a search site is created in either (or both) of two ways:

- **Manually.** Folks who've created Web pages, or who've discovered pages they want the world to know about, fill in a form on the search site's Web site to add new pages (and their descriptions) to the database.

- **Through a *crawler* (or spider, or worm).** All of these creepy-crawly names describe programs that systematically contact Web servers (at regular intervals), scan the contents of the servers, and add information about the contents of the servers to the database. (They "crawl" around the Web, like spiders—get it?) It takes the crawler a few weeks to complete each of its information-gathering tours of the Web.

Where a search site's database has been created by a crawler, the tool tends to deliver results that are more complete and up-to-date, whereas manually-built databases tend to contain more meaningful categorization and more useful descriptive information.

Also, most search sites with crawler-built databases do not offer you a way to search by browsing through categories—a valuable technique you'll pick up later in this hour. All search sites, however, support the main search method: entering a *search term*.

 NEW TERM **Search term.** A *search term* is a word or phrase you type in a text box on a search site's main page, to tell the search site the type of information you're looking for. You learn all about search terms in Hour 10, "Searching for Information."

> Because search sites search a database and not the actual Web, they will sometimes deliver results that are out of date. You may click a link that a search site delivered to you, and find that the page to which it points no longer exists. That happens when a page has been moved or deleted since the last time the search site's database was updated.
>
> When this happens, it's no big whoop. Just click Back to go back to the list of results, and try another link.

Despite differences and strengths and weaknesses among the available tools, the bottom line is this: Any of the major search sites may locate a page or pages that meet your needs, any may not. If you can't find what you want through one tool, try another. Because each tool has its own database, and each tool applies a different technical method for searching its database, no two search sites turn up exactly the same results for any given topic.

Where Are the Major Search Sites?

There are about a dozen general purpose search sites out there, and many, many more specialized search sites (more about those in upcoming hours).

Table 9.1 lists the major players. You can visit any search site by entering its URL.

TABLE 9.1 THE TOP SEARCH SITES

Tool	URL
Yahoo!	www.yahoo.com
Excite	www.excite.com
AltaVista	www.altavista.com
Lycos	www.lycos.com
Infoseek	www.infoseek.com
Snap	www.snap.com
WebCrawler	www.webcrawler.com

Note that a few of the search sites listed in Table 9.1 are also Web portals (see Hour 6, "Revisiting Places You Like"), pages that are popular as home pages because they provide easy access to searching, news, and other popular services. Two other popular portals not only offer searches, but actually let you use several different popular search sites, all from the portal page. These are

- Netcenter: `home.netscape.com`
- MSN: `home.microsoft.com`

For example, right from the MSN portal, you can submit a search term to MSN's own search engine, or to Infoseek, AltaVista, and other popular search sites (see Figure 9.3).

FIGURE 9.3

Some Web portals, such as the MSN portal shown here, provide one-stop access to multiple searches.

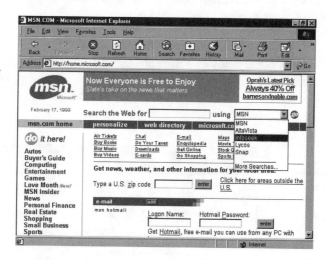

There's a confusion about search sites, created by some ISPs and browser sellers. In part to simplify their sales pitch for novices, these folks sometimes tout their products as "featuring all the best search sites," or words to that effect. That implies that a search site is a feature in a browser, or a service provided by an ISP.

That claim is, oh, what's the word... hooey. A search site is a Web page, and anyone with a browser can use it. Browsers sometimes include features that can make accessing search sites easier, but no browser has a real built-in search engine, and no ISP can claim ownership of any of the important search sites.

To Do: Check Out the Search Sites

Before beginning to use search sites, take a peek at a few. While visiting these pages, watch for helpful links that point to

- Instructions for using the search site.
- A text box near the top of the page, which is where you'd type a search term (see Hour 10).
- Links to categories you can browse.
- Reviews and ratings of recommended pages.
- "Cool Sites"—a regularly updated, random list of links to especially fun or useful pages you may want to visit just for kicks.
- Other search engines.

1. Go to Yahoo! at www.yahoo.com, and observe that Yahoo! features a search term box at the top, plus a menu of categories below, for searching by category (Figure 9.4). Note also the graphical buttons at the top of the page, for displaying Cool Sites and such.

FIGURE 9.4

Step 1: Go to Yahoo! and look around.

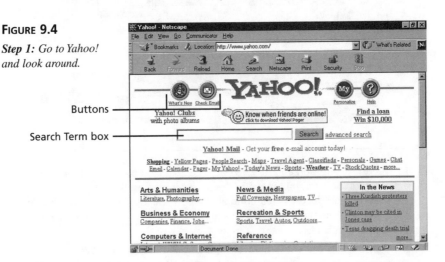

2. Jump to AltaVista at www.altavista.com. What familiar search site features do you see? (Figure 9.5.)

3. Explore any of the other tools listed in Table 9.1 (Figure 9.6).

FIGURE 9.5

Step 2: Check out AltaVista.

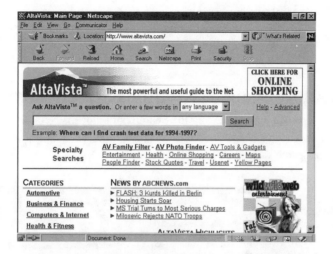

9

FIGURE 9.6

Step 3: Explore other sites, like snap.com.

Getting to Know Your Browser's Searching Features

Most major browsers have a Search button on their toolbars, or a Search item somewhere within their menus. To use your browser's search features productively, you need to understand what they do.

In general, a Search button (or menu item) is preconfigured to take you to a particular search site; the button doesn't really help you search, it just makes opening a search site convenient.

If your browser has a search button, that doesn't mean you're required to use it. You can enter a URL to go straight to any search tool, no matter what browser you use.

About Netscape Navigator's Search Button

In Netscape Navigator, clicking the Search button opens Netscape's all-in-one Net Search page (see Figure 9.7). From this page, you can submit a search term to any of five different search sites. (See Hour 10 to learn more.)

FIGURE 9.7

Netscape Navigator's Search button opens this page, which offers fast access to five different search sites.

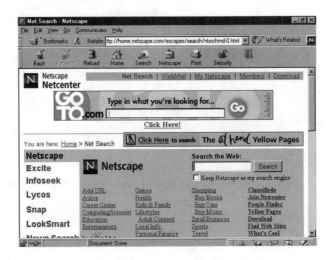

Finding More Through Netscape Navigator's What's Related Button

In version 4.5, Netscape Navigator introduced a new search capability never before seen in a browser: a What's Related button. While viewing any Web site, you can click the What's Related button to display a short list of links you can click to go to other sites that may contain similar information. One item on that list is labeled Detailed List; click that one to see a longer list of related pages. (See Figure 9.8.)

It's a nifty idea, and using it can't hurt you, so give it a try. But I'd advise you not to rely upon the What's Related button as a substitute for real Internet searching.

FIGURE 9.8

Netscape Navigator's What's Related button shows a list of links to pages that may have content that's related to the content on the page you were viewing when you clicked the button.

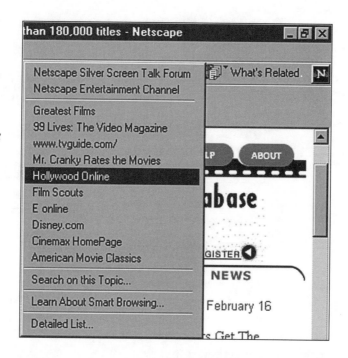

The button doesn't really go out and search for other, related pages (although it may give you a link to a hit list or category listing in another tool, such as Yahoo!). All it really does is figure out which sites lots of folks went to immediately after viewing the site you're viewing. Those sites may really be related, but they may not be.

Maybe more importantly, it's been suggested that What's Related encourages a herd mentality, making it too easy for people to follow one another's footsteps instead of blazing their own trails. But it's new, so who knows? Do what you want to do.

About Internet Explorer 5's Search Button and Explorer Bar

Clicking the Search button on Internet Explorer's toolbar opens the Explorer bar, a pane in the left side of the browser window (see Figure 9.9). The Explorer bar is also used in Internet Explorer for displaying your Favorites (when you click the Favorites button on the toolbar) and History list.

In the Explorer bar, a search term box appears, along with radio buttons for choosing whether to use a Web-searching tool (see Hour 10) or a people-searching tool (see Hour 12, "Finding People").

FIGURE 9.9

Internet Explorer 5's Search button opens a search box in the Explorer bar.

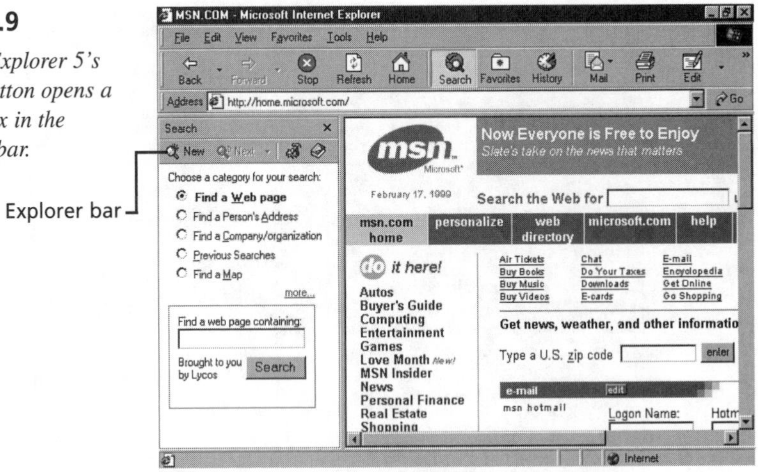

Explorer bar

Whichever tool you choose, anything you do with that tool—whether clicking through categories or using a search term—happens in the Explorer bar. When you finally open a page from your search, that page appears in the main window, to the right of the Explorer bar. You can continue searching in the Explorer bar, or click the X button in the Explorer bar's upper-right corner to close it.

> The Explorer bar can be a handy feature, but it can also be a pretty cramped place to work with searches. Always remember that you're not required to use the Search button; you can enter a search site's URL in Internet Explorer to work in that tool, full-screen.

Simple Searching by Clicking Categories

These days, all of the major search sites accept search terms. But a few also supply a directory of categories, an index of sorts, that you can browse to locate links to pages related to a particular topic. Tools that feature such directories include Yahoo!, Excite, and Infoseek.

> Directory browsing is something of a sideline for other search sites, but it's the bread and butter of Yahoo!. When you want to search in this way, Yahoo! is almost always your best starting point.

Why Use Categories Instead of a Search Term?

When you're first becoming familiar with the Web, forgoing the search engines and clicking through a directory's categories is not only an effective way to find stuff but also a great way to become more familiar with what's available on the Web. As you browse through categories, you inevitably discover detours to interesting topics and pages that you didn't set out to find. Exploring directories is an important part of learning how the Web works and what's on it.

Also, the broader your topic of interest, the more useful categories are. When you use a search term to find information related to a broad topic (cars, dogs, music, plants), the search site typically delivers to you a bewildering list containing hundreds or thousands of pages. Some of these pages will meet your needs, but many will be pages that merely mention the topic rather than being *about* the topic.

Some links a search term delivers will match the term, but not your intentions; a search on "plant" will likely turn up not only botany and houseplant pages, but others about power plants, folks named Plant, and maybe the Plantagenet family of European lore. Categories, on the other hand, help you limit the results of your search to the right ballpark.

Using a Directory

Everything in a directory is a link; to find something in a directory, you follow those links in an organized way.

You begin by clicking a broad category heading to display a list of related subcategories (see Figure 9.10). Click a subcategory heading, and you display its list of sub-subcategories.

You continue in this fashion, drilling down through the directory structure (usually through only two to five levels), until you eventually arrive at a targeted list of links to pages related to a particular topic. You can explore those page links one by one, and after finishing with each, use your Back button to return to the search site's list and try another link.

FIGURE 9.10

A subcategory list in Yahoo!.

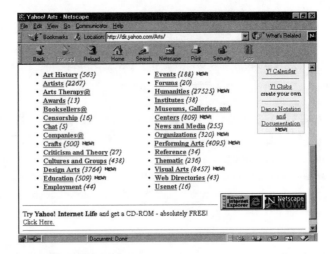

To Do: Exploring Categories

1. Go to Yahoo! at www.yahoo.com (Figure 9.11).

FIGURE 9.11

Step 1: Go to Yahoo!.

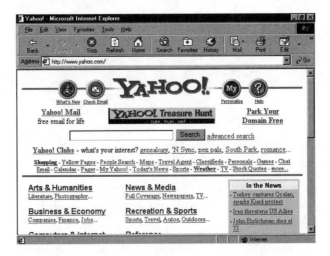

2. In the list of categories, click Entertainment (Figure 9.12).
3. In the list of subcategories that appears, click Amusement and Theme Parks (Figure 9.13).

FIGURE 9.12

Step 2: Click on Entertainment.

Categories

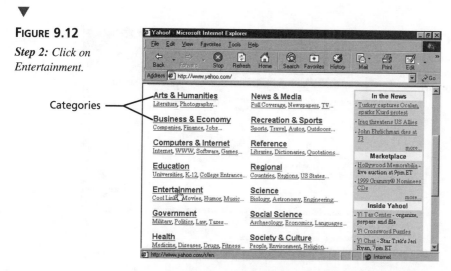

FIGURE 9.13

Step 3: Click on Amusement and Theme Parks.

Subcategories

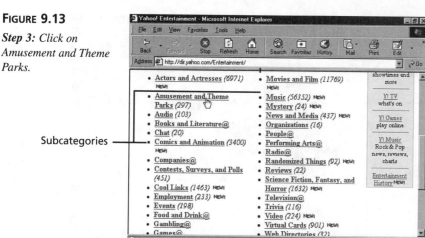

4. Scroll down to reveal links leading to pages about amusement parks. You can click one of the subcategories above to see more options, or visit one of the pages below (Figure 9.14).

5. Click Back until you return to the top Yahoo! page. Observe that you can try any path or page and then back out by as many levels as you want to so that you can try a different path (Figure 9.15).

▼

FIGURE 9.14

Step 4: Choose a sub-category or visit a site, like Adventure City.

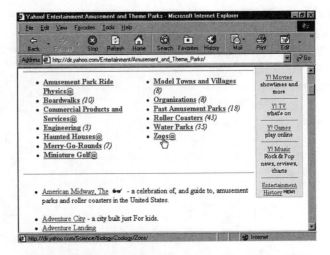

FIGURE 9.15

Step 5: Click Back until you return to the top and try a different path.

6. Explore on your own, clicking down through the directory and then back up again with Back (Figure 9.16).

▼

FIGURE 9.16

Step 6: Explore on your own.

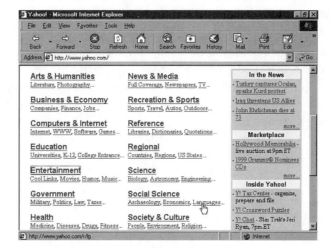

Summary

A search site is a Web page. You can get to a search site by entering its URL, or by using your browser's Search button. Virtually all search sites support searching with search terms (see Hour 10), but some also enable you to find pages by browsing through a directory.

Q&A

Q Why would I ever need more than one search site? Can't I just pick my favorite, and always use it?

A Every search site has a different database, and uses a different technical method for extracting results from that database. Although there will be overlap, you'll never see the same results from two different search sites.

Sure, if you have a search site you're comfortable with, it makes sense to try it first. But to ensure the best hope of finding exactly what you're looking for, it's important that you know how to get to several different search sites, and how to operate each one.

Portals like MSN and Netcenter can make trying the same term in multiple search sites easier, as can Internet Explorer's search sites in its Explorer bar. You learn how in Hour 10.

Q I like exploring Yahoo!'s directory, but find it tiresome after exploring one branch to Back my way back upward a few levels to try another route. Is there a shortcut?

A If you look carefully at any listing in Yahoo!, you'll notice that a complete path appears in a large heading at the top, showing the full list, left to right, of the category and subcategories under which the list you're viewing appears. You can click on the name of any subcategory in that path to jump directly back to that subcategory's listing.

HOUR 10

Searching for Information

Clicking categories, as you learned to do in Hour 9, "Getting Started with Searching," can be a very productive way to search. But often, a more powerful method is called for, one that delivers to you a custom-made list of links related to any topic you can imagine.

That's what search terms do. In this hour, you learn how to use search terms, and how to phrase them carefully to produce precisely the results you need.

At the end of the hour, you'll be able to answer the following questions:

- What's a *search term*?
- How do I use a simple search term to produce a list of *hits*, Web pages related to the term?
- How do I phrase more complex search terms, for power-searching?
- How can I conveniently use multiple search tools all from one place?
- How can I search for information just among the contents of a particular site?

Understanding Searches

Each of the search tools described in Hour 9, and just about any other you might encounter on the Web, has a text box featured prominently near the top of its main page (see Figure 10.1). That text box is where you will type your search terms. Adjacent to the box, there's always a submit button, almost always labeled "Search."

Typing a search term in a text box and then clicking the submit button to send the term to the search tool is known as *submitting a search term.* Such searches are sometimes also described as *keyword* searches, because the search term serves as a key to finding matching pages.

FIGURE 10.1

The text box you see near the top of any search tool page is where you type a search term.

Search term box

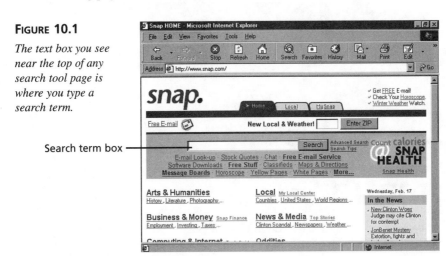

When you submit a search term, the search tool searches through its database of information about pages, locating any entries that contain the same combination of characters in your search term. Although the contents of the various search tool databases differ, the record for each page typically contains the page's URL, title, a brief description, and a group of keywords intended to describe the page's contents. If your search term matches anything in that record, the search tool considers the page a match.

After searching the whole database (which takes only a moment or two), the search tool displays a list of links to all of the pages it determined were matches: a *hit list.*

| NEW TERM | **Hit list.** A *hit list* is a list of links, produced by a search engine in response to a search term you have entered. Each link is a "hit": a page that contains a match for your search term. |

Each hit in the list is a link (see Figure 10.2). You can scroll through the hit list, reading the page titles and descriptions, to determine which page might best serve your needs, then click the link to that page to go there. If the page turns out to be a near miss, you can use your Back button to return to the hit list and try a different page, or start over with a new search.

FIGURE 10.2

Excite organizes the hit list from best matches to worst, and gives each a confidence rating.

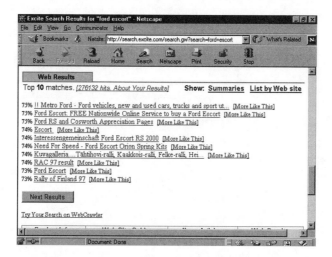

A hit list may show no hits at all, or it may have hundreds. Zero hits is a problem, but hundreds or even thousands of hits really isn't. Remember, most search engines put the best hits at the top of the list, so even if your hit list has thousands of links, the links you want may appear somewhere within the top 20 or so.

Regardless of the number of hits, if you don't see what you want somewhere in the first 30 to 50 links, you probably need to start over with a new search term. And if your first search turned up hundreds of hits, use a more specific term in your second try.

Some tools organize the hit list in smart ways, attempting to put the best matches at the top of the list so you see them first, and weaker matches lower in the list.

For example, suppose you use *Godzilla* as your search term. A particular search tool would tend to put at the top of the hit list all pages that use the word "Godzilla" in their titles or URLs because those are the pages most likely to be all about Godzilla. Matches to keywords or the page's description come lower in the list, since these may be pages that simply mention Godzilla, but aren't really *about* Godzilla. Even lower in the list, a tool might show links to "partial" matches, pages to which only part of the search term, such as those containing the word "God" or the partial word "zilla."

In addition to organizing the hit list this way, some search engines put a confidence rating next to each hit. The rating—usually expressed as a percentage—indicates how well the page matches your search term, with 100% being a perfect match (see Figure 10.3.)

FIGURE 10.3

Some search tools display a rating next to each hit, to tell you how close a match it is to your search term. A 100% rating means that your exact search term appears on the page.

┌─────Rating

71% Toy Soldier Homepage - The No.1 magazine for toy soldier collectors & enthusiasts
http://www.toy-soldier.com/
Search for more documents like this one

69% Untitled Document - THE FIRST PEEK AT GODZILLA By ALLEN SALKIN He ain't so big.
The new Godzilla -- seen here in the first public look at the topsecret movie monster -- is only 8 inches
tall in toy form.
http://www.fortunecity.com/tattooine/ellison/86/post.html
Search for more documents like this one

In Internet Explorer, you can search straight from the address box. How you do it depends on which version of Internet Explorer you use.

In IE5, you just click in the address box, type a search term (instead of a Web site address), and press Enter. In IE4, you click in the address box, type the word *find* followed by a search term, and press Enter.

Either way, the search term is automatically forwarded to a search site (selected at random by Microsoft), and the hit list appears.

This isn't the greatest way to search: You don't pick the search site, and you can't take advantage of directories or any special search options. But when you're in a *big* hurry…

Phrasing a Simple Search

You can get awfully artful and creative with search terms. But nine times out of ten, you needn't get too fancy about searching. You go to the search site, type a simple word or phrase in the text box, click the submit button, and wait a few moments for the hit list to show up.

If the list shows links that look like they hold what you're after, try 'em. If not, try another search term.

You can use multiple words in a search term; for example, someone's full name (*Michael Moriarty*) or another multi-word term (*two-term presidents*). But when you use multiple words, some special considerations apply. See "Phrasing a *Serious* Search," later in this hour.

10

Here are a few basic tips for improving your search success:

- **Use the simplest form of a word.** The search term *Terrier* will match references to both "Terrier" and "Terrier*s*." However, the term *Terriers* may fail to match pages using only "Terrier." Some search sites are smart enough to account for this, but some aren't. So try to use the simplest word form that's still specific to what you want.

- **Use common capitalization.** Some search sites don't care about capitalization, but some do. So it's always a good habit to capitalize words as they would most often be printed, using initial capitals on names and other proper nouns, and all lower-case letters for other words. Be careful to observe goofy computer-era capitalizations, such as AppleTalk or FrontPage.

- **Be as specific as possible.** If it's the German Shepherd you want to know about, use that as your search term, not dog, which will produce too many hits, many unrelated to German Shepherds. If the most specific term doesn't get what you want, then try less specific terms; if *German Shepherd* fails, go ahead and try *dog*. You may find a generic page about dogs on which there's a link to information about German Shepherds.

- **Try partial words.** Always try full words first. But if they're not working out, you can use a partial word. If you want to match both "puppies" and "puppy," you can try *pup* as a search term, which matches both.

When you use a search term in Yahoo! (www.yahoo.com), the hit list typically shows not only pages, but Yahoo categories related to the search term. You can try one of the pages, or start exploring related category headings from the head start the search provides.

To Do: Try a Simple Search

1. Go to AltaVista at www.altavista.com (Figure 10.4).

FIGURE 10.4

Step 1: Go to AltaVista.

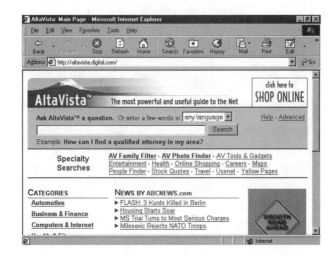

2. Click the search term box, and type *DaVinci* for a search term (Figure 10.5).

FIGURE 10.5

Step 2: Type DaVinci into the search term box.

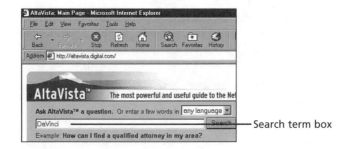

Search term box

3. Click the submit button, labeled Search (Figure 10.6).

FIGURE 10.6

Step 3: Click the Search button.

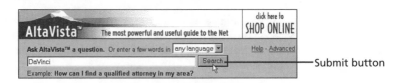

Submit button

4. Click any link in the hit list, to see where it leads (Figure 10.7).

FIGURE 10.7

Step 4: Try out a link.

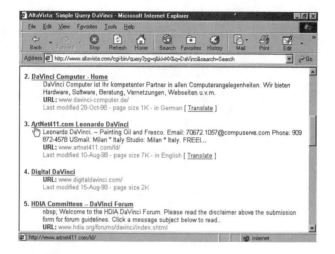

5. Click Back to return to the hit list (Figure 10.8).

10

FIGURE 10.8

Step 5: Return to the hit list.

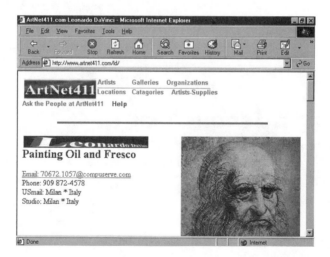

6. Scroll to the bottom of the page, and observe that there are links for moving ahead to more pages of the hit list (Figure 10.9).

FIGURE 10.9

Step 6: Scroll down to the bottom of the page.

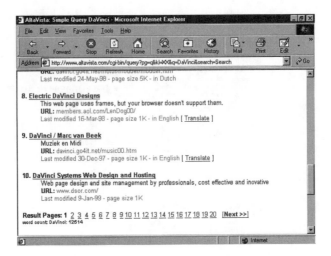

Observe that the search term box appears on every page of the hit list. You can start a new search at any time, from any page of the hit list, by entering a new search term.

Some search sites display the search term box only on the top page; to start a new search in those, just click Back until you return to the top page.

Phrasing a *Serious* Search

Sometimes, in order to phrase a very specific search, you need multiple words. And when you use multiple words, you may need to use *operators* to control the way a search site works with those words.

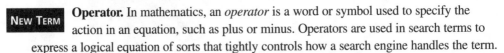

NEW TERM **Operator.** In mathematics, an *operator* is a word or symbol used to specify the action in an equation, such as plus or minus. Operators are used in search terms to express a logical equation of sorts that tightly controls how a search engine handles the term.

Using Multiple Words in a Search Term

In a search term, you can use as many words as you need in order to make the term specific.

For example, suppose I want to learn about Boxer dogs. I could use the search term *Boxer*. While that term might turn up some hits about Boxer dogs, those hits may be buried among hundreds of other links about prizefighters, China's Boxer Rebellion, Tony Danza (actor and ex-boxer), and people named Boxer. So to make my search more specific, I use two words:

Boxer dog

Now the search engine will look for pages that contain both "Boxer" and "dog," which greatly increases the chances that hits will be about Boxer dogs, since most pages about all those other "boxers" I mentioned earlier will not also be about "dogs." I still might see a link to a page about George Foreman's dog, if he has one. But the hit list will be a lot closer to what I want.

If my hit list is still cluttered with the wrong kind of pages, I might remember that a Boxer is a breed of dog, so a page about Boxer dogs probably also uses the term "breed" prominently. So I might try a third term to further narrow the hit list:

Boxer dog breed

Get the idea? Now, if you get *too* specific, you may accidentally omit a few pages you want—there may be Boxer dog pages that don't use "breed" anywhere that would show up in a search database. So it's best to start off with a happy medium (a term that's specific but not overly restrictive), see what you get, and then try subsequent searches using more or less specific terms, depending on what's in the hit list.

10

A few search engines support *natural language queries*. In a natural language query, you can phrase your search term as you might naturally phrase a question; for example, you might use the search term *Who was the artist Leonardo DaVinci*, and the search site applies sophisticated technology to determine what you're asking.

Natural language queries are a good idea, and they're worth experimenting with. But in my experience, their results are usually not as good as you'd probably get with a really smartly phrased search term.

Using Operators to Control Searches

Whenever you use multiple words, you're using operators, even if you don't know it. Operators are words you use between the words in a multi-word search term to further define exactly how the search site will handle your term. Using operators in this way is sometimes described as *Boolean logic*. There are three basic operators used in searching:

- **And.** When you use *and* between words in a search term, you tell the search engine to find only those pages that contain *both* of the words—pages that contain only one or the other are not included in the hit list.

- **Or.** When you use *or* between words in a search term, you tell the search engine to find all pages that contain *either* of the words—all pages that contain either word alone, or both words, are included in the hit list.

- **Not.** When you use *not* between words in a search term, you tell the search engine to find all pages that contain the word before not, then to remove from the hit list any that also contain the word following not.

Table 10.1 illustrates how *and*, *or,* and *not* affect a search site's use of a term.

TABLE 10.1 HOW OPERATORS WORK IN SEARCH TERMS

Search Term	What a Search Tool Matches
Dodge and pickup	Only pages containing both "Dodge" and "pickup"
Dodge or pickup	All pages containing either "Dodge" or "pickup," or both words
Dodge not pickup	All pages that contain "Dodge" but do not also contain "pickup" (gets all the Dodge pages, then eliminates any about pickups)
Dodge and pickup and models	Pages that contain all three words
Dodge or pickup or models	Pages that contain any of the three words
Dodge not Chrysler	Pages that contain "Dodge" but do not also contain "Chrysler" (gets all the Dodge pages, then eliminates any that also mention Chrysler)

Before using operators in search terms, check out the options or instructions area of the search site you intend to use (see Figure 10.10). Most search sites support *and*, *or,* and *not*, but some have their own little quirks about how you must go about it. For example, Excite and AltaVista prefer that you insert a plus sign (+) at the beginning of a word rather than precede it with *and*.

Another powerful way to use multiple words is to do an *exact phrase match*, which most search sites support. In an exact phrase match, you surround the multi-word term with quotes to instruct the search to match only pages that show the same words as the term, in the same order.

For example, suppose you want to know about the film *Roman Holiday*. A search on *Roman Holiday* will probably match any page that uses both of those words anywhere, in any order, together or separately. That'll still get you some good hits, but a lot of bad ones, too. A search on *"Roman Holiday"* (in quotes) matches only pages that use the exact phrase Roman Holiday, so the hit list will be much better targeted to what you want.

FIGURE 10.10

Click the Advanced Search link near Yahoo!'s search term box to learn how Yahoo! supports operators and other advanced search techniques.

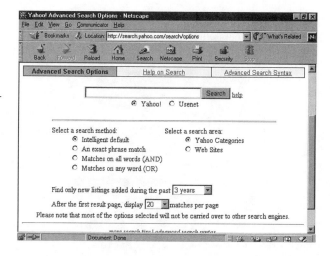

When you use multiple words and don't include operators, most search engines assume you mean to put "and" between words. (See, you are using operators, even if you don't know it.)

For example, if you use the term candy corn, most search engines assume you mean "candy and corn" and match only pages that contain both words.

Some engines will apply and first, then use or. The "and" hits go to the top of the hit list, and the "or" hits go to the bottom, as lower-rated hits.

To Do: Try a Power Search

Try out multi-word searches using the operators *and* and *or*:

1. Go to the search site of your choice, enter the search term *star or trek,* and click the search button (Figure 10.11).

2. Examine the results. You should see many pages about *Star Trek,* but if you go far enough into the results, you'll see other kinds of "stars" and other topics that include the word "trek."

3. Return to the search term box, and submit the search term star and trek (Figure 10.12).

▼

FIGURE 10.11

Step 1: Enter a search term that uses "or" into a search site.

FIGURE 10.12

Step 3: Submit a new search using "and".

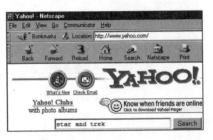

4. Examine the results. Just about every hit should be about *Star Trek* (Figure 10.13).

FIGURE 10.13

Step 4: Examine the results.

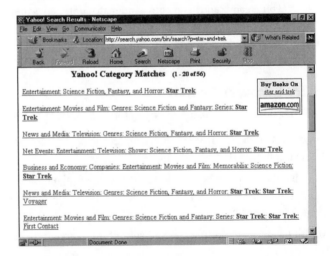

5. Finally, try the exact phrase *"Star Trek"* (including the quotes). Does the hit list look different from the one you got in step 4? (Figure 10.14.)

▼

FIGURE 10.14

Step 5: Try entering an exact phrase with quotation marks around two words.

In high school, they warned you that you'd need algebra one day. If you ignored that warning (like I did), then you've forgotten all of that stuff about grouping parts of equations in parentheses.

If you remember algebra, then note that you can apply those techniques for super searches. For example, suppose you wanted to find pages about pro boxers (the kind that hit each other). You'd need a hit list that matched all pages with "boxer" or "prizefighter," but eliminated any that matched "dog" (to weed out the Boxer dog pages). You could do that with either of the following algebraic terms:

(boxer or prizefighter) not dog

(boxer not dog) or prizefighter

If you can apply these techniques, drop your old math teacher a note of thanks for a job well done.

Using Multiple Search Sites from One Place

As I mentioned in Hour 9, Web portals and some other sites offer one-stop access to multiple search sites. When you access multiple search sites this way, you usually can't see and use the full range of options and tools each individual search page offers. However, you can quickly and easily submit the same search term to one tool after another.

Fast Multi-Tool Searching in Navigator

In the Net Search page that appears when you click Navigator's Search button (see Figure 10.15), you can search by clicking on the name of a search site in the column on the left, typing your search term in the box, and then clicking the Search button.

FIGURE 10.15

Portals like Netcenter enable you to quickly run searches in multiple search sites.

Search sites—

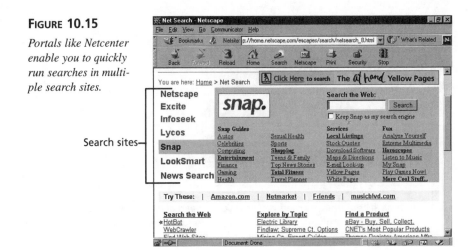

Big deal, you say? Well, after using the hit list from the first tool, you can click Back to return to Netcenter, where you'll see the search term still in the box. You may then click the name of another search site in the left column, then click the search button—there's no need to retype your search term.

Fast Multi-Tool Searching in Internet Explorer 5

In IE5, you can begin your multi-tool search by clicking the Search button, which displays IE5's searching tools in the Explorer bar (see Figure 10.16).

Type a search term in the box, click the Search button that appears next to the search term box, and the hit list from one search site appears in the Explorer bar beneath the search term box.

After examining the hit list and visiting any hits you want, you can click the Next button at the top of the Explorer bar to submit the exact same search term to another search site. You can keep clicking Next to submit the term to many different tools, one at a time. (See Figure 10.17.)

Your copy of IE5 has a list of search sites it submits the term to, in a particular order, each time you click Next.

- To choose the next tool to use, click on the tiny arrow on the right side of the Next button, and choose a tool from the list that appears.

- To select the search sites IE5 uses, and to choose the order in which they're used, click the Customize button at the top of the Explorer bar. A set of choices for customizing the Search Settings appears (see Figure 10.18).

FIGURE 10.16

Start an IE5 multi-tool search by clicking the Search button on IE5's toolbar to open the search sites in the Explorer bar.

Explorer bar

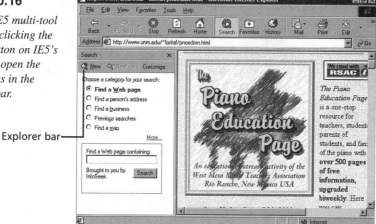

FIGURE 10.17

When you search from the Explorer bar, the hit list appears there, too.

Next button

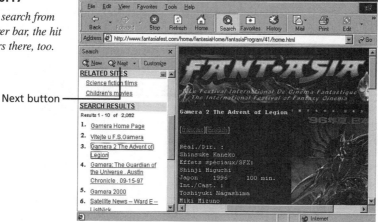

10

Figure 10.18

Click the Customize button to display options for choosing which search sites to use and the order in which to use them.

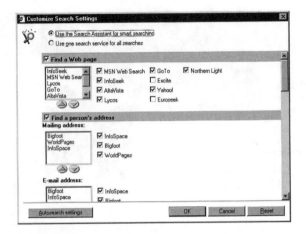

About Site Searches

The major search sites mentioned in this hour and Hour 9 are for finding information that may reside anywhere on the Web. Because they have that enormous job to do, they can't always find everything that's on a particular server.

However, large Web sites often provide their own search tools, just for finding stuff on that site alone. For example, Microsoft's Web site is huge, encompassing thousands of pages. So Microsoft supplies a search tool (you can open it from a SEARCH link atop most pages) just for finding stuff at Microsoft. Even fairly small sites may have their own search tools; Figure 10.19 shows one for *Discover* magazine.

You use a site's search tool just as you would any search site, by entering a search term. Many such search tools even support multi-word searches and operators—but always check the instructions accompanying the search tool to find out whether it supports fancy searches.

FIGURE 10.19

Discover *magazine supplies its own search tool just for finding stuff on its site.*

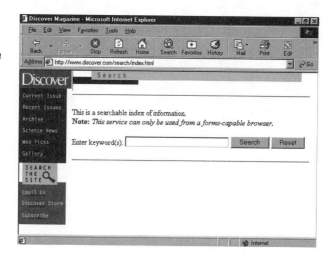

Summary

Most of the time, a search is a snap. Just type a likely sounding word in any search tool's text box, click the submit button, and wait for your hits. But the more you know about narrowing your searches by choosing just the right word, using multiple words, and using operators, the better your odds of always finding exactly what you're looking for.

Q&A

Q When searching for a name, like "Bill Clinton," should I use that old last-name-first gag and use *Clinton, Bill* as my search term?

A It doesn't matter. Search tools pretty much ignore commas, so whichever way you do it, the tool sees *Bill and Clinton* and comes up with the same hits. By the way, if you're searching for who I think you're searching for, note that A) He's not the only Bill Clinton in the world, and B) He sometimes goes by William, not Bill. The term *President Clinton* is a better choice.

Q In some search tools, like AltaVista, I see options for searching "Usenet." What's that all about?

A Some search engines can search not only the Web, but also the contents of Internet newsgroups, which are sometimes collectively (and inaccurately) called Usenet. You'll learn about newsgroups, including searching them, in Hour 15, "Reading and Posting to Newsgroups."

10

HOUR 11

Finding Programs and Files

The huge, diverse group of people that use the Internet have only one thing universally in common: They all use a computer. So it's no surprise that computer programs and files are the most common "things" you can acquire through the Internet. You can find online all kinds of Internet software, other kinds of programs (like games or word processors), documents (such as books or articles), and other useful files such as utilities and plug-ins.

To find a particular file or program you want, you can apply the search techniques you've already picked up in Hours 9, "Getting Started with Searching" and 10, "Searching for Information." But in this hour, you'll learn how to use search techniques that are better focused and faster so you can find exactly the files you want. You'll also learn all about *downloading* the files you'll find, and about preparing those files for use on your computer.

At the end of the hour, you'll be able to answer the following questions:

- What's downloading?
- What kinds of files can I download and use on my computer?
- Where are the sites that can help me find and download files, and how do I use them?
- What's a compressed archive—or *Zip* file—and what must I do with it before it will work on my computer?
- What's a computer virus, and how can I avoid catching one when downloading files?

What's Downloading, Anyhow?

Downloading is the act of copying a computer file from a server, through the Net, to your computer so you can use it there, just as if you had installed it from a diskette or CD-ROM. (Incidentally, you can also *upload*—send a file *to* a server—but you'll learn about that in Hour 19, "Tools for the Serious User: FTP and Telnet.")

Click a Link, Get a File

Whether you've thought about it or not, when you're on the Web, you're really downloading all the time. For example, every time you open a Web page, the files that make up that page are temporarily copied from the server to your computer.

But here we're talking more deliberate downloading: You locate a link in a Web page that points to a file or program you want (see Figure 11.1). To download that file, you click the link, then follow any prompts that appear. It's really that simple.

Observe that most of the file links in Figure 11.1 have the filename extension .zip. That extension indicates that these files are compressed archive files, also known as *Zip* files. You'll learn more about Zip files later in this hour.

The easiest and usually best way to find and download files from the Internet is by using a Web link, as described in this hour. However, there is another important way to download files, *FTP*, which may be useful to you when the file you want is not available through a link in a regular Web page.

You'll learn about FTP in Hour 19.

FIGURE 11.1

You download files from the Web simply by clicking links that lead to files, such as those shown here.

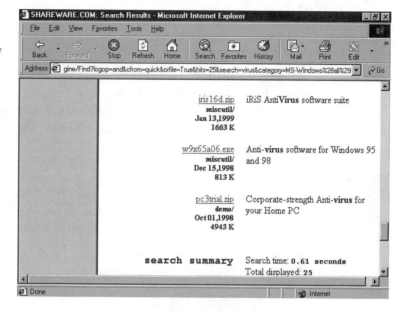

SHAREWARE.COM: Search Results - Microsoft Internet Explorer

File   Edit   View   Favorites   Tools   Help

Back   Forward   Stop   Refresh   Home   Search   Favorites   History   Mail   Print   Edit

Address   gine/Find?logop=and&cfrom=quick&orfile=True&hits=25&search=virus&category=MS-Windows%28all%29   Go

iris16d.zip **miscutil/** Jan 13,1999 1663 K	iRiS AntiVirus software suite
w9x65a06.exe **miscutil/** Dec 15,1998 813 K	Anti-virus software for Windows 95 and 98
pc3trial.zip **demo/** Oct 01,1998 4943 K	Corporate-strength Anti-virus for your Home PC

search summary   Search time: 0.61 seconds
Total displayed: 25

Done   Internet

How Long Does Downloading Take?

11

The larger the file, the longer it will take to download. That's why the size of the file is usually shown somewhere in or near the link for downloading it (refer to Figure 11.1). The size is expressed in kilobytes (K or KB) for smaller files, or in megabytes (M or MB) for larger files. One M equals 1,024K.

How long does it take to download a file of a given size? That depends on many factors, including the speed of your Internet connection, and how busy the server is. But over a connection of 28.8 kbps, a 1 MB file typically downloads in around 10 minutes, give or take.

You might expect that downloading a file through a 56K connection would take half as much time as doing so through a 28.8K connection, but that's never the case.

Even in the best case, current regulations limit the download speed over phone lines to 53K, even if the modem handles 56K. More importantly, a noisy phone or other factors can make a 56K modem perform way below its top speed.

Finally, other factors—pauses in the downloading caused by overly busy servers, the speed of your computer's hard disk, and so on—can affect download speed.

You'll find lots of great stuff to download that's smaller than 1 MB. However, many programs or multimedia files can be much, much larger. A download of the entire Internet Explorer program from Microsoft's Web site takes several hours, even through a fast, 56K connection.

With experience, you'll develop a sense of how long downloading a file of a given size takes on your system. Once you have that sense, always carefully consider the size of the file, and whether you want to wait that long for it, before starting the download.

To Do: Download a File

Just for practice, and to understand what to do once you locate a file you want, download the Adobe Acrobat reader, a program that enables you to display documents in the Adobe Acrobat (.pdf) file format, which are common online. If you already have an Adobe Acrobat reader, or just don't want one, you can cancel the download before it finishes.

1. Go to Adobe's Web site at www.adobe.com, scroll to the bottom of the page, and click the button labeled Get Acrobat Reader (Figure 11.2).

FIGURE 11.2

Step 1: Click the Get Acrobat Reader icon.

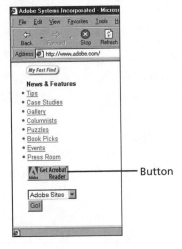

2. Click the link for free Adobe Acrobat Reader (Figure 11.3).

3. Complete the choices on the form, then click the Download button (Figure 11.4).

FIGURE 11.3

Step 2: Click on free Adobe Acrobat Reader.

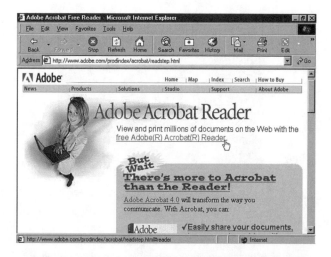

FIGURE 11.4

Step 3: Fill in the form, and click Download.

11

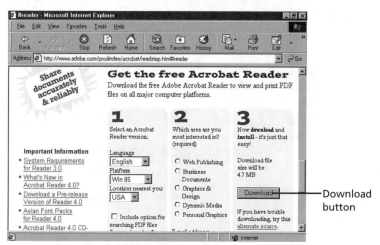

Download button

4. The exact dialogs you'll see differ by browser and computer type, but typically, a dialog opens to ask whether you want to just save the file to disk after downloading, or immediately open or run the file once it's downloaded. Usually it's smartest to choose the Save option, then to open the file later (Figure 11.5).

FIGURE 11.5

Step 4: Save the file to disk.

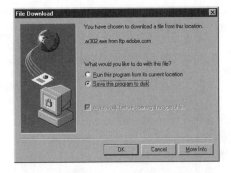

When a link leads to a media file, such as a sound or video clip (see Hour 7, "Playing Online Video, Music, and Broadcasts"), and you choose the Open option (rather than Save to disk) when downloading, as soon as the file has been downloaded, your browser can play the file automatically.

5. The next dialog you may see prompts you to select the location (folder or desktop) and filename for the downloaded file (Figure 11.6). Choosing a location is a good idea, so that you can easily locate and use the file after downloading. Don't mess with the filename, though—if you don't supply a new filename, the file will be stored on your computer under its original name, which is usually best.

FIGURE 11.6

Step 5: Choose the location where to save the file.

6. After you deal with any dialogs that appear, the download begins, and a status message appears. The status message usually features a Cancel button, so you can quit the download before it finishes if you want to (Figure 11.7).

Figure 11.7

Step 6: The status message appears.

When the download is complete, the status message disappears. You can continue browsing, or go use the file you just downloaded, which you can find in the folder you selected in the dialog described in step 5.

In the download status message, some browsers also display an estimate of how much longer the download will take to finish. Although that estimate can be handy, it's just a guess, and should not be taken as an exact prediction of how long the download will take.

11

Choosing Files You Can Use

You can download any type of computer file. But not every file or program you find online works on every type of computer.

"Duh!", you may think. But you'd be surprised how often people forget this. Web browsing enables different kinds of computers to all look at the same online content, so after awhile people tend to forget that off the Web, PCs, Macs, and other types of computers each use different kinds of files and programs.

When you search for files and programs, you must make sure that the ones you choose are compatible with your computer type, and often also with your operating system (Windows 3.1, Windows 95/98/NT, DOS, Mac OS 7 or OS 8, UNIX flavor, and so on).

The Two File Types: Program and Data

Although there are dozens of different types of files, they all generally fall into either of two groups:

- **Program files.** A program file contains a program—a game, a word processor, a plug-in, a utility, and so on. Program files are almost always designed to run on only one type of computer and operating system. For example, a program file designed for a Mac typically will not run in Windows. However, many programs are available in similar but separate versions, one for each system type.

- **Data files.** A data file contains information that can be displayed, or used in some other way, by a program. For example, a word processing document is a data file, to be displayed by a word processing program. Like program files, some data files can be used only by a particular program running on a particular computer type. But most data file types can be used on a variety of systems.

> Popular files are usually available from multiple servers, spread across the continent or globe. Often, a downloading page will refer to the servers as *mirror sites* because they all offer an identical copy of the file, a "mirror image."

Common Data File Types on the Net

When you encounter a link to a file, you'll usually have no trouble telling what system the file is made for.

Often, before arriving at the link, you will have navigated through a series of links or form selections in which you specified your system type, so that when you finally see links to files, they all point to files that can run on your system. In other cases, the link itself—or text near the link—will tell you the system requirements for the file.

 System requirements. The computer type, operating system, and (for a data file) program required to use a particular file. Some files you'll encounter have special hardware requirements as well, such as a particular amount of memory.

Even when the link doesn't fill you in, you can often tell a file's system requirements by its filename extension, the final part of the filename that follows the period. (For example, in the filename MONTY.DOC, the extension is DOC.) Table 11.1 shows many of the most common file types online.

> Data files can often be converted and used by programs other than those in which they were created. For example, nearly all full-featured word processing programs can convert Microsoft Word (.doc) files so you can read or edit them. Most spreadsheet programs can handle an Excel or Lotus 1-2-3 file.
>
> If you lack the required program for using a particular kind of data file, check out any similar program you already own to see whether it can convert a file of that type.

TABLE 11.1 COMMON FILE TYPES YOU'LL FIND ONLINE FOR DOWNLOADING

Extension	Type of File	Requirements
.exe, .com	Program file (a game, utility, application, etc.)	Runs on one (and only one) type of system. Always read any text near the link to be sure that a particular .exe or .com file will run on your computer.
.doc	Word document	Can be opened and edited in either the Windows or Mac version of Word, or Windows 95/98's WordPad program.
.pdf	Adobe Acrobat document	Can be opened in the Adobe Acrobat Reader program (available for a variety of systems) or in a browser equipped with an Adobe Acrobat plug-in. Can also be converted and displayed by some word processing programs.
.xls	Excel spreadsheet	Can be opened and edited in either the Windows or Mac version of Excel.
.txt, .asc	Plain text file	Can be opened in any word processor or text editor (such as Windows' Notepad) on any system, and displayed by any browser.
.wri	Windows Write document	Can be displayed by Windows Write (in Windows 3.1) or WordPad (in Windows 95/98/NT).
.avi, .mp3, .mov, .qt, .mpg, .au, .mid, .snd	Various types of media files	Can be run by various player programs, or by your browser if it is equipped for them (see Hour 7).
.zip	*Archive* containing one or more compressed files	Must be decompressed (*unzipped*) before the files it contains can be used; see "Working with Zip Files" later in this hour.

11

Very few program files are designed to run on both Macs and PCs. However, if you use a PC, you should know that some programs work in multiple PC operating systems. For example, there are programs written to run in both Windows 3.1 and Windows 95/98, and sometimes also DOS, as well.

By and large, programs written just for DOS or Windows 3.1 will also run in Windows 95 or NT, although the reverse is never true. And any Windows 95 program will run in Windows 98 or NT, but some NT programs will not run in Windows 95. A very few, specialized utility programs written for Windows 98 will not run in Windows 95.

If you use a PowerPC-based Mac, you know that you can run some Windows programs on your Mac. You probably also know that those programs do not run as well there as native Mac programs.

A program always runs best on the system for which it was written, so favor choices that match what you have. For example, if you use Windows 95, and you're given a choice between Windows 3.1 and Windows 95 versions of a file, favor the Win 95 version. And even if you have a PowerPC-based Mac, always favor true Mac files over PC versions.

Finding Sites That Help You Find Files

Where you begin looking for a file depends upon the manner in which that file is offered on the Web, or rather, in what way that file is licensed for use by those other than its creator. Most software falls into one of the following four groups:

- **Commercial.** The programs you can buy in a box at the software store. Many software companies have Web sites where you can learn about their products and often download them as well. Typically, you fill in an online form to pay for the software, then download it.

- **Demo.** Demo software is commercial software that has some features disabled, or automatically stops working—*expires*—after you use it for a set number of days. Demo software is distributed free on commercial and shareware sites, and provides a free preview of the real thing.

- **Shareware.** Shareware is software you're allowed to try out for free, but for which you are supposed to pay. After the trial period (usually 30 days), you either pay the programmer or stop using the program. Some shareware expires or has features disabled, like demo software, so you won't continue using it without paying.

- **Freeware.** Freeware is free software you can use all you want, as long as you want, for free.

Appendix A, "Fun Web Sites to Visit," shows the URLs of a great selection of sites for getting shareware, freeware, and commercial software.

All-Purpose Shareware Sites

Sites for downloading shareware appear all over the Web. Many popular shareware programs have their very own Web sites, and links to shareware products can be found on thousands of pages, such as Yahoo!'s shareware directory at

www.yahoo.com/Computers_and_Internet/Software/Shareware/

But when you're looking for a shareware, freeware, or demo program to do a particular job, you'll have better luck if you visit a Web site designed to provide access to a wide range of products, sites such as

- **Shareware.com**, whose easy-to-remember URL is shareware.com (see Figure 11.8).

- **Download.com**, (can you guess the URL?).

These sites are very much like the search tools you used in Hours 9 and 10, providing search term boxes, directories, and other tools for finding files. But the hits they produce are always either links to files that match your search, or links to other Web pages from which those files can be downloaded.

11

Shareware.com and Download.com are good places to find all sorts of software, including Internet client software, such as a new browser, FTP client (see Hour 19), or Web authoring tool (see Hour 23, "Creating Web Pages and Multimedia Messages").

But a more efficient way to find and download Internet client software is to go to the Tucows directory at www.tucows.com, which is a special directory of Internet client software.

The key to using Shareware.com, Download.com, and similar file-finders is to make sure that your search specifies both of the following:

- The kind of file or program you seek: email, word processing, game, paint program—whatever you want.

- Your computer type and operating system: Windows 95/98, Mac OS8, and so on.

If you include this information in your search, the hit list will show only files and programs of the kind you want, and only those that run on your particular system.

> Note that sites like Shareware.com don't actually store on their own servers the thousands of files to which they offer links. Rather, they find and show you links that lead to files stored on other servers and mirror sites for those other servers.

FIGURE 11.8

Shareware.com, a search engine for finding shareware, freeware, and demo software.

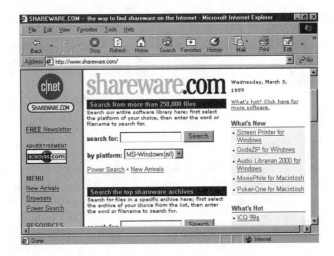

> If it's mainstream, commercial software you want to buy—you know, the stuff you buy in a box at the software store—check out one of the online software shops, such as Beyond.com (beyond.com) or MicroWarehouse (warehouse.com).

For practice, try finding a solitaire game for your system at Shareware.com, in the following To Do.

To Do: Find a Program on Shareware.com

1. Go to Shareware.com at www.shareware.com, type *solitaire* in the box labeled Search For, choose your system type from the By Platform list, and then click the Search button (Figure 11.9).

FIGURE 11.9

Step 1: Type in soli-taire at Shareware.com and choose an operat-ing system.

2. Read the descriptions of the solitaire programs for your system type, choose a pro-gram that you'd like to have, and click its filename (Figure 11.10).

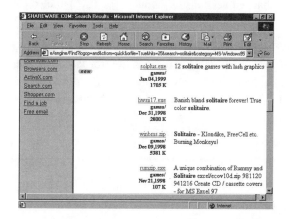

FIGURE 11.10

Step 2: Choose a pro-gram that looks inter-esting and click on it.

11

3. A new list of links appears, each pointing to the identical file stored on a different server. Click one to start the download (Figure 11.11).

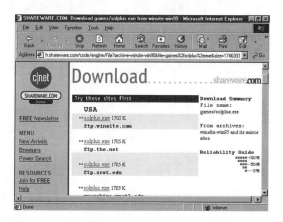

FIGURE 11.11

Step 3: Choose a site from which to down-load the program.

If you use Windows 95 or 98, and a search for Windows 95/98 programs doesn't get you what you want, try another search for any "Windows" file of the type you want. For example, in Shareware.com, you'd choose MS-Windows (all) from the list of system types.

Such a search will turn up both Windows 95 and Windows 3.1 hits. You can substitute a Windows 3.1 program when no Windows 95 program is available.

Commercial Software Sites

As a Web user, you have a lot to gain by frequenting the Web sites of any commercial software companies whose products you use regularly. There, you can not only learn about new and enhanced versions of products you use, but also pick up tips, free enhancements, product support, and fixes for common problems.

In particular, it's important to know about the Web site of the maker of the operating system you use on your computer: Microsoft's site (for Windows users) and Apple's (for Mac OS folks). On these sites, you can find all sorts of free updates and utilities for your operating system, fixes for problems, and news about upcoming new releases and enhancements.

Microsoft and Apple offer so many downloads that each provides its own search tools and directories for locating the file you need. The best place to start:

- For Apple files, is at `www.apple.com/support/` (see Figure 11.12).
- For Microsoft files, is at `www.microsoft.com/msdownload/` (see Figure 11.13).

FIGURE 11.12

Apple's support site offers a wealth of free files for Mac users.

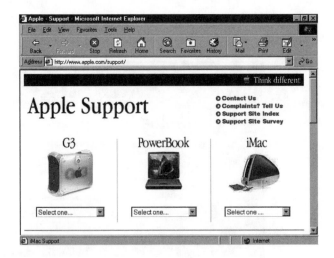

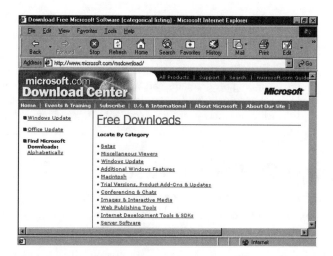

FIGURE 11.13

See Microsoft's free downloads page to pick up all sorts of handy freebies.

Working with Zip Files

The larger a file is, the longer it takes to download. So some files online are *compressed*—converted into smaller files—to cut the download time. After downloading, you must decompress a compressed file to restore it to its original size and use it.

Also, most application programs are made up not just of one fat file, but of a collection of program and data files. A single compressed file can pack together many separate files, so they can all be downloaded together in one step. When you decompress a compressed file containing multiple files—which is sometimes called an *archive*—the files are separated.

There are several forms of compression used online, but by far the most popular form is called Zip, a compressed file created by a program called PKZip. A Zip file uses the extension .zip, and it must be decompressed—*unzipped*—after downloading before you can use the file or files it contains.

You need a special program to unzip Zip files. If you don't already have one, the most popular shareware unzippers are

- For Windows, WinZip, which you can download from www.winzip.com.
- For Mac, ZipIt, which you can download from
  www.awa.com/softlock/zipit/zipit.html.

After installing an unzipping program, you can decompress any Zip file by opening the program, choosing the Zip file you want to decompress, and then choosing Extract from a toolbar or menu.

11

One special type of .exe program file is called a *self-extracting archive,* which is a compressed file or files, just like a Zip file.

Unlike a Zip file, however, a self-extracting archive file does not require an unzipping program. Instead, it decompresses itself automatically when you open it (usually by double-clicking). Most large applications offered online, such as Web browsers, download as self-extracting archives.

Watching Out for Viruses

A few years back, in the movie *Independence Day*, Jeff Goldblum stopped an intergalactic invasion by uploading a computer virus into the aliens' mothership and thereby scrambling the alien system.

NEW TERM **Computer virus.** Program code secretly added to or attached to a file or email message that makes mischief when the file or message is opened. Often, the virus is designed to reproduce and spread itself from the file it travels in—its host file— to other files.

Computer viruses are created by sorry, sick people who get a thrill out of cheap little tricks—viruses that display silly messages on your screen—or major attacks—viruses that crash whole computer systems.

If you saw *Independence Day*, you may wonder, "If Jeff Goldblum puts a virus on the Internet, and I happen to download a file containing that virus, what might happen to my computer? Would I still be able to conquer Earth? Can I get Jeff to come over and fix it?"

Viruses are like lightning: On one hand, your odds of getting struck are not really that high, so there's no need to fret; on the *other* hand, there's no sense standing on a hill in a storm, holding a golf club skyward. Protect yourself.

You can catch a virus from files you download, *and* from email messages (and files attached to email messages). You'll learn about email viruses in Hour 16, "Emailing Through the Web, Stopping Junk Mail, and Other Tips."

To play it safe, try to limit your downloading choices to commercial sites or reliable shareware sources (such as Shareware.com). Big suppliers regularly scan files for viruses. In addition to exercising caution about where you download files from, you should also install and use a virus scanning program, such as Norton Antivirus, which can find viruses in files and, in some cases, kill the virus while saving the file.

If you intend to scan for viruses, DO NOT open or run a file you have downloaded until AFTER you have used your antivirus software to check it for viruses.

Remember: A virus in a file does no harm until you open the file (or run the program, if the file is a program). So you can download anything safely, then scan it with the virus program before you ever open or run it. If the virus program detects a bug it cannot remove, just delete the file to delete the virus.

You can learn more about viruses, and find links to shareware and commercial virus scanners, from the AntiVirus Resources page at

www.hitchhikers.net/av.shtml

Summary

Finding the files you need begins with starting at the right site: a commercial software site, a shareware search site, and so on. When you start in the right place, and understand the simple steps required to select, download, and (sometimes) unzip files, getting any files you want is a snap.

11

Q&A

Q **While a file is downloading, can I do other things on my computer, like browse other pages or run another program?**

A Most browsers built for Windows 95/98, or Mac 07 or 0S8, permit you to continue browsing during a download. When using one of these browsers—which include the Windows 95/98/NT versions of Internet Explorer and Navigator—you can explore another page, or even start another download, while one download is in progress. The more memory you have in your computer, the better this works. (Don't even *try* it if your computer has less than 32 MB of RAM—it'll act like you're standing on its lungs.)

However, regardless of how much memory you have, I always recommend that you leave your computer alone while downloading. Go get coffee, or play with the kids or something, until the download is complete. Using your computer for any other task—even an offline one—slows down both the download and whatever else you're doing, and raises the likelihood that the download might fail partway through, forcing you to start the download over again.

HOUR 12

Finding People

Using mainly the search techniques you've picked up in the preceding three hours, you can find people on the Internet—or rather, the email addresses, mailing addresses, or telephone numbers through which particular people can be reached.

This people-finding power is one of the Internet's most valuable and controversial capabilities. Applied properly, it can aid research, locate missing persons, track down deadbeats delinquent in their child support payments, reunite old friends, and even help adult adoptees find their birth parents, if they want to. Abused, this capability aids stalkers and overaggressive direct marketers. Unfortunately, as is always the case with freedom of information, there's no practical way to preserve the benefit of this capability without also enabling its abuse.

At the end of the hour, you'll be able to answer the following questions:

- Where on the Web are search tools I can use to find the addresses, phone numbers, or email addresses of folks I want to contact?
- How do I use a people-finding search tool on the Web?

- How do I use the people-finder that's built in to Internet Explorer 5?
- How can I also use a people-finding search tool from within my email program?

Throughout this book, I show screen images to illustrate an activity. But in this hour, although I show you how to perform people searches, I never show the *results* of a people search. Showing those results would invade the privacy of whomever the search found.

Finding the People-Finding Sites

As with all types of search tools, every people-finder on the Web draws from a different database of names and contact information. Note that these tools don't find only people who have Internet accounts; they search public telephone directories, and so can show you addresses and telephone numbers of people who wouldn't know the Internet if it snuck up and bit 'em.

For any particular name, a search using one tool may turn up no hits, while a search with a different tool may hit pay dirt. It's important to know where several different search tools are, so that if one tool fails, you can try another. Figure 12.1 shows a typical people-finder page.

FIGURE 12.1

InfoSpace is one of several handy people-finders on the Web.

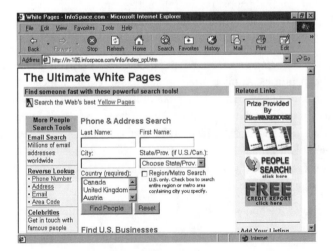

If there's a possibility the person you seek has his or her own home page on the Web, using a special people-finding tool may not be necessary. It's usually a good idea to first perform an ordinary search with a tool like AltaVista or Excite, using the person's name (plus maybe the city or town they live in, to help narrow the search) as your search term (see Hour 10, "Searching for Information").

Such a search will likely turn up that person's home page, if they have one (along with any references to other folks who have the same name, of course), and if you visit the home page, you'll likely find contact information on it.

You use these tools like any other search tool: Enter as much as you know about the person—name, city, and so on—and the tool finds matches in its database. But that database contains only contact information, so your search won't turn up all sorts of references that have nothing to do with contacting someone.

Some of the better people finders include the following:

- Yahoo!'s People Search, at `people.yahoo.com`
- Excite's US People Finder (for addresses and phone numbers), at `www.excite.com/reference/people_finder/`
- Excite's E-mail Lookup (for email addresses), at `www.excite.com/reference/email_lookup/`
- Bigfoot, at `www.Bigfoot.com`
- Four11, at `www.Four11.com`
- InfoSpace, at `www.infospace.com`

12

Depending on the people-finder you use and the options you choose, you may find a person's mailing address, phone number, or email address (or all three). Of course, you haven't learned how to use email yet, but that's OK—you'll learn all about it in the next hour.

For now, if a search turns up an email address of a person you want to contact, just jot it down. A little over an hour from now, you'll know how to use it to send a message to that person.

To Do: Find Yourself in Yahoo!'s People Search

Since you're probably already familiar with Yahoo!, Yahoo!'s People Search is a great first place to try finding someone.

1. Go to Yahoo!'s People Search at `people.yahoo.com` (Figure 12.2).

FIGURE 12.2

Step 1: Go to Yahoo!'s People Search site.

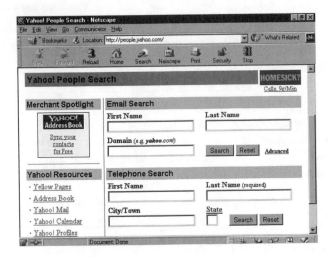

2. Fill in the boxes in the Telephone Search form: First Name, Last Name, City, and so on, and then click the button labeled Search (Figure 12.3).

FIGURE 12.3

Step 2: Fill in the Telephone Search form and click Search.

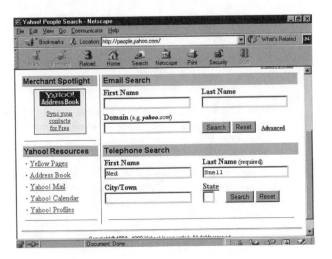

▼   3. On the list of matching names (not shown) click Back to return to the People Search page.

4. Now fill in the boxes under Email Search, and click the Search button (Figure 12.4).

FIGURE 12.4

Step 4: Fill in the Email Search form and click Search.

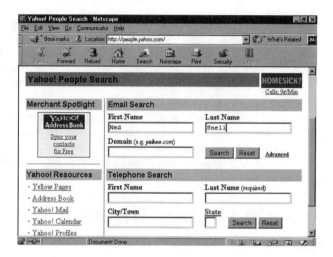

5. Just for fun, click Back to try another Email Search, but this time, leave some boxes empty, to see how these tools will show you more names to choose from when you don't have complete information about a person (Figure 12.5).

FIGURE 12.5

Step 5: Try it again leaving some boxes empty.

12

▲

If you found yourself in your Yahoo! searches, you may be wondering, "How did my phone number, email address, or other information get on the Web?"

Most of the information in the search tool databases— including names, addresses, and phone numbers—comes from public telephone records. By agreeing to have your name, address, and phone number listed in the phone book, you've agreed to make it public, so there's nothing to prevent it from winding up in a Web database. Some databases may also obtain records from other online databases (such as your ISP's user directory), or even from online forms you've submitted from Web pages.

So even if you have an unlisted telephone number (which phone companies call "unpublished"), a record about you may find its way into a database from another source. That's just one reason you must be careful about how and when you enter information about yourself in an online form (see Hour 8, "Protecting Your Privacy (and Other Security Stuff)").

Using People-Finders Through Your Email Program

There is a family of people-finding directories, known collectively as LDAP directories, that are specifically and solely for finding email addresses, both in North America and worldwide.

NEW TERM **LDAP.** *Lightweight Directory Access Protocol*, a standard followed by some people-finders so that a single dialog box in an email program can be used to search any LDAP directory.

Some LDAP directories, such as the aforementioned Bigfoot (`www.Bigfoot.com`) and Four11 (`www.Four11.com`) are accessible through a Web page. But these and several other LDAPs may also be accessed from within some email programs. This enables you to search for an email address from within your email program—which is, after all, the place you need email addresses.

Now, I know we haven't covered email yet—that's in the next hour. However, since this hour is about finding people, it's a good place to quickly show how an email program can also be a people-finder.

The two email programs included in the big two Internet Suites—Netscape Communicator's Messenger and Internet Explorer's Outlook Express—both support LDAP searches, from within their *address book*, a utility that helps you keep track of email addresses.

Searching an LDAP directory from within your email program is just like using a people-finder on the Web: You fill in a name and other information in a form. The only difference is getting to that form. Instead of opening a Web page, you go online, open your email program, and navigate to the LDAP search form as follows:

- In Messenger, choose Communicator, Address Book to open the Address Book (see Figure 12.6). In the column labeled Directory, choose one of the LDAP directories listed. Type the name to search for in the Show Names Containing box, then click the Search For button.

- In Outlook Express, click the Address Book button on the toolbar to open the Address Book, then click the Find People button in the Address Book's toolbar. A search dialog opens (see Figure 12.7). Use the top list in the dialog to choose the LDAP directory to search, fill in the other boxes in the dialog, and then click Find Now.

FIGURE 12.6

Searching an LDAP directory from within Netscape Messenger's Address Book.

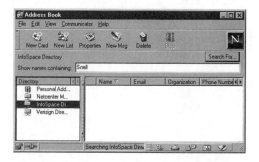

FIGURE 12.7

Searching an LDAP directory from within Outlook Express's Address Book.

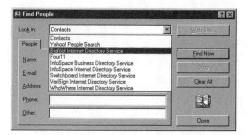

12

People-Finding from Internet Explorer 5

Besides searching the Web, Internet Explorer's built-in search facility (see Hour 10) can optionally search LDAP directories. The following To Do shows how.

To Do: Use Internet Explorer 5 to People-Search

1. In IE5 while looking at any Web page, click the Search button on the toolbar (Figure 12.8).

FIGURE 12.8

Step 1: Click the Search button in Internet Explorer 5.

Search button

2. In the Explorer bar, click the radio button next to Find a Person's Address (Figure 12.9).

FIGURE 12.9

Step 2: In the Explorer bar click the radio button next to Find a Person's Address.

3. Open the list under Search For, and choose the type of information you're looking for: mailing address or email address (Figure 12.10).

FIGURE 12.10

Step 3: Choose either email or mailing address in the Search For box.

4. Fill in as much as you know about the person, then click the Search button (Figure 12.11).

FIGURE 12.11

Step 4: Fill in info about the person you're searching for.

5. If you want, you can customize the way IE5's people-searcher works, choosing which directories it uses and in which order. Click the Customize button, then choose options in the form that appears on the right (Figure 12.12).

FIGURE 12.12

Step 5: If desired, customize the search settings.

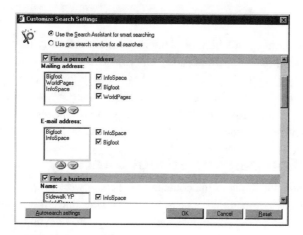

12

Other Folk-Finding Tips

The all-around easiest ways to find people online are those I've already described. But if those don't pay off for you, try the following methods.

Try an Advanced Search

People-finders are designed first and foremost to be easy to use. For that reason, many do not display their most advanced tools at first. They present an easy-to-use, quick form for general-purpose people-searching, but also supply an optional, advanced form for more sophisticated searches. The advanced form comes in handy when the basic form doesn't dig up the person you want.

For example, on Yahoo!'s people-finder page, you'll see a link labeled Advanced, which brings up the Advanced search page shown in Figure 12.13.

FIGURE 12.13

In addition to their basic, easy-to-use form, some people-finding tools also offer an advanced form for more sophisticated searches.

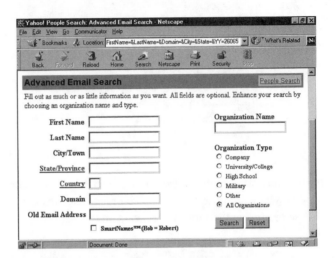

Besides providing you with more options for more narrowly identifying the person you're looking for, the Advanced search provides a check box for "SmartNames." When this check box is checked, Yahoo! searches not only for the exact name you supplied, but also for common variations of that name. If you entered "Edward," the search might match records for "Edward," "Ed," and "Eddy," too. This increases the chances of finding the right person when you're not sure which name form the person uses.

Use a Company or School Directory

Do you know the name of the company the person works for, or a school he or she attends? Many companies, colleges, and universities have their own Web sites, and those Web sites often contain employee and student directories you can browse or search (see Figure 12.14). Just search for and go to the Web site, then browse for a directory.

Try Name Variations

Might the person you're looking for sometimes use a different name than the one you've been using as a search term? Try alternative spellings (Sandy, Sandi) or nicknames. Try both the married name and birth name of people who may have married or divorced recently. You may even want to try a compound name made out of both the birth name and married name (Jacqueline Bouvier Kennedy); I know both men and women who use compound or hyphenated married names.

FIGURE 12.14

Like many companies and schools, the University of Minnesota offers on its Web site a searchable directory of students and faculty.

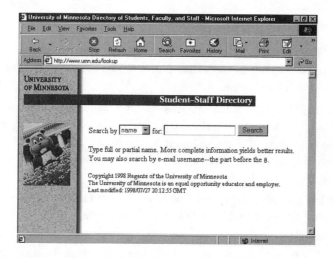

Use an Online Service Directory

If you use an online service and think the person you seek may use the same online service you do, try your online service's own directory of its users. You can access the directory from within the service's interface for non-Internet content.

Note that in most cases only the online service's customers can access its user directory. For example, you cannot use America Online's member directory unless you are also on America Online.

Use Old Communications to Start the New Ones

Do you know either the mailing address or phone number of the person, and just want his or her email address? Don't be shy: Call or write, and just ask for the person's email address so you can conduct future communication online. Life's too short.

Summary

You know from earlier hours that you can find all sorts of information and files online. But until this hour, you may not have realized how easy it is to use the Internet to find an old friend or other contact you need. Most often, finding someone on the Web is a simple matter of opening a people-finding search tool and typing a name.

And if your search turns up an email address, you have a very powerful way of getting touch with that person; see Hour 13, "Sending and Receiving Email."

12

Q&A

Q **When my people searches turn up email addresses, those addresses appear to be links: They're underlined, and shown in the same color as other links. What are they links to?**

A These links are called "email links" or "mailto" links, and they contain an email address. Some browsers are equipped to automatically open your email program when you click a mailto link in a Web page (see Hour 13). If your browser is so equipped, you can click a mailto link and immediately begin composing a message addressed to that person.

Q **I was looking for Carla Jones, and I found three people with that name. How do I figure out which Carla Jones is the one I want?**

A Well, first you should try new searches, supplying as much information as you reliably know about the person. For example, include the state where the person lives; doing so may exclude the other choices. Try running your searches on different tools; another tool may display more detailed information, enabling you to choose the right Carla.

If you still have several choices, send a polite letter or email message (never phone) to all of the Carlas, identifying yourself and the context in which you know Carla, and requesting that the right Carla reply. The wrong Carlas will ignore your message, and the right Carla will contact you (if she wants to).

In your note, say as little as possible, and be tactful. For example, if Carla is an old flame, consider the possible effect of your note on the boyfriends or husbands of the *wrong* Carlas when describing your relationship.

PART IV

Communicating with Email and Newsgroups

Hour

HOUR 13

Sending and Receiving Email

Web browsing is the hottest Internet activity, but email may be the most widely used and most productive one.

Using Internet email—which has become such an everyday fixture that many people now call it plain "mail"—you can easily exchange messages with anyone else on the Internet. An email message typically reaches its addressee within minutes (or at most, an hour or so), even on the opposite side of the globe. It's faster than paper mail, easier than faxing, and sometimes just plain fun.

It's so easy, in fact, that I know people who haven't written a dozen paper letters in a decade but who write email daily. It's a great way to keep up with friends and communicate with business contacts. In fact, there are some businesspeople so tied to their email that if you contact them in any way *other* than email, you may not get an answer.

At the end of the hour, you'll be able to answer the following questions:

- How do I recognize an email address?
- How do I set up my email program?
- How do I display a message so I can read it?
- How do I compose and send an email message?
- How do I receive messages others have sent to me?
- How can I reply to a message I've received, or forward that message to someone else?
- How can I keep track of all the email addresses I use?

Understanding Email Addresses

The only piece of information you need to send email to someone is that person's Internet email address. An email address is easy to spot: It always has that "at" symbol (@) in the middle of it. For example, you know at a glance that

sammy@fishbait.com

is an email address. In most email addresses, everything following the @ symbol is the domain address (see Hour 4, "Connecting to the Internet") of a company, Internet service provider, educational institution, or other organization. The part before the @ is the name (or user ID) of a particular employee or user. For example, the addresses

SallyP@genco.com

mikey@genco.com

Manager_of_Sales@genco.com

obviously belong to three different people, all of whom work for the same company or use the same Internet service provider (whatever Genco is).

Each online service has its own domain, too: For example, America Online's is aol.com, and Microsoft Network's is msn.com. So you can tell that the email address

neddyboy@aol.com

is that of the America Online user named "neddyboy."

Online service users usually can omit the @ symbol and anything that follows it when sending to other users on the same service. For example, suppose you want to send email to

`allieoop@aol.com`

If you use a regular ISP or any online service other than America Online
(aol.com), you would use the address as shown. However, if you use America
Online, you can address the message simply to

`allieoop`

Setting Up Your Email Program

There are many different email programs out there. Internet suites such as Internet
Explorer and Netscape Communicator include an email program—but you must take
care when installing these programs not to optionally omit the email component of the
suite. Choosing the "full" installation option when setting up a suite ensures that you
include all of the suite's client programs.

In the suites, the email programs are called:

- **Messenger,** in Netscape Communicator. You can open Messenger from within the
  Navigator browser by choosing Communicator, Messenger. See Figure 13.1.

- **Outlook Express,** in Internet Explorer. You can open Outlook Express from within
  the Internet Explorer browser by choosing clicking the Mail button on the toolbar
  and choosing Read Mail from the menu that appears. See Figure 13.2.

Don't confuse the free Microsoft email program Outlook Express with
another Microsoft program, Outlook (no "Express").

Like Outlook Express, Outlook is an email program. But Outlook also does
many other things Outlook Express does not do, such as personal scheduling
and contact management. And of course, Outlook is not free. Most people
who use Outlook buy it as a part of Microsoft's Office suite.

13

If you don't already have an email program, you can apply the file-finding techniques
from Hour 11, "Finding Programs and Files," to search for one, or check out the Tucows
directory of Internet software at `www.tucows.com`.

FIGURE 13.1

Netscape Messenger, the email program that's included in the Netscape Communicator suite.

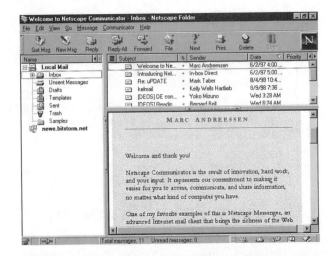

FIGURE 13.2

Outlook Express, the email program that's included with Microsoft Internet Explorer.

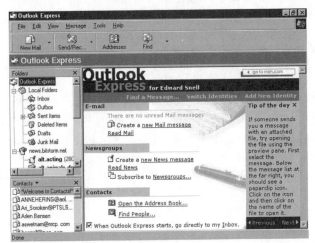

Among the links you'll likely find in any search for email programs are links to various versions of a program called Eudora, one of the most popular email programs outside of the suites. If you simply want to go straight to learning about and downloading Eudora (which is available for both Mac and Windows, in a freeware version called Eudora Light and a commercial version, Eudora Pro), visit the site of Eudora's maker at www.eudora.com.

If you use an online service, such as America Online or CompuServe, you may not be able to easily choose just any email program you want to email; you may be required to use the online service interface—the tool you use for accessing the service's non-Internet content—to send and receive email.

However, using an online service interface for email is similar to using an Internet email program, as described in this hour. And from the online service interface, you can send email both to others on your service and to anyone on the Internet.

You need not configure email, as described next, for an online service. Email configuration is handled automatically when you sign up for the service and install its software.

Configuring Email

After installing an email program, you need to configure it before you can use it. All email programs have a configuration dialog of some kind (or a series of dialogs) in which you can enter the information required for exchanging email. You'll find the configuration dialogs:

- **In Netscape Messenger,** by choosing Edit, Preferences to open the Preferences dialog. In the list of Categories, choose Mail & Newsgroups. Complete the configuration settings in the Mail & Newsgroups category's Identity and Mail Servers subcategories (see Figure 13.3).

- **For Outlook Express,** by completing the Mail dialogs of the Windows Internet Connection Wizard (see Hour 4). If you open Outlook Express without having configured it first, the Connection Wizard opens automatically to collect configuration information from you.

FIGURE 13.3

In Netscape Messenger, configure email settings in the Mail & Newsgroups category of the Preferences dialog box.

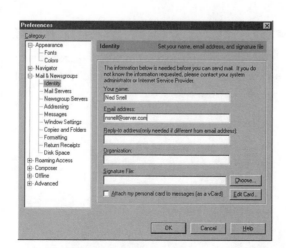

13

The automated setup routines supplied with programs such as Netscape
Communicator and Internet Explorer not only set up your browser and
Internet connection, but can optionally collect the information required to
configure their email components (Messenger and Outlook Express). See
Hour 4.

If you open Messenger or Outlook Express without first having configured
them, a dialog opens automatically, prompting for the configuration information.

The configuration dialogs for most email programs require most or all of the following
information, all of which your Internet service provider will tell you:

- Your full name. (Okay, so you don't need your ISP to tell you this one.)
- Your full email address. (Some configuration dialogs make you indicate the two
  parts of your address separately: the *username*—the part of the email address
  preceding the @ symbol—and your *domain*—the part of the email address
  following the @ symbol.)
- The address of your service provider's *outgoing mail server*, sometimes called the
  SMTP server.
- The address of your service provider's *incoming mail server*, sometimes called the
  POP3 server. The POP3 address is sometimes (but not always) identical to the
  SMTP address.

Also, to ensure that no one but you gets your email, most ISPs require you to choose and
use an email password. Some email programs let you enter that password in the configuration dialog so you needn't type a password each time you check your email.

Getting Around in Your Email Program

Before jumping right into sending and receiving messages, it's a good idea to learn how
to get around in your email program, move among its *folders* (lists of messages), and display messages you select from a folder.

When working with email, the only time you need to be connected to the Internet is when you actually send messages—transmit them to the Internet—or receive messages—copy them from the Internet to your computer. You can be online or offline while composing messages, reading messages you've received, or managing your messages.

You'll learn more about using email offline in Hour 20, "Working Smarter by Working Offline."

Choosing a Folder

Netscape Messenger and Outlook Express divide their messaging activities into a family of folders. In each folder, you see a list of messages you can display or work with in other ways. The folders are

- **Inbox**. The Inbox folder lists messages you have received.
- **Outbox** (called Unsent Messages in Messenger). The Outbox folder lists messages you have composed but saved to be sent later.
- **Sent**. The Sent folder lists copies of all messages you've sent, for your reference.
- **Deleted** (called Trash in Messenger). The Deleted folder lists messages you've deleted from any other folder.

Outlook Express and Messenger both handle two different jobs: Email and newsgroups. Each therefore has folders not only for email, but also for newsgroups. Before performing an email activity in one of these programs, always be sure first that you're in an email related folder, such as Inbox, and not a newsgroup folder.

You'll learn about using newsgroups in Hour 15, "Reading and Posting to Newsgroups."

13

To switch among folders in either Outlook Express or Messenger, click a folder name in the panel along the left side of the window (see Figure 13.4).

FIGURE 13.4

Select a folder to choose the messages you want to work with.

Folders

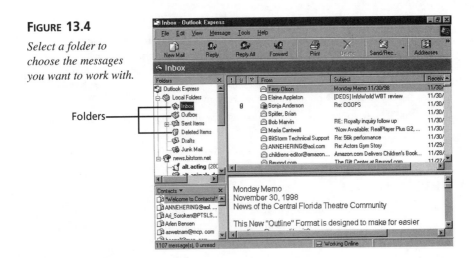

Displaying a Message

From the list displayed by each folder, you can display any message. You do this in either of two ways (the steps are the same in both Outlook Express and Messenger):

- Single-click the message in the list to display it in the preview pane (see Figure 13.5) in the bottom of the window.
- Double-click the message in the list to display it in its own message window (see Figure 13.6).

In general, the preview pane is best when you're simply scanning messages, and need to move quickly from one to the next. Use a full message window to read a long message, or to read a message you will reply to or forward (as described later in this hour).

Composing and Sending a Message

Once you have something to say, and the email address of someone to whom you want to say it, you're ready to go.

Writing Your Message

In most email programs, you compose your message in a window that's very much like a word processing program, with a special form at the top for filling in the address and subject information—the message's *header*. Below the form for the header, you type your message text in the large space provided for the message *body*.

FIGURE 13.5

Single-click a message in a folder to display the message in the preview pane.

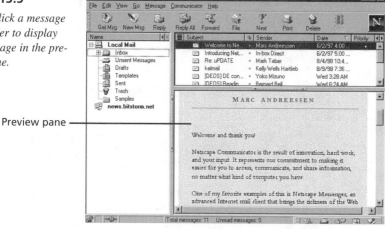

Preview pane —————

Message window

FIGURE 13.6

Double-click a message in a folder to display the message in a message window.

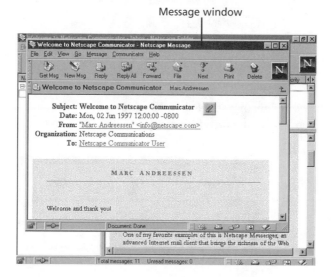

13

NEW TERM **Body** and **Header.** The *body* of a message is the text, which you compose in the large pane of the message window. The address information you type—including your recipient's email address and the subject of the message—is called the *header* of the message.

The following To Do shows how to compose a simple email message. Following the To Dos, the next section describes how you send that message.

To Do: Compose a New Message in Outlook Express

1. Click the New Mail button (Figure 13.7).

New Mail button

FIGURE 13.7

Step 1: Click the New Mail button in Outlook Express.

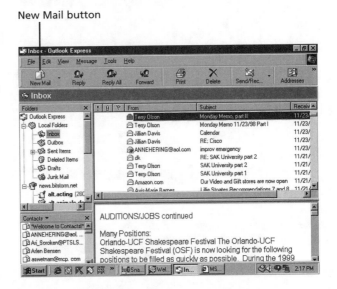

2. In the To line (near the top of the window), type the email address of the person to whom you want to send a message (Figure 13.8).

FIGURE 13.8

Step 2: Type in the recipient's email address.

To line

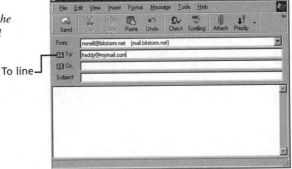

3. Click in the Subject line, and type a concise, meaningful subject for your message (Figure 13.9). (The subject appears in the message list of the recipient, to explain the purpose of your message.)

FIGURE 13.9

Step 3: Type in a subject for the message.

Subject line ——

4. Click in the large panel of the new message window and type your message, just as you would in a word processor (Figure 13.10).

FIGURE 13.10

Step 4: Type in your message.

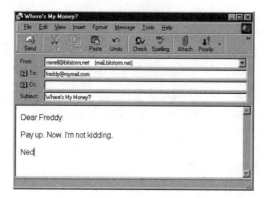

> As a general rule, you cannot use text formatting (fonts, bold, italic, underlining, and so on) in an email message, so for now, stick to simple text. In Hour 23, "Creating Web Pages and Multimedia Messages," however, you learn how to do some fancy message formatting. But you also learn that you must take care when dressing up messages, because many email recipients cannot display fancy formatting.

13

To Do: Compose a New Message in Netscape Messenger

1. Click the New Msg button (Figure 13.11).
2. Follow steps 2, 3, and 4 of the preceding To Do for composing a message.

New Msg button

FIGURE 13.11

Step 1: Click the New Msg button in Netscape Messenger.

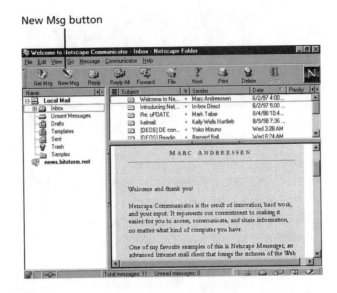

You can send one message to multiple recipients in several different ways. For example, you can "cc" (carbon copy) your email to recipients other than your primary addressee(s). See Hour 16, "Emailing Through the Web, Stopping Junk Mail, and Other Tips."

Sending a Message

After the header (To and Subject) and body (what you have to say) of the message are complete, you send your message on its way. In most programs, you do so simply by clicking a button labeled Send in the toolbar of the window in which you composed the message.

What happens immediately *after* you click Send depends upon a number of different factors:

- The email program you use
- Whether you're online or off
- How your program is configured

The message may be sent immediately out through the Internet to its intended recipient. If you're offline when you click Send, your email program may connect you to the Internet automatically to send the message. Otherwise, you must connect before sending.

However, instead of sending your message the instant you click Send, your email program may instead send the message to your Outbox (or Unsent Messages) folder, to wait. After clicking Send, you can open your Outbox or Unsent Messages folder to see if the message is there. (See Figure 13.12).

FIGURE 13.12

In some programs, messages are sent to wait in the Outbox or Unsent Messages folder, then finally go out to their recipients at a later time.

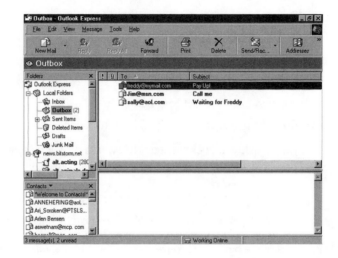

Why does this happen? Well, actually it's pretty smart. This Outbox scenario enables you to do all your email composing offline, saving as many messages as you want in your Outbox folder. Then, when you're all done, you can send all of the messages in one step.

In Hour 20, you'll learn how to make the most of this "delayed send" scenario, along with other offline techniques.

You'll also learn how to configure both Outlook Express and Messenger to do what you want: Either send messages right away, or send them to the Outbox or Unsent Messages folder for sending later.

13

Here's how to send waiting messages:

- In Outlook Express, click the Send/Recv button (it may be labeled "Send/Receive" in your copy) to send all messages in the Outbox folder.

- In Netscape Messenger, click the Get Msg button (short for Get Messages) to send all messages in the Unsent Messages folder.

If you are offline when you click the Send/Recv (Send/Receive) or Get Msg button, Outlook Express and Messenger connect you to the Internet automatically to send your messages.

The Send/Recv and Get Msg buttons not only send all waiting messages, but also receive any new messages sent to you. See "Receiving Messages," later in this hour.

Receiving Messages

When others send messages to you, those messages go to your service provider's mail server, and wait there until you choose to receive messages. To receive messages:

- **In Messenger,** click the Get Msg button on the toolbar.
- **In Outlook Express,** click the Send/Recv (or Send/Receive) button on the toolbar.

If you are offline when you click the Send/Recv or Get Msg button, Outlook Express and Messenger connect you to the Internet automatically to retrieve your new messages.

As I mentioned earlier, your ISP provides you with a special password you use only when receiving email (you don't need it to send email). When you click the button to receive mail, a dialog may appear to prompt for your password. Just type your password and press Enter to continue receiving email.

In the configuration dialogs of some email programs, you can type your email password; this enables the email program to automatically enter your password for you when you receive messages, saving you a step. This feature is handy, but should only be used if your computer is located where no one else might try to retrieve and read your email if you leave your desk while connected to the Internet.

Your email program contacts your ISP, and checks for any new messages addressed to you. If there are none, the words "No new messages on server" appear in the status bar at the bottom of the window. If there are new messages, the messages are copied to your PC and stored in your Inbox folder, where you can read them any time, online or off.

In the message lists displayed by most email programs, the messages you have not yet read appear in **bold** (see Figure 13.13).

FIGURE 13.13

Messages listed in the Inbox in bold type are those you have not read yet.

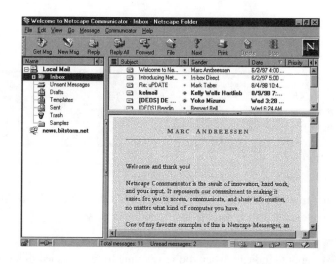

 Messages you receive can contain computer viruses, particularly (but not exclusively) when those messages have files attached to them and/or they come to you from strangers. See Hour 16 to learn how to protect yourself.

Replying and Forwarding

Most email programs provide you with two easy ways to create new messages by using other messages you have received: *reply* and *forward*.

NEW TERM **Replying** and **Forwarding.** *Replying* means sending a message back to someone from whom you have received a message, to respond to that message. *Forwarding* is passing a copy of a message you've received to a third party, either because you want to share the message's content with the third party or because you believe that, although the message was originally sent to you, the third party is a more appropriate recipient for it.

To reply or forward, you always begin by opening the original message. From the message window's toolbar, you then click a button or menu item with a label like one of the following (see Figure 13.14):

- **Reply.** Reply creates a reply to the person who sent you the message.
- **Reply All.** Reply All creates a reply to the person who sent you the message and to everyone else in the email's recipient list.
- **Forward.** Forward creates a new message containing the entire text of the original message, ready for you to forward.

13

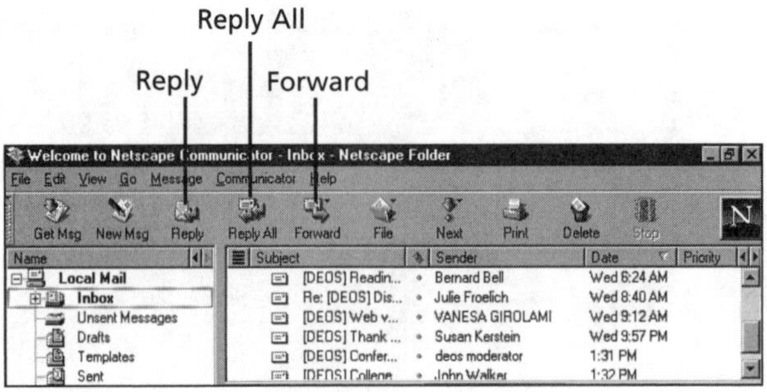

FIGURE 13.14

The Reply, Reply All, and Forward buttons offer different ways of responding to messages you've received.

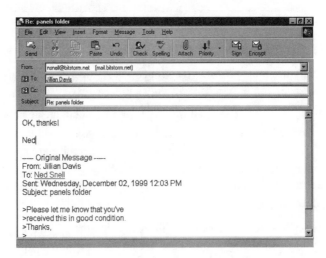

Reply All

Reply   Forward

Whichever button you click, a new message window opens. In the body of the message, a complete quote of the original message appears (see Figure 13.15).

NEW TERM **Quote.** A *quote* is all or a portion of a message you've received, included in a reply to indicate what you're replying to, or included in a forward to carry the message you're forwarding.

You can edit the quote, cutting out any parts that aren't relevant and inserting your own comments above, below, or within the quote.

FIGURE 13.15

A reply or a forward includes a quote from the original message.

In the message window of a reply, the To line is automatically filled in for you, with the address of the person from whom you received the message (or multiple addresses, if you chose Reply All). The Subject line is filled in with the original message's subject, preceded by Re:, to indicate that your message is a reply to a message using that subject. To complete the reply, all you have to do is type your comments above, below, or within the quote, and then click Send.

In the message window of a forward, the To line is empty, so that you can enter the address of the person to whom you want to forward the message. (As with any message, you can enter multiple To recipients, and Cc recipients as well.) The Subject line is filled in with the original message's subject, preceded by FW: (*forward*). To complete the forward, address the message, type your comments above, below, or within the quote, and then click Send.

Using an Address Book

Most folks find that there's a steady list of others to whom they email often. Keeping track of those all important names and addresses, and using them, is easier when you use your email program's *address book*.

 Address Book. A directory you create, containing the names, email addresses and often other information (mailing address, phone, notes) about your contacts.

When an addressee's information is in your address book, you needn't type—or even remember—his or her email address. Instead, you can simply choose the person's name from the address book, and your email program fills in the address for you. Some address books also support *nicknames*—short, easy-to-remember names you type in the To line of a message instead of the full email address.

Adding to Your Address Book

In both Outlook Express and Messenger, the easiest way to add to your address book is to copy information from messages you've received. For example, if you've received a message from Sue, you can use that message to quickly create an address card you can use to send messages to Sue.

To create a new address book entry from a message, begin by displaying the message in its own window. Next...

- **In Netscape Messenger,** from the message window's menu bar, choose Message, Add Sender to Address Book. A New Card dialog opens (see Figure 13.16). Make sure the name and email address boxes on the Name tab have been filled in, and complete any of the other, optional boxes you want. Click OK to save the new entry.

- **In Outlook Express,** from the message window's menu bar, choose Tools, Add to Address Book, Sender. Make sure the name and email address boxes on the Name tab have been filled in, and complete any of the other, optional boxes and tabs you want. Click OK to save the new entry.

13

FIGURE 13.16

When you use a message you have received to add someone to your address book, that person's name and email address are entered for you, automatically.

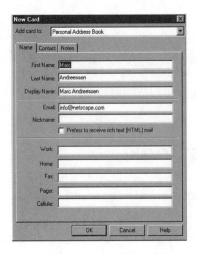

To create an address book entry from scratch (without beginning from a message you've received):

- **In Outlook Express,** choose Tools, Address Book, click the New button, then choose New Contact from the menu that appears.
- **In Netscape Messenger,** choose Communicator, Address Book, then click the New Card button.

Addressing a Message from the Address Book

To use an address book entry to address a message (in Netscape Messenger or Outlook Express), begin by opening the new message window as usual. Then open the address book list:

- **In Netscape Messenger,** by clicking the Address button.
- **In Outlook Express,** by clicking the little icon in the To line that looks like an open address book.

In the list, click the name of an addressee, and click the To button to add the addressee to the To line (see Figure 13.17).

When done choosing recipients, click OK to close the address book, and complete the Subject and body of your message.

FIGURE 13.17

Use your Address book to fill in the To line.

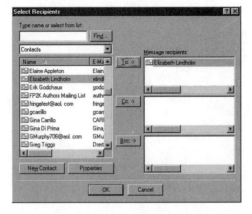

Summary

Wow! You learned a lot this hour. As you saw, the hardest part about email is getting yourself set up for it. Composing, sending, and receiving messages is a breeze, and techniques that can make you even more productive—such as using an Outbox or Address Book—are also pretty easy, and always optional.

Q&A

Q Can I look over messages I've already sent, to recall what I wrote to someone?

A Sure. Most email programs include a Sent(or Sent Messages) folder, in which a copy of every message you send is saved. If you need to refer later to a message you've sent, find its copy in your Sent folder.

Q Can I send a file, like a picture or a program, through email?

A A file sent through email is called an "attachment" because it's attached to a regular email message. You learn how to attach files to messages in Hour 16.

13

HOUR 14

Joining a Mailing List

The Internet boasts two different facilities commonly described as *discussion groups* that differ only in the medium on which the discussion takes place. In the first type of discussion group, *mailing lists*, you read the discussion in email messages you receive, and contribute to the discussion by sending email. In the second type of discussion group, *newsgroups*, you read messages on, and send messages to, a *news server* (more about newsgroups in Hour 15, "Reading and Posting to Newsgroups").

Regardless of the type you use, discussion groups are a great way to keep up with news about any imaginable topic, and to engage in conversation and debate with others online who share your interests.

The great thing about mailing lists (besides the fact that they are perhaps the best way to get in-depth, authoritative info on a topic) is that you already know most of what you need to know to use them; you know how to send and receive email. All you need to learn is where and how to find the mailing lists that interest you, how to sign up, and how to quit a mailing list if you lose interest in it. Once you sign up, getting the latest, greatest news and discussion on any topic is as easy as retrieving your daily email. And asking experts a question is as easy as sending an email message.

At the end of the hour, you'll be able to answer the following questions:

- What are the two kinds of mailing lists, and the two different email addresses I need to use most mailing lists?
- How can I find the addresses for mailing lists covering topics that interest me?
- How do I join a mailing list and contribute to it?
- What rules of online courtesy—*netiquette*—must I observe when contributing to a mailing list?

The Two Types of Mailing Lists

For a mailing list to work, someone has to handle its management and administration: mostly signing up new members and removing members who have asked to be removed.

In a few mailing lists, that administration task is handled by a real person. However, most mailing lists are managed not by a person, but by a *Listserv*. Sometimes, the mailing lists managed by people are called *manual* mailing lists, to distinguish them from the lists automated by Listservs.

NEW TERM   **Listserv.** A program that automatically manages a mailing list. Actually, there are several different programs that manage mailing lists, including Listserv, Listproc, and Majordomo. But the term Listserv is often used generically to refer to all such programs, and often to the lists they manage, as well.

Finding a Mailing List

The first step in using mailing lists is finding one that interests you. When visiting Web pages devoted to your favorite topics, you'll often see mention of related mailing lists, along with the email address required for signing up: the *subscription address*.

You can also visit any of several Web pages that help folks find mailing lists related to a particular subject. A good first stop is Liszt (`www.Liszt.com`), a search tool dedicated to helping you find and use mailing lists (see Figure 14.1).

You can browse through Liszt's categories to find a list, or use its search engine to find lists related to a search term you enter.

FIGURE 14.1

Use Liszt to browse for a mailing list, or search for one.

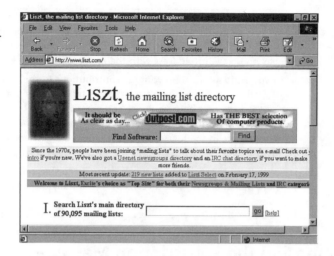

Besides Liszt, other good places to find mailing lists (and instructions for using them) include the following:

- The list of Publicly Accessible Mailing Lists at www.neosoft.com/internet/paml
- The List of Lists, at catalog.com/vivian/interest-group-search.html
- Yahoo!'s directory at www.yahoo.com/Computers_and_Internet/Internet/ Mailing_Lists/

If the address of Yahoo's mailing list directory looks like too much typing, try this. From Yahoo's top page (www. yahoo.com), click on the Computers & Internet category. On the page that appears, click on Internet. On the next page, choose Mailing Lists.

Subscribing to a Mailing List

To use any mailing list, you need to know two different email addresses:

- The address of the person, or program, that manages the list. This address might be called the "management" or "subscription" address.
- The list address, an email address to which you send all of your contributions to the list, the comments or questions you want all others in the list to see.

14

> Sorry, sorry... Hate to break into an easy topic like mailing lists with a big fat Caution. But I really want to alert you to the one major mailing list mistake: Mixing up the *list* address with the *management* address, and vice versa.
>
> If you accidentally send your list contributions to the management address, the others on the list won't see them. And if you send management commands to the list address, those commands will not be carried out. Worse, the message containing those commands might show up in the mailing list of everyone in the list, which won't win you any friends.
>
> Never forget: Contributions to the discussion go to the list address, commands for managing your subscription go to that other address (subscription, management, whatever), which is usually the same one you used to subscribe.

Composing the Subscription Message

When you're ready to sign up, you send to the subscription address a simple email message that contains the command required to subscribe. Unfortunately, the command differs from list to list.

Most references to mailing lists—including those you'll turn up in the directories described earlier—include subscription instructions. Those instructions typically tell you the command you must send, and also *where* in the email message—the Subject line or the message body—you must type that command.

Command instructions use a *syntax diagram* to tell you what to type. Even manually managed lists generally require a particular command syntax, although they're more forgiving of command mistakes than automated lists are.

NEW TERM **Syntax diagram.** A *syntax diagram* shows what you must type in order to properly phrase a command to control a computer program, such as a Listserv. In a syntax diagram, the exact words you must type are shown in normal type, while any parts of the command you must add are surrounded by brackets or shown in italics.

For example, to phrase the command indicated by the syntax diagram

subscribe *lastname firstname*

or

subscribe [lastname] [firstname]

I would type

subscribe Snell Ned

Notice that I replace any portions in italics or brackets with the information indicated, and that I do not type the brackets.

To subscribe to a list, read the instructions to find the following:

- The syntax diagram for subscribing
- The part of the message in which to type the command (either the Subject line or body)
- The subscription address

Compose an email message containing only the command indicated by the instructions, and send it to the subscription address. Figure 14.2 shows a typical subscription message in which the command appears in the message body.

FIGURE 14.2

You subscribe to a mailing list by typing a subscription command in an email message and sending it to the list's subscription address.

When composing your message, don't type anything the instructions don't ask for. If the instructions tell you to put the command in the message's Subject line, leave the message body blank. If the command belongs in the message body, leave the Subject line blank, and put nothing but the command in the body. (Many lists don't care whether you follow this rule, but since you can't predict which lists *do* care, it's best to follow the rule always.)

> Because many automated list management programs manage more than one list, the subscription command syntax often includes the name of the list, so the program knows which list you're subscribing to; for example:
>
> subscribe *listname firstname lastname*

Reading the Welcome Message

14

Shortly after you send your subscription message, you'll receive a reply message from the list. An automated list may reply within a minute or two; after sending a subscription message to an automated list, stay online, wait a few minutes, and then check your email—the reply will probably be there. (Some automated and manual lists may take a day or more to reply, so be patient, and don't resend the subscription message if you don't get an immediate reply.)

If you did not phrase your subscription message properly, the reply reiterates the subscription command syntax and usually includes instructions. You must compose and send another subscription message, carefully following any instructions in the reply.

Once you subscribe successfully, you receive a Welcome message like the one shown in Figure 14.3.

Always, always, always read *and save* the Welcome message, if for no other reason than that it contains the instructions for *unsubscribing*—quitting—the mailing list if you choose to do so later.

FIGURE 14.3

A Welcome message tells you that you've subscribed, and also supplies general instructions.

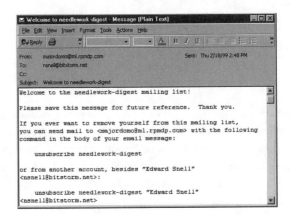

The Welcome message contains lots of very valuable information, particularly:

- A syntax diagram for phrasing the command to *un*subscribe. If and when you decide you no longer want to receive messages from the list, you'll need to send this command to the subscription address.

- The list address to which you must send all of your contributions, and the management address (which is usually the same as the subscription address, but not always).

- Syntax for other commands you can use to manage the way messages come to you. For example, many lists let you send a command to temporarily pause—stop sending you messages—if you go on vacation or want messages paused for any other reason.

- Any other rules or policies all members of the list are required to observe. These typically include the basic rules of netiquette (see "Observing Proper Netiquette," later in this hour).

> Sometimes, the Welcome message includes instructions to send a reply to the Welcome, to confirm your subscription. In such cases, you're not officially subscribed until you send a reply as instructed.

Always read and save the Welcome message, so you can refer to it when you need to know a command or policy or want to unsubscribe. If your email program lets you organize your messages in folders, create a special folder for Welcome messages, so they're easy to find and you don't accidentally delete them when cleaning up your Inbox. You may also want to print the Welcome message and file it.

Shortly after you receive the Welcome message (and reply to it, if so instructed), you'll begin receiving email messages from the list. How many and how often depends on the list, but it's not unusual to receive a dozen or more messages per day. Read anything that looks interesting; ignore (or delete) the rest.

> Some mailing lists are purely informational. They're designed not as a discussion forum, but to keep you abreast of news and developments in a particular company or other organization.
>
> Usually, such lists don't have list addresses to which you can contribute. It's a one-way conversation; you just subscribe, and then read whatever shows up.

To Do: Subscribe to a List

Just for kicks, subscribe to a list. This To Do shows how to subscribe to the Ballroom list, which is devoted to ballroom and swing dancing, but if you've already found the address of another list you really want to subscribe to, feel free to substitute that one. (Also, if you go with the Ballroom list, I'll give you a chance to bail without subscribing, when the time comes.)

1. In your email program, start a new message (Figure 14.4).
2. In the To line, enter the Ballroom list subscription address (Figure 14.5):

   `listserv@mitvma.mit.edu`

14

FIGURE 14.4

Step 1: Start a new message.

FIGURE 14.5

Step 2: Fill in the subscription address.

FIGURE 14.6

Step 3: Type in the subscribe command.

4. Send the message. After a few minutes, check your email. You will probably have received a Welcome message, prompting you to reply if you really want to subscribe (Figure 14.7).

5. To start receiving messages about ballroom dancing, reply to the message as instructed. To avoid subscribing, don't reply; the Welcome message expires in 48 hours.

▼

FIGURE 14.7

Step 4: Send the message and wait for the reply.

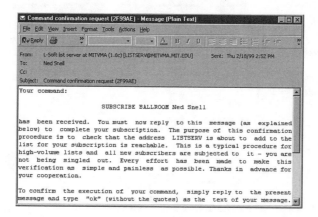

▲

Mailing lists can send dozens of messages a day, which can clutter up your Inbox and make it hard to find other messages. If your email program supports a facility called *filtering*, you can set up a separate folder where all messages from the list are stored automatically as soon as they're received, leaving your Inbox for other mail. See Hour 16, "Emailing Through the Web, Stopping Junk Mail, and Other Tips."

Contributing to a Mailing List

You are not required to contribute to a mailing list. Many people simply read and enjoy the messages they receive, and never add their own comments or questions.

If you do feel inspired to contribute, just send a message to the list address. If the contribution is related to a previous message, use your email program's Reply feature to reply to the group, and include in the reply a quote of any portion of the original message that's relevant to your comment or question. See Figure 14.8.

When using Reply to send a message to a mailing list, always double-check the To line in your message to be sure that it shows the correct list address. Many lists are configured so that when you click Reply, the message is addressed not to the list, but to the individual sender of the message. In such cases, you'll want to type the actual list address in the To line (or choose that address from your Inbox).

14

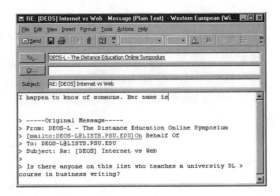

FIGURE 14.8

You can use your email program's Reply button to reply to a specific message you receive from a list.

Observing Proper *Netiquette*

How you communicate with private friends in email is between you and your friends. But once you begin contributing to discussion groups—mailing lists and newsgroups— you're participating in a public forum, and have an obligation to follow a code of conduct that keeps the conversation pleasant and productive for all.

Netiquette—the unofficial code of online conduct—can be boiled down to the Golden Rule: Do unto others. As you gain experience, you'll begin to notice things others do that bug you, such as quoting too much or writing sloppily. Obviously, those are the things you must remember not to do yourself.

Here are the basics of being a good cyber-citizen, particularly in discussion groups. Note that none of this stuff is law; if you skip a rule, the cyber-police will not show up at your door. (Although there are a few strictly managed lists that will kick you out if you break certain rules—another reason to read and follow the Welcome message!) Like all forms of courtesy, netiquette is often not strictly required, but always highly recommended.

- **Don't shout.** SOME FOLKS LIKE TO TYPE ALL MESSAGES ONLY IN CAPITAL LETTERS, and some others overuse capital letters FOR EMPHASIS! Capitalize like a person, and use your word choices and phrasing for emphasis, saving the all-caps trick for rare, EXTREME EMPHASIS.

- **Stay on topic.** Nothing's more aggravating than subscribing to a list and then receiving all sorts of messages that veer off on tangents. If your message does not pertain directly to the discussion group's stated topic, don't send it.

- **Keep current.** Newcomers to a list or group, or folks who only drop in occasionally, tend to ask questions that have already been asked and answered a dozen times, which annoys the regulars. Keep up with the conversation so you know what's going on. Read the FAQ, if one is available.

NEW TERM **FAQ.** *Frequently Asked Questions*, a file that contains a general list of common questions and answers pertaining to a particular list, newsgroup, Web page, or other topic.

By reading FAQs (pronounced "faks" so that computer book authors can make stupid puns with "fax"), you can come quickly up to speed on the background information shared by others in the group.

When a FAQ is available for a mailing list, you'll find instructions for obtaining the FAQ in the Welcome message.

- **Don't use sarcasm.** It's very difficult to communicate sarcasm effectively in a written message. Often, exaggerated messages intended as sarcasm are taken literally by those who read them, and confusion or arguments ensue.

- **Keep personal discussions personal.** Before sending any message, ask yourself: Would this message interest the whole list, or is it really a personal message to just one member? If the message is really for one person, you can find that person's email address in the header information quoted in all list and newsgroup messages, and send your comment or question directly to that person, in private.

> Avoid small, conversational contributions that add little information. For example, if someone posts a message with a great idea in it, don't send a reply to the group just to say "Great idea!" No one wants to go to the trouble of receiving and opening a message with so little to say.

- **Don't over-quote.** When replying, cut quotes down to just what's necessary to show what you're replying to. When a series of replies builds up and nobody cuts the quotes, each message can be pages long even if it contains only one new sentence. Try to leave enough information so that a newcomer to the conversation can tell what's being discussed, but cut everything else.

- **Write and spell well.** In the name of speed and efficiency, some folks boil their msg.s down to a grp. of abbrev.'s &/or shorthnd, or write toooo quikly and slopppilly. Do your readers the courtesy of writing whole words and complete sentences, and fix mistakes before you send.

- **Neither *flame* nor counter-flame.** A *flame* is an angry tirade or attack in a message, the kind that flares when a debate grows into a spat. No matter how hot the argument gets, try to keep your cool. When flamed personally, don't rise to the bait: Flame wars only escalate, and no one ever wins.

14

Some folks flame others for breaches of netiquette, but that's hypocritical. Take responsibility for your own online behavior, and let others worry about theirs.

- **Fit in.** Usually, I'm no fan of conformity. But every mailing list and newsgroup has its own, insular culture. After reading messages for awhile, you'll pick up a sense of the general technical level of the group, whether they're experts or novices (or both) on the topic at hand, the overall tone, catchphrases, vocabulary, and so on.

  By all means, be yourself—any group needs fresh ideas, new personalities. But try to be yourself within the style and culture of the group, to ensure that you can be understood by all.

Adding Personality with Smileys and Shorthand

Over the years, a system of symbols and shorthand has developed to enable folks to be more expressive in their messages: *Smileys* and *shorthand*. You'll see both used online often, in discussion groups and in email.

Although I show you smileys and shorthand next, I'm doing so mainly to help you understand them in messages you receive. Except for the occasional, simple smiley face, I don't recommend using these in your contributions to discussion groups.

There are many newcomers online today who don't know smileys or shorthand, so if you use these, many of your readers won't understand you. Try to put all of your meaning in your words, so everybody gets the message.

Smileys

Smileys are used to communicate the tone of a message, to add an emotional inflection. (In fact, smileys are sometimes called *emoticons*—emotional icons.) They're little pictures, usually of faces, that are built out of text characters.

To see the picture, you tilt your head to the left. For example, tilt your head to the left (or tilt this book to the right) while looking at the smiley below, which is made up of three characters: a colon, a dash, and a close parenthesis:

:-)

Looks like a little smiling face, doesn't it? Folks follow a statement with this smiley to indicate that the statement is a joke, or is made facetiously; for example:

Just for that, I'm leaving you everything in my will. : -)

There are many different smileys, some so obscure that only the real Net jocks use or understand them. But you're likely only to see the basics, including the basic smile shown earlier and also:

: - (—Frown

; -) —Wink

: - 0 —Surprise

8 -) —Smile with glasses or bug-eyed

: ' - (—Crying

: - D —Laughing

> Some folks omit the nose from their smileys; for example:
>
> :) ;)   :0

Shorthand

Shorthand abbreviations are used to carry a common phrase efficiently, to save space and typing. Some of these are commonly used offline, every day, such as ASAP (As Soon As Possible). Another shorthand expression used commonly online is IMO (In My Opinion) and its cousin, IMHO (In My Humble Opinion). For example:

The Godfather is the greatest film of the '70s, IMHO.

Other popular shorthand expressions include the following:

BTW—By The Way

B4—Before

FWIW—For What It's Worth

IBTD—I Beg To Differ

IOW—In Other Words

LOL—Laughing Out Loud (generally used to declare that a statement is laughable)

OTOH—On The Other Hand

ROTFL—Rolling On The Floor Laughing (generally used to declare that a statement is extremely laughable)

14

Summary

Mailing lists are easy. Once you understand the difference between the list address and the management address, and learn how to phrase a subscription command, the rest is a cinch. And they are a great way to keep up with the latest, most authoritative info about a particular topic.

But not the only way. Mailing lists aren't for everyone, or for every topic—it all depends on what you want. Personally, I subscribe to just a few lists, on topics I have a very deep and daily interest in. For more casual interests, I prefer newsgroups (coming up next, in Hour 15, "Reading and Posting to Newsgroups"). I must manage so much work-related email traffic that the steady flow from a mailing list gets in my way, if the topic isn't central to my day. Once you learn about newsgroups, you'll be in a position to decide which type of Internet "discussion group" you prefer for each of your interests.

Q&A

Q I've seen forms in Web pages that say I can fill them in to get on a mailing list related to the page's topic. How are those Web-based mailing lists different from the regular ones?

A Some lists you subscribe to through the Web are not "Web-based." The Web page merely supplies a convenient front-end to an otherwise normal mailing list.

You subscribe by filling in a Web page form, but then the Web page passes your form entries—name and email address—to a list management program, which emails you the usual Welcome message. From there, using the list is pretty much like using any other mailing list.

Mailing lists you subscribe to through Web forms are usually the informational type—designed to keep you posted about news and events in an organization—rather than the type intended for interactive discussion.

There are Web-based discussion groups, however, which are more like newsgroups (see Hour 15) than mailing lists. You learn about Web-based discussion groups in Hour 16.

HOUR 15

Reading and Posting to Newsgroups

Mailing lists are a great way to keep up with a subject, but not always an efficient way. Some mailing lists can post 20 or more new messages a day, and many of those are trivial. Sure, you want to keep up with the subject, but you don't want to be buried in email every day.

Newsgroups carry pretty much the same discussions that mailing lists do. In fact, many mailing lists and newsgroups that cover the same topic carry the very same conversation; they're hooked together so that all messages sent to either the mailing list or the newsgroup show up in both. But unlike mailing lists, newsgroups don't come to you—you go to them. Whenever you want to catch up on the news, you access the newsgroup through your newsgroup program (*newsreader*), scroll through the list of current messages, and read just the ones that interest you.

At the end of the hour, you'll be able to answer the following questions:

- What are newsgroups?
- How do I set up my newsreader?
- How do I find and open a newsgroup?
- How do I navigate among and read the messages in a newsgroup?
- How do I contribute to a newsgroup?
- How do I search for and display newsgroup messages through my browser?

Getting Started with Newsgroups

When you know how to use an email program, you know 90 percent of what you need to know to use newsgroups. Reading a message, composing a new message, and replying are all very similar in an email program and a newsreader.

Where a newsreader differs, of course, is that it retrieves messages from and posts messages to Internet newsgroups, sometimes known as discussion groups or, collectively, as Usenet. The newsgroups and their messages are stored on a family of servers called *news servers* or *NNTP servers*.

 Post. Sending a message to a newsgroup is known as *posting*, because you're publishing the message in a public forum, just as if you had "posted" a paper note on a bulletin board.

Your ISP or online service has a news server you are authorized to use for reading and contributing to newsgroups. Access to one news server is all you need; the messages sent to any news server on the Internet are automatically copied—at regular intervals—to all news servers.

On any news server, you can open any newsgroup and read any current message posted to that newsgroup, no matter which news server the message was originally posted to. That's why a newsgroup on an ISP's server in New York has messages from folks in Canada, California, and the U.K.

Before you can open newsgroups and display their messages, you must configure your newsreader to contact your ISP's news server, and you must download the complete list of newsgroups from the server.

15

In general, all news servers carry the same newsgroups and current messages—but not exactly.

First, a few ISPs or online services do not carry all newsgroups, omitting those they deem potentially offensive to their customers, such as sex-oriented groups. A few ISPs carry only newsgroups specifically requested by their subscribers, instead of all of the thousands of groups out there. And some ISP's servers carry special newsgroups of local interest that are not copied to other news servers.

Beyond those differences, note that it takes a day or so for a message posted to one server to be copied to all of the others. At any given time, a new message may be on some servers, but not yet on others.

Finally, no news server keeps messages forever. After a set number of days, a newsgroup message is automatically deleted from the server. Each server has its own schedule for removing these old—*expired*—messages, so a message that's been deleted from one server may remain on others.

Configuring Your Newsreader

As with other types of Internet programs, there are many different newsreaders out there. In the Big Two Internet suites, the programs are the same ones you use for email: Netscape Messenger and Outlook Express. You just have to switch these programs from email mode to newsgroup mode.

To switch either program to newsgroup mode, you simply click your news server's name near the bottom of the folder list (see Figure 15.1). Observe that choosing the server changes the toolbar buttons and menu choices from those used for email to those you need for newsgroups.

You can open Outlook Express directly in newsgroup mode from Internet Explorer 5 by clicking the Mail button on IE5's toolbar, then choosing Read News from the menu that appears. You can open Netscape Messenger directly in newsgroup mode by choosing Communicator, Newsgroups from within any Communicator component (such as Navigator).

If you use an online service, such as America Online or CompuServe, you may not be able to choose your own newsreader; you may be required to use the online service interface—the tool you use for accessing the service's non-Internet content—to access newsgroups.

FIGURE **15.1**

To use Netscape Messenger (shown here) or Outlook Express for newsgroup activities, click your news server's name in the folder list.

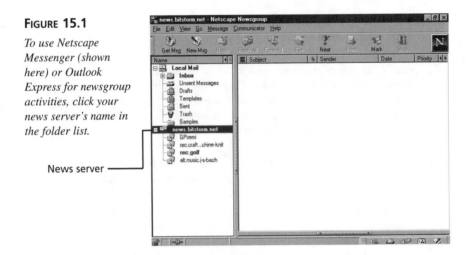

News server

All newsreaders have a configuration dialog in which you enter the information required for communicating with your ISP's news server. That dialog always requires the address of your ISP's news server. If your newsreader is not part of a suite (and thus cannot copy configuration information from the email component), the configuration dialog also requires your email address and full name.

You'll find the configuration dialog:

- **For Netscape Messenger,** by choosing Edit, Preferences to open the Preferences dialog. In the list of Categories, choose Mail & Newsgroups (see Figure 15.2). Complete the configuration settings in the Mail & Newsgroups category's Newsgroup Servers subcategory.

- **For Outlook Express,** by completing the News dialogs of the Connection Wizard (see Hour 4, "Connecting to the Internet"). If you choose your news server folder in Outlook Express without having configured first, the Internet Connection Wizard opens automatically.

Instead of using the Internet Connection Wizard, you can configure newsgroup access in Outlook Express by choosing Tools, Accounts, then clicking the Add button on the Internet Accounts dialog.

FIGURE 15.2

Use the Preferences dialog to configure newsgroup access in Netscape Messenger.

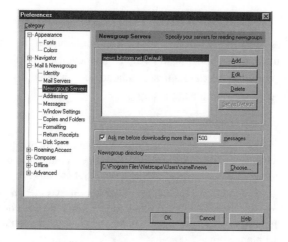

15

Downloading the Newsgroups List

Once your newsreader knows how to contact the server, you must download the complete list of newsgroups, which usually takes just a few minutes. If you open some newsreaders (including Netscape Messenger and Outlook Express) without first having downloaded the list, a prompt appears, asking whether you want to download the list.

If your newsreader does not prompt you, find a button or menu item for downloading the list:

- **In Netscape Messenger,** make sure you are in newsgroup mode by clicking the name of your news server or choosing Communicator, Newsgroups. Choose File, Subscribe, and on the dialog that appears, click the Refresh List button.

- **In Outlook Express,** click the name of your news server, then click the Newsgroups button. On the dialog that appears, click Reset List.

> The list of newsgroups changes periodically, adding new groups and removing others. Netscape Messenger, Outlook Express, and some other newsreaders detect automatically when the list changes, and display a prompt asking whether you want to update your list.
>
> If your newsreader does not detect changes in the list, it's smart to re-download the full list once a month or so, to keep current.

Finding and Subscribing to Newsgroups

Once the list has been downloaded to your computer, you can find and subscribe to any newsgroups you want. While exploring Web pages devoted to topics that interest you, you'll probably come across the names of related newsgroups. But newsgroups are easy to find, with or without a Web page's help.

Unlike mailing lists, you are not required to subscribe to a newsgroup in order to use it. All subscribing really does is add the group to an easy-access list in your newsreader, to make visiting it convenient.

Most people have a small list of groups they visit often, so subscribing makes sense. But in most newsreaders, you can pick a newsgroup out of the full list, or enter the group's name in a dialog, to open the list without subscribing.

Newsgroups are perhaps the one Internet activity where names are a reliable indicator of content. Newsgroups are organized under a system of names and categories. The leftmost portion of the name shows the top-level category in which the group sits; each portion further to the right more narrowly determines the subject of the group.

For example, the top-level category `rec` contains *rec*reational newsgroups, those dedicated to a recreational—rather than professional—discussion of their topics. So the hypothetical newsgroup name

`rec.sports.basketball.womens`

indicates that the discussion focuses on a recreational interest in women's basketball. There are thousands of `rec` groups, many `rec.sports` groups, several `rec.sports.basketball` groups, and just one `rec.sports.basketball.womens` newsgroup. See how it works?

Some of the other major top-level categories include the following:

- `alt`—*Alt*ernative newsgroups, those in which the most free-wheeling conversations are accepted
- `biz`—Business newsgroups and ads
- `comp`—*Comp*uter-related newsgroups
- `k12`—Education-related groups
- `misc`—*Misc*ellaneous
- `sci`—*Sci*ence-related groups

To Do: Choose, Subscribe to, and Open Groups in Netscape Messenger

1. Connect to the Internet, open Netscape Messenger, and click the news server's name in the left-hand column (Figure 15.3).

FIGURE 15.3

Step 1: Click on the news server's name in the left-hand column of Netscape Messenger.

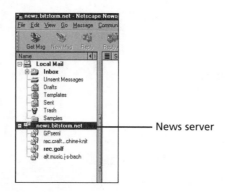

— News server

2. Choose File, Subscribe (Figure 15.4).

FIGURE 15.4

Step 2: Choose File, Subscribe.

3. In the All tab, display the group's name in the Newsgroup box (Figure 15.5). There are several ways to do this:

- If you know the exact name of the group you want to subscribe to, type the name in the box.

- Use the list to scroll to the group name, then click it. In the list, the groups are presented alphabetically and also organized by category; display a category's subcategories or groups by clicking the plus sign (+) that precedes it.

▼   • Click the Search tab, and enter a search term to locate group names contain-
                       ing the term. Click the name of the group you want to subscribe to.

FIGURE 15.5

*Step 3: Display the
group's name in the
Newsgroup box.*

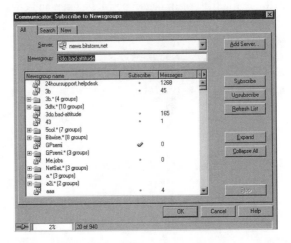

4. When the name of the group you want to subscribe to is highlighted, click the
   Subscribe button, then click OK (Figure 15.6).

FIGURE 15.6

*Step 4: Click the
Subscribe button.*

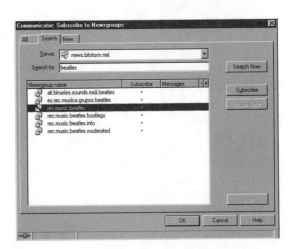

5. Subscribed newsgroups are listed under your news server's name. If you don't
   see newsgroups listed under your server, click the plus sign (+) to the left of the
   server name to display them. To open a newsgroup, click its name in the list
▼   (Figure 15.7).

FIGURE 15.7

Step 5: Click the news-group name to open a list of messages.

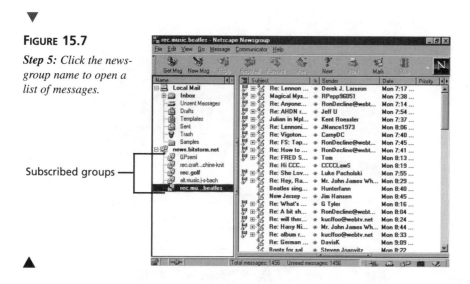

Subscribed groups

To Do: Choose, Subscribe to, and Open Groups in Outlook Express

1. Connect to the Internet, open Outlook Express, and click the news server's name in the left-hand column (Figure 15.8).

FIGURE 15.8

Step 1: Click the news server's name in Outlook Express.

News server

▼ 2. Click the Newsgroups button (Figure 15.9).

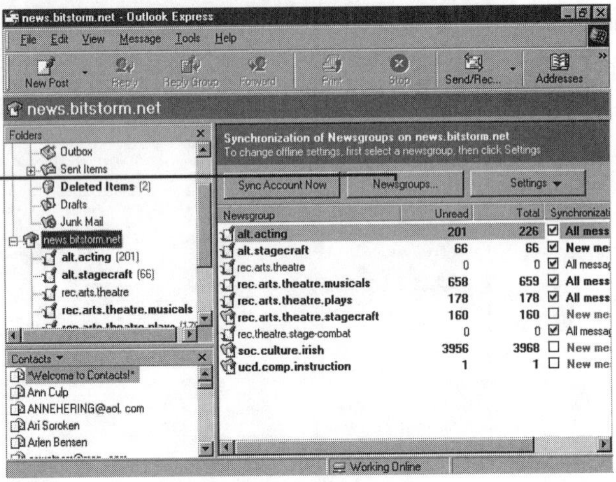

FIGURE 15.9

Step 2: Click the
Newsgroups button.

Newsgroups button —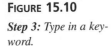

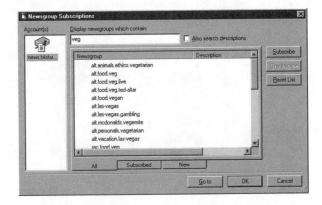

3. Type a word related to the topic for which you want to find a list (Figure 15.10).

FIGURE 15.10

Step 3: Type in a key-
word.

4. When you see in the list the name of a group you want to subscribe to, click it to select it. Click the Subscribe button to subscribe to the selected newsgroup, and then click OK (Figure 15.11).

5. To show messages in the list, double-click the group's name (Figures 15.12 and 15.13).

▼

▼
FIGURE 15.11

Step 4: Highlight a group and click Subscribe.

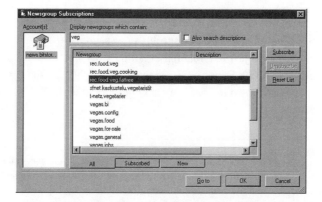

FIGURE 15.12

Step 5: Double-click the group's name.

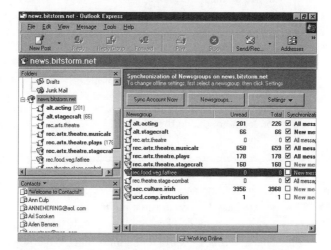

FIGURE 15.13

Step 5: When you open a newsgroup, the list of current messages appears.

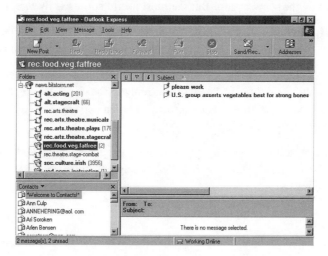

15

▲

Reading Newsgroup Messages

Once you open and display a newsgroup's message list (peek ahead to Figure 15.14), reading messages is just like reading email messages in an email program. In Netscape Messenger or Outlook Express, you single-click an item in the list to display it in the preview pane (as shown in 15.14), or double-click it to display the message in its own window.

The message lists you see in an email program generally show messages that have been copied to your computer. But in most newsreaders, the messages in the list you see when you open a newsgroup are not on your computer; they're on the news server.

All that's been copied to your computer are the message *headers*, to make up the list. When you display any particular message, that message is then copied to your computer. Because the messages aren't copied until you request them, you must stay online while working with newsgroups.

Some newsreaders—including Netscape Messenger and Outlook Express—support *offline news reading*. You can configure them to automatically download messages from newsgroups so you can read them later, offline. You learn how to do this in Hour 20, "Working Smarter by Working Offline."

The tricky part about reading news messages is organizing the list in a way that works for you. Most newsreaders let you arrange the messages in myriad ways: Alphabetically by subject, by author, by date, and so on. (The options for sorting the message list in Netscape Messenger, Outlook Express, and most other Windows and Mac newsreaders appear on the View menu.) But the most useful sorting is by *thread*.

NEW TERM **Thread.** In a newsgroup, a *thread* is one particular conversation—a message and all replies to that message (and replies to those replies, and so on).

In effect, threads group messages by subject. Two messages can have the same subject but not the same thread, if neither is a reply to the other (or a reply to a reply to the other). If you sort messages by thread, and then by subject, you'll get all threads on a given subject grouped together.

When you sort messages by thread (see Figure 15.14), you can follow the flow of the conversation, click your way in order, through the messages to see how the discussion has progressed.

In most newsreaders, when messages are sorted by threads, the replies to a message do not appear automatically in the list; instead, a plus sign (+) appears next to the message's listing, to indicate that there are sub-messages—replies—to that message. To display the replies, click the plus sign.

15

FIGURE 15.14

You can organize your newsgroup message list by thread, to better follow the flow of individual conversations.

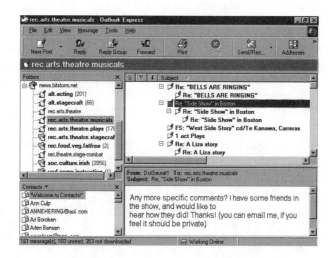

Composing and Replying to Messages

You compose and reply to messages in a newsreader exactly as you do in an email program. The only differences are in the message header, because instead of addressing a message to a person, you're addressing it to a newsgroup.

The only other important difference between sending email and newsgroup messages is the terminology you see applied on buttons and menu items:

- In email, you click Send to send a message; in a newsreader, it's either Send or Post.
- In email, you click Reply to reply to a message; in a newsreader, it's either Reply or Respond.

The easiest way to deal with that difference is to start in the right place. For example, when you want to compose a new message (not a reply) and post it to a newsgroup, begin by opening that newsgroup, then clicking your newsreader's button for composing a new message (it's New Msg in Netscape Messenger, New Post in Outlook Express). When the message window opens, you'll see that it's preaddressed to the currently open newsgroup.

When replying, open the message to which you want to reply, and then click the Reply (or Respond) button on the message window in which that message appears. In the message window that opens, the message is preaddressed to the appropriate newsgroup, the subject line is correctly phrased to add the reply to the same thread as the original message, and the original message is quoted in the message area (see Figure 15.15). Just add your comments, and edit the quote as necessary.

After completing a new message or reply, send the message by clicking the button or menu item labeled Send or Post.

When you choose to reply, most newsreaders provide the option of replying to the newsgroup or sending an email reply directly to the author of the message you're replying to. The email option is handy when your reply is really intended only for the author, not the whole group.

FIGURE 15.15

Start a new message or reply while viewing the message list of a newsgroup, and that message is preaddressed to the open newsgroup.

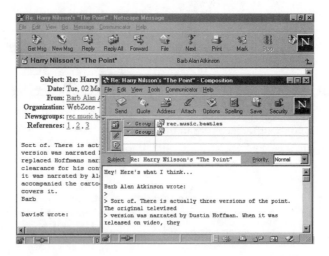

As in a mailing list (see Hour 14, "Joining a Mailing List"), always be mindful of your netiquette when posting to a newsgroup, and resist using smileys and shorthand.

Finding and Reading Newsgroup Messages Through Your Browser

Many Web browsers can display newsgroup messages. Note, however, that you cannot use a Web browser to contribute to a newsgroup (except in one special case, described in a moment), so you'll still need a newsreader to really get into newsgroups.

A Web browser's display capability comes in handy when a search tool turns up a newsgroup message. Newsgroup messages show up in a search tool's hot list as links; if your browser can display newsgroup messages, clicking one of those links displays the message. (In some suites, the newsreader and the browser are linked so that clicking a link that leads to a newsgroup message automatically opens the newsreader to display the message.)

Links to newsgroup messages may be turned up by several of the everyday search tools (see Part III, "Finding What You're Looking For"). One Web-based search tool, DejaNews, is specifically for finding and displaying newsgroup messages through the Web. The following To Do shows how to use DejaNews to find and read newsgroup messages.

Note that DejaNews is a special Web-based interface to newsgroups, including most of the regular "Usenet" newsgroups *and* a family of "discussion groups" unique to DejaNews. So even if you have a newsreader, when you open any message in DejaNews, it appears in your browser. DejaNews also lets you post messages from your browser, by displaying a form you can fill in with your post.

To Do: Find and Display a Newsgroup Message in DejaNews

1. Open your Web browser, and go to DejaNews at www.dejanews.com (Figure 15.16).

FIGURE 15.16

Step 1: Open up www.dejanews.com *in your Web browser.*

▼   2. In the Find box, type a term for a topic you're interested in, and click the Find button (Figure 15.17).

FIGURE 15.17

Step 2: Enter a search term and click Find.

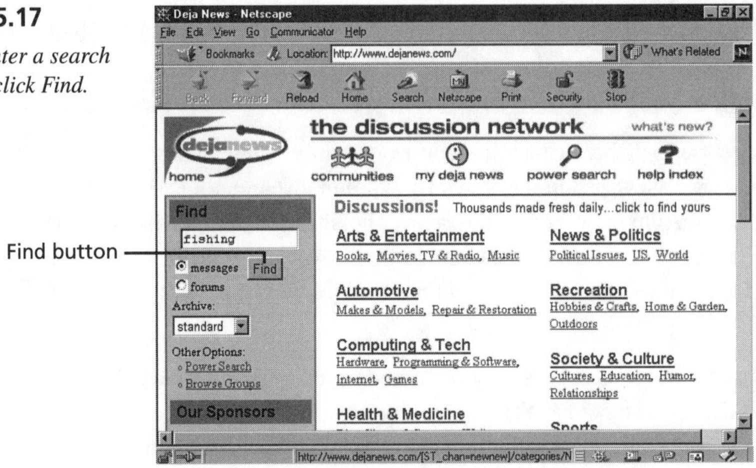

Find button ——

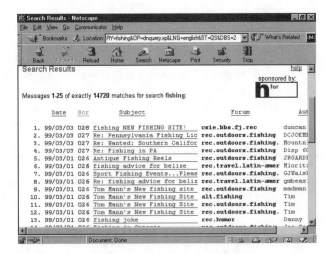

3. Click a link. The message appears in your browser (Figures 15.18 and 15.19).

FIGURE 15.18

Step 3: Click a link.

▼

Figure 15.19

Step 3: Read the message.

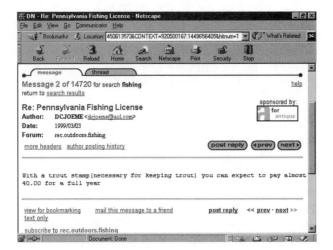

Summary

If the Web is like a library, newsgroups are like a barber shop or beauty salon: The information you get from the former is generally more reliable and complete, but the information you get from the latter—while often pure opinion—is usually more personal, immediate, and fun.

Perhaps the best way to stay informed about any topic is to make sure you frequent both related Web pages *and* related newsgroups, and use what you learn in each to balance the other.

Q&A

Q I heard that some newsgroups and mailing lists are "moderated" and some aren't. What does that mean?

A Those lists have a "moderator," a person who reads every message and tries to ensure that messages follow some general rules set forth for the group (usually the rules of netiquette; see Hour 14). If you break the rules in a group, the moderator may send you a warning or two. In a mailing list, if you break rules repeatedly, the moderator may kick you off the list.

Of course, some folks object to moderators, saying that a moderator inevitably imposes his or her values on the whole group, preventing a truly free-flowing dialog from taking place. There are many "unmoderated" newsgroups; for example, many of the "alternative" newsgroups (those whose names begin with "alt") are unmoderated. There are fewer unmoderated mailing lists, but of course, some moderators are so lenient that the list seems unmoderated anyway.

Personally, I don't pay much attention to whether a list or group is moderated or not. But if you're particularly bothered by petty squabbles and off-color remarks, you may find that the moderated lists and groups are more to your liking.

HOUR 16

Emailing Through the Web, Stopping Junk Mail, and Other Tips

The first three hours of this part of the book showed you all of the important ways you can communicate with others through the Internet. But just so you know you're fully informed, this final hour in this part describes a few important (and/or fun) messaging activities that aren't essential, but may very well come in handy.

At the end of the hour, you'll be able to answer the following questions:

- Can I send and receive email without an email program?
- How can I send a message to a friend who's online the same time I am, so they can see the message the instant I send it?
- Can I make a phone call from my computer, through the Internet, to a real telephone in another state or country?

- How do I use email to send and receive pictures, documents, and other types of files?
- What can I do about all the ads and other junk email I keep getting?

Using the Web for Email

An email program like Outlook Express or Netscape Messenger is the best way to send and receive email. But through several different sites online, you can send and receive email to and from your Web browser (using a different email address than the one you use with your email program).

You use Web-based email (sometimes called Webmail) entirely within your browser. To send a message, you fill in the blanks in an online form that offers spaces for the recipient's address, the message's subject, the message body, and so on. Messages you receive are displayed to you in a Web page only you can see, or in a box that pops open atop a Web page.

Why use this Web-based email? How 'bout:

- If you spend most of your time online in your browser, you don't have to switch to another program for email.
- You can set up a decoy address to help stop junk email from cluttering your mailbox. See "Stopping Junk Email ('Spam')" later in this hour.
- You can use Web-based mail as a secondary email address; for example, you can give your regular email address to business associates, and give your Web email address to friends. This helps you easily separate different kinds of communication.
- If you travel and you want to get your email while on the road, but you don't want to bring your computer along, you can read your Web-based email from any computer with Web access—say, the computer of relatives you're visiting, or a computer in a library. As long as you remember your Web email account name (or username) and password, you can get your email through anybody's computer and Internet account.

If you need several email addresses on one Internet account—say, one for each member of your family or separate business and personal email accounts—most ISPs and online services will set you up with two or more addresses for no extra charge. But if your Internet provider won't set up all the addresses you need for free, Web-based email makes a great alternative.

There are many free Web email sites online (see Figure 16.1). But the easiest way to set up for Web email is to visit one of the Web portals, most of which list free Web-based email among the services they offer to entice you to visit their sites often.

FIGURE 16.1

Web-based email is a free, handy way to communicate.

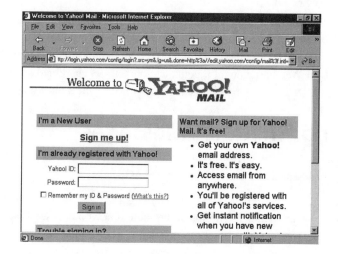

16

To sign up for Web-based email, visit any of the following sites:

- Yahoo!, at www.yahoo.com
- Excite, at www.excite.com
- Netcenter, at home.netscape.com
- Hotmail, at msn.com

On the site, look for a link to "Email." Click it, and follow the instructions that appear. (The precise steps for signing up for and using a Web-based email service vary by service.)

When considering Web-based email, keep in mind the following tips:

- Messages are not generally stored on your computer in the sort of easy-to-organize, easy-to-look-at-later way that they are in an email program. On some systems, they may be deleted as soon as you've read them (although they may be viewed for a time from your Web cache files, like any other recently viewed page), or they may be available for reading for a limited time, after which they "expire" and are deleted automatically. That limitation makes Web email best suited to very casual email activities, not important ones. Think of Web email like a message on your answering machine (once you hear it, you erase it), and regular email like paper letters you can file and keep forever.

- Most Web-based email is free because it's supported by advertising you'll see every time you use it. If you're trying to reduce the number of times a day somebody tries to sell you something (like I am), you may want to think twice about Web email.

- To sign up for Web email, you typically must fill in a form on which you may or may not be asked to reveal various kinds of information about yourself. Revealing that information increases your exposure to unwanted, junk email messages, both on your Web-based email account and on your regular email account (if you reveal your regular email address in the form). See "Stopping Junk Email" later in this hour.

Sending "Instant" Messages

If you use Netscape for browsing, you can take advantage of a service called AOL Instant Messenger (even if you don't use AOL).

Instant Messenger lets you see, from among a list you set up yourself (a "Buddy List"), which of your friends are online at the same time you are (see Figure 16.2). You can exchange typed messages with those friends—but unlike email, those messages show up instantly. The moment you send a message to a friend who's online, he or she sees it, and vice versa. So you can carry on a live, interactive conversation (much like chat, only more private).

FIGURE 16.2

AOL Instant Messenger lets you exchange live messages with friends who are online the same time you are—even if neither of you uses AOL.

The easiest way to sign up for Instant Messenger is to install Netscape Communicator. From Navigator's menu bar, choose Communicator, AOL Instant Messenger Service, and then follow the prompts to sign up.

Note that AOL Instant Messenger is not the only such service available. Another is Yahoo! Pager, which you can learn about at pager.yahoo.com (see Figure 16.3).

FIGURE 16.3

Yahoo! Pager is another service, similar to AOL Instant Messenger.

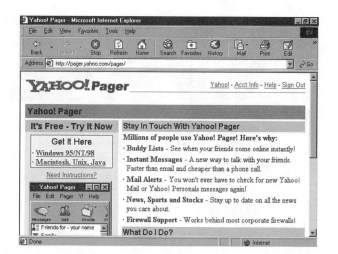

16

Making Better (but Not Free) Internet Phone Calls

Internet conferencing gives you the effect of a long-distance phone call (or even a video-phone call) for no extra cost atop whatever you already pay for Internet access (see Hour 17, "Voice and Video Conferencing"). The only problem is that both you and your conversation partner must have computers and Internet accounts, and often even the same conferencing program. Wouldn't it be better if you could use your computer and Internet connection to call any telephone, anywhere in the world?

Well, you can—except it's not free. Services are now coming online that connect your computer to any phone, anywhere, for a per-minute charge like any other long-distance carrier. You talk through your computer's sound card (talking into a connected microphone, listening through your PC speakers or headphones), and the person on the other end uses the phone as usual.

One such service is Net2Phone (see Figure 16.4). You can learn more about Net2Phone at www.net2phone.com.

To use the service, you visit the Net2Phone Web site, download and install the required Net2Phone software (available for Windows and Mac), and fill out some online forms to sign up.

FIGURE 16.4

The Net2Phone service lets you call any phone in the world from your computer and Internet connection.

Is it a good deal? I can't say; it depends on where you call, what you usually pay for calls through your regular phone, and how rates change (on your own phone and Net2Phone) between the time I write this and the time you read it. You have to check it out—and check out any other, competing services that may come along in the meantime—to make your own choice.

Attaching Files to Email Messages

Once new Internet users get the hang of using their Web browsers and email programs, nothing causes more frustration than file attachments.

NEW TERM **Attachment.** A file (any type—a picture file, word processing document, anything) that's attached to an email message so that it travels along with the message. The person who receives the message can detach the file from the message and use it.

The following To Do shows how to attach a file to an email message in Outlook Express. You'll send that message to yourself, so you can also learn how to detach and use a file attachment you receive. Note that the steps are similar in Netscape Messenger.

In Hour 11, "Finding Programs and Files," you learned about the risk of catching a computer virus from programs and other files you download from the Internet. Well, you can pick up a virus just as easily from an email attachment.

If you're like most people, most email attachments you receive come from people you know, so you may think that those files are safe. But what if your friend is just passing on a file they received from someone else, maybe a stranger? That's one way email viruses spread; innocent, well-meaning people catch them and spread them around.

You can use most major virus protection programs, such as Norton AntiVirus and McAfee VirusScan, to check email attachments for viruses. Just save the attachment as a file separate from the message (as described in step 5 of the following To Do), then scan the file for viruses.

DO NOT open the file (by double-clicking its file icon or right-clicking it and choosing Open or Run) until *after* you have scanned it for viruses and determined that it's safe.

16

To Do: Attach a File to an Email Message

1. Compose and address your message (to yourself) as you normally would. Then click the Attach button (Figure 16.5).

2. Use the dialog to navigate to and select the file to attach, then click the dialog's Attach button (Figure 16.6).

FIGURE 16.5

Step 1: Click the Attach button in a new message.

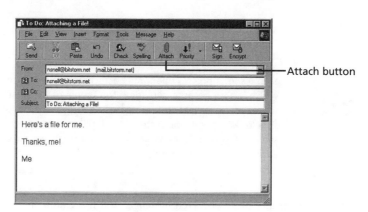

▼

FIGURE 16.6
Step 2: Find the file, then click the Attach button.

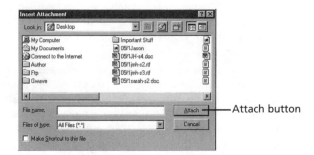

—Attach button

3. Send the message (Figure 16.7). If you do not immediately receive it, click Send/Recv again to receive the message.

FIGURE 16.7
Step 3: Send the message.

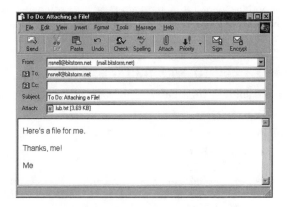

Step 4 shows how to open a file attachment directly from the message, which is okay because you know the source of the file (you). But as a rule, unless you're *very* confident about the source of a file attachment, you should skip step 4, and instead do step 5 to separate the file from the message. Then you can use your virus-scanning software to check the file for viruses *before* you open it.

4. In the header of the received message, you'll see an icon and a filename representing the attached file. To view the file, double-click the icon (Figure 16.8).

FIGURE 16.8

Step 4: To read the attachment in the received message, double-click the file's icon.

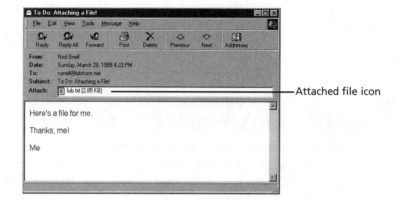

Attached file icon

16

5. If you want to save the file separately from the message (for use later), right-click the icon, and choose Save As (Figure 16.9).

FIGURE 16.9

Step 5: To save the file, right-click and choose Save As.

If you have your email program configured for formatting fancy, HTML-based messages (see Hour 23, "Creating Web Pages and Multimedia Messages"), when you attach a picture file (such as a photo you've scanned) to a message, you may see the actual picture displayed in the message instead of an icon.

Not to worry: Anyone you send to who has a similarly configured email program will see the picture the same way, and anyone who does not have such an email program will receive the picture as an attachment.

Keep in mind that big file attachments can dramatically increase the length of time it takes you to send a message, *and* the length of time it takes the recipient to receive messages. Avoid sending really large files (over 300K), and before sending an attachment to someone you haven't sent to before, send a message describing the file and its size, asking if it's OK to send it.

Stopping Junk Email ("Spam")

Within a few weeks after you begin using the Internet, you'll make an unpleasant discovery: The same sort of take-no-prisoners direct marketing types who telemarket you at suppertime and stuff offers in your mailbox have found you online. Over time, you'll see an ever-increasing number of ads, offers, chain letters, pyramid schemes, and other such scams in your Inbox. This mountain of unwanted crapola is collectively known as *spam*.

NEW TERM **Spam.** Unsolicited email sent out to a large group of strangers for purposes of advertising products and services, promoting political causes, or making mischief. (Senders of spam are called *spammers*.) The name may derive from the fact that the messages multiply the way the word "spam" does in an old *Monty Python* skit, but the term's origin is unconfirmed.

It's easy and cheap for an advertiser to automatically crank out an email ad to thousands—millions, even—of Internet users all at once. These messages often have subject lines designed to entice you into reading the message (FREE $$$) or to trick you into doing so (MESSAGE FROM AN OLD FRIEND). As the Internet population has grown, so has the spam problem.

The next few pages offer advice for dealing with the spam problem.

I should say right up front that nothing today can prevent or eliminate spam altogether—the problem is too pervasive. But by following the advice in this chapter, you can reduce spam to a tolerable amount. Until and unless it's outlawed, spam will remain as sure a fact of life as death, taxes, and telemarketing.

How They Get You

The more widely known your email address is, the more spam you'll get—it's that simple. So a logical first step in stopping spam is being very careful about how and when you reveal your email address.

Unfortunately, you cannot fully enjoy the Internet while keeping your email address a secret. Many online activities, such as shopping or posting to newsgroups, create an online record of your email address. In fact, anytime you send email, an unscrupulous spammer may harvest your address by intercepting messages on their way across the Net.

Still, you can effectively reduce the extent to which your address is known by making some smart surfing choices. In particular, be careful about:

- **Forms.** Be very careful how and when you fill out online forms or surveys. A growing number of Web sites request that you complete a form to "register" in order to use the site; the form data is almost always used for marketing, and often for spam. On any site where you might complete a form, look for a link to a "Privacy Policy"; some Web sites promise in that policy not to spam you or to sell your information to spammers. See Hour 8, "Protecting Your Privacy and (Other Security Stuff)."

Some folks use a secondary email address—such as a Web-based email address—on all forms and other activities that are not part of their personal communications. That way, any spam resulting from filling in forms goes to the secondary address, where it's easier to ignore.

You still need to check messages on the secondary address from time to time, in case you do get a legitimate message there, and to clean out old messages. But at least you can minimize the day-to-day spam intrusion.

- **Newsgroup postings.** When you post to a newsgroup, a spammer can easily learn two things about you: your email address, and that you're interested in the newsgroup's topic.

That's valuable direct marketing information; if you post a message to a newsgroup about a particular kind of product, you can expect to receive spam trying to sell you such a product. If you post to a sex-related newsgroup, you will soon receive spam selling phone sex or other sex-related stuff. You can *read* newsgroup messages anonymously—but when you post, you reveal your address. So watch where you post.

Again, all of the suggestions offered here are ways to *reduce* spam—nothing yet can truly eliminate it. So even if you never visit a sex-related newsgroup and never, ever post to one, you probably will receive spam from sex-related advertisers, from time to time.

It's not your fault; receiving such messages does not necessarily mean that you did something to bring it on yourself. It's just that the merchants of sex and the merchants of get-rich-quick schemes are the two most aggressive kinds of spammers, and they both spam anyone—and everyone—they can find.

- **Cookies.** Cookies are files on your computer stored there by a Web site, such as an online store, to record information about you that the page can access next time you visit. Unfortunately, the cookies on your computer—which may contain your email address and other personal data—may be read not only by the servers that put them there, but by other servers you visit, who may use that information for spam. See Hour 8 to learn how to control cookies.

- **Mailing lists.** When you subscribe to mailing lists, your name and email address (and your interest in the list's topic) are recorded in a database that may be accessed and copied very easily by a spammer, particularly if the list is managed by an automated program. (Some mailing lists let you keep your address private; read the list's Welcome message for information about a CONCEAL command.) See Hour 14, "Joining a Mailing List."

A newsgroup covering the same topic is a safer choice, as long as you don't post to it. If you contribute to the discussion, the mailing list is still less spam-risky than the newsgroup.

Stopping spam is a little trickier for users of online services than for users of ISPs. The online services derive some of their revenue from advertisers, for providing access to you. So they're not too keen on letting you block those ads.

Experts on AOL and spam advise users to avoid posting messages on AOL's forums, and to use Internet newsgroups instead. Despite the spam exposure risk in newsgroups, AOL's forums are notoriously harvested by spammers.

Report 'Em!

The people who run Internet servers are generally described as system administrators (*sysadmins*) or as system operators (*sysops*). These folks usually hate spam as much as you do, because it dramatically increases the traffic on their servers, taking up room needed for legitimate communications. There are two times you should contact sysops about spam:

16

- If you do not want to receive spam, always let the sysop of your Internet provider know how you feel. He or she may be able to take steps to minimize (but not eliminate) spam to your account. You can email your sysop by sending a message to the technical support address for your account.

- You can report spammers to the sysops of *their* Internet providers, who may then cancel their accounts or issue a warning. To address the message, take the part of the spammer's email address following the @ symbol, and put system@ or sysop@ or support@ in front of it. For example, if you get spam from jerko@serv.com, address messages to

      support@serv.com

      system@serv.com

      sysop@serv.com

reporting that the user named Jerko is sending spam. This technique won't work all the time, because spammers are savvy about hiding their real server names. But it's a start.

In Newsgroups, Spoof 'Em!

Ultimately, having to restrain yourselffrom posting to newsgroups can severely hamper your ability to enjoy the Net. Here's a technique that some folks use to post to newsgroups while foiling spammer's efforts to cull their addresses: *spoofing*.

NEW TERM **Spoofing.** Also known as *munging*, the practice of scrambling your return email address in newsgroup postings just enough so that if it's harvested by one of the programs spammers use, the resulting spam will never reach you (it'll be sent to the spoofed address, not your real one).

A properly spoofed email address fools the automated harvesting programs that spammers use, but enables real folks on the group to still send you messages. For example, suppose your address is

shirley@aol.com

You can use your newsreader's configuration dialogs to change the Reply to address to

`shirleytake_out_this_part@aol.com`

If you use a signature at the bottom of your messages to identify yourself, change the address there, too. You can even add a note to your signature telling readers of your postings how to decode your address to send you email. The programs spammers use aren't smart enough to decode the address or read the note.

To spoof your newsgroup return address in Outlook Express, choose Tools, Accounts from the menu bar. On the dialog that appears, click the News tab, then click Properties. In the box labeled Email Address, type the spoofed address (see Figure 16.10).

Spoofing your newsgroup return address in Netscape Messenger is not recommended, because doing so also spoofs your return address on your email messages. That makes it difficult for people to make legitimate replies to your email messages.

FIGURE 16.10

Use this dialog in Outlook Express to spoof your return address on newsgroup postings.

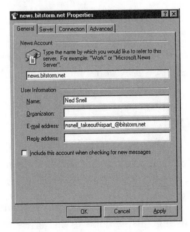

At this writing, spoofing works pretty well. But inevitably, spammers will smarten up their harvesting programs so that they recognize and decode spoofed addresses. Spoofing is only one step in reducing spam; you still need to do the other stuff described here, too.

Never Reply! Never! *Never!*

Many spam messages include "removal" instructions, telling you that if you reply to the message and include the words "REMOVE ME" or a similar phrase in the subject line, you'll receive no further messages.

In some cases, doing so may work. But in many cases, the "REMOVE ME" bit is actually a trick intended to make you verify your email address, so that the spammer knows he has a live one. In such cases, following the removal instructions won't remove you from the spammer's list, and may even *increase* the amount of spam you get.

Some folks also try to stop spam by sending angry replies to spammers. This approach never works. Often, the "From" line in the spam is left empty, or filled with a dummy or spoofed email address, so a reply won't even reach the real spammer. When angry replies do reach spammers, spammers ignore them. (They know full well that they are bothering some folks. They don't care. If they must annoy a million people in order to make a sale to two or three, they're happy with that.)

The moral? Never do anything an unsolicited email tells you to do, even if the instruction claims to be for your benefit. Never.

Filter 'Em Out!

If you can't stop the spam from coming, your next best bet is to avoid having to look at it. A variety of programs and techniques *filter* your incoming email to remove unwanted messages.

NEW TERM   **Filter.** Settings in your email program (or a special utility) that automatically delete or move messages under specified circumstances. For example, if there's a person whose messages you never want to read, you can configure a filter so that all messages from that person's email address are deleted automatically upon receipt; you'll get them, but they'll be gone before you ever see them.

Filters cannot completely remove spam. In order to set up filters to delete all spam messages, you'd have to know the address of every spammer. No complete master list of spammers exists (new folks start spamming every day, and slippery spammers change addresses often), but you can pick up lists of many of the worst offenders, and then import or manually copy the lists into your email program so you can create filters to block messages from them.

Use the following URLs to learn about and download lists of spammers for filtering:

- The BadMail from Spam List: `www.webeasy.com/spam/`
- The Network Abuse Clearinghouse: `www.abuse.net/`

- Multimedia Marketing Group: `www.mmgco.com/nospam/`
- The Blacklist of Internet Advertisers: `www-math.uni-paderborn.de/%7Eaxel/BL/#list`

> You can pick up utilities that combine a filtering system with a spammers database, for fast and easy configuration of anti-spam filters. Check out
>
> SpamNet at `www.spamnet.com`
>
> SpamKiller at `novasoft.base.org`
>
> SpamBlaster (Mac) at `www.gooware.com`
>
> eFilter at `www.eflash.com`

Finding Filters in Your Email Program

Most full-featured email programs have their own built-in filtering systems you can apply to manage incoming mail and, to a limited extent, control spam.

If you don't have a list of spammers, or if creating filters for a long list is too difficult, you can deal with spam by creating filters for your legitimate contacts.

It works like this: If you have a steady group of people you communicate with regularly, create a filter that automatically stores all messages from those people in a separate folder. When you receive email, all of the important messages are automatically stored in the folder, while all of the spam stays in your Inbox, where you can ignore it. (You'll still want to scan your Inbox from time to time to check for legitimate messages from folks you haven't added to your filters.)

You can find the filters dialogs:

- **In Messenger,** by choosing Edit, Message Filters.
- **In Outlook Express,** by choosing Tools, Message Rules.

> In Outlook Express, you can choose Tools, Message Rules, Mail to open a dialog on which you can set up all sorts of rules for how incoming messages are handled (see Figure 16.11).
>
> But when all you want to do is prevent certain senders from sending you email, just choose Tools, Message Rules, Blocked Senders List, click Add, and type the address of the person from whom you will no longer accept email.

FIGURE 16.11

Email programs use filters (which Outlook Express, shown here, calls Rules) to automatically deal with certain incoming messages in whatever way you choose.

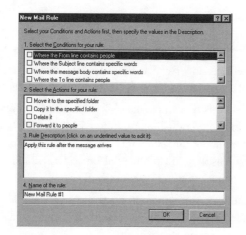

16

The Last Resort: Move

When all else fails, if you're still getting too much junk mail, there's one reliable (albeit temporary) solution: Change ISPs, or ask your current ISP to change your email address.

When you change your email address, spam directed to your old address can't reach you. (Be sure to inform all of your legitimate email partners of your new address, and instruct your old ISP not to forward email to your new address.) If your address has found its way into lots of spam databases, you can get a clean start this way.

Eventually, spammers will find you. But if you start clean with a new address, and then diligently apply the steps you learned in this hour, you may be able to keep the spammers at bay for a time.

Summary

Before this hour, you knew everything you *had* to know about messaging on the Internet. Now that you know how to stop spam, send Web-based messages, and so on, you know even *more* than you really have to. Doesn't that make you feel special?

Q&A

Q At the start of the hour, you mentioned outlawing spam. Is that going to happen?

A There are many efforts underway to control or eliminate spam through legislation, but it's impossible today to say which, if any, of these efforts will succeed.

One of the most promising campaigns seeks not to enact new laws against spam, but to extend an existing law—the prohibition of junk faxes—to also cover email. You can learn more about that campaign on the Web page for CAUCE, the Coalition Against Unsolicited Commercial Email (www.cauce.org), which also provides links to many other anti-spam resources.

If you really want to do something productive about spam, let your congressperson know how you feel. You can find your congressperson's email address from the Web page at www.house.gov/writerep/.

PART V
Beyond Browsing

Hour

Hour 17

Voice and Video Conferencing

With an Internet conferencing program, you can have a live conversation—very much like a telephone call—with anyone else on the Internet who uses the same conferencing program. Depending on what you pay for Internet service and how far away your caller is, conducting such "Internet telephone calls" may be substantially cheaper than making a long-distance telephone call because it costs you nothing beyond what you already pay for your Internet account. You can, in effect, make a one-hour call to France for free if your French friend has an Internet account and conferencing software.

But conferencing programs do more than just carry a conversation. You can have a text-based chat (like a chat client), draw and type messages on a collaborative whiteboard, and even add video to the conversation.

At the end of the hour, you'll be able to answer the following questions:

- What can I do with Internet conferencing tools?
- What hardware do I need to conduct a voice or video conference?

- How do I set up and configure NetMeeting, Microsoft's free conferencing program?
- How do I make a call?
- How do I accept a call from someone else?
- What advanced conference features can I use?

Understanding Conferencing and "Internet Phone Calls"

Conferencing is a very different animal from the Internet activities you've explored thus far. Before venturing into conferencing, it's useful to understand a little more about how it works.

How It Works—and Doesn't Work

Most Internet activities are *standardized*; that is, they're based on agreed-upon rules than enable different programs and systems to interact. For example, you can send a message with one email program and your recipient can read it in another. The difference in programs doesn't matter because all Internet email programs follow the same standards.

Conferencing has yet to be completely standardized (although standardization efforts are underway). For that reason, those with whom you share a conference often must use the same conferencing program you do, or a program on a short list of programs that are compatible with the one you use.

Obviously, this is a severe limitation. You cannot simply dial up any friend on the Internet and have a conference. Rather, you must first contact your conferencing partners by phone or email and agree upon what conferencing software you will use when you call one another. In effect, you must establish your own standard for your community of conferencing partners.

Getting a Program

Your best shot for a good all-around conferencing program today is Microsoft NetMeeting (See Figure 17.1). Why? Because it's free, it's widely used (so there are plenty of others with whom you can communicate), and it's easy to get. The To Dos and figures in this hour use NetMeeting as an example.

NetMeeting is included in the full installation (all options included) of Internet Explorer 4 and 5, and you may also download NetMeeting separately from the Web. (You do not have to use Internet Explorer to use NetMeeting.) To learn more about NetMeeting, or to download it, visit the following site:

www.microsoft.com/netmeeting/

17

FIGURE 17.1

Microsoft's NetMeeting, a free, all-purpose conferencing program.

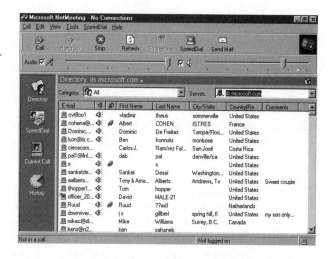

 If your partners use a variety of programs, nothing is preventing you from installing several different conferencing programs and using different programs to talk to different folks.

Other popular conferencing programs include the following:

- **Internet Phone:** www.vocaltec.com
- **CU-SeeMe:** www.wpine.com
- **PowWow:** www.tribal.com/powwow

You can find other conferencing programs for download in the Tucows Internet software directory at www.tucows.com.

Hardware You Need

The most popular form of conferencing with these products is *voice conferencing*, which entails speaking and listening just as you would in a telephone call.

 In addition to voice conferencing, some programs also support *video conferencing*, in which you see the person with whom you're speaking (and they see you), and *text conferencing*, in which conversations are carried out through typed messages.

See "Advanced Conferencing Techniques" near the end of this hour.

To have a voice conference, you must have the following equipment installed and configured in your computer:

- A sound card.
- A microphone, either attached to your sound card or built into your computer. In a voice conference, you speak into the mic.
- Speakers or headphones, either attached to your sound card or built into your PC. You'll hear your partner's words through the speakers or headphones.

Microphone headsets (which cost about $30) are becoming a popular accessory for conferencing. You get a pair of headphones with an added microphone on a rod near your mouth (you know, like pilots and telemarketers wear), letting you talk and listen privately, hands-free.

The cord on a microphone headset has two plugs: One goes into your sound card's microphone input, and the other goes into its speaker or headphone input.

The sound quality of voice conferences is highly variable. An Internet voice conference never sounds as clear as a phone call, even on the best equipment. Still, it's important to know that the better your equipment, the clearer the call will sound.

In particular, the more expensive 32-bit sound cards (standard on nearly all new PCs made since around 1996) will enable a much clearer conversation than cheaper 16-bit or 8-bit cards you may find on some older PCs or notebooks (although those will work). An external microphone connected to your sound card is usually preferable to any built-in mic. Built-in mics tend to be low-quality and pick up too much background noise from the computer.

Most recent sound cards support *full-duplex* communications. That is, when you're having a voice conference through them, you can talk and listen at the same time, just as you would in a phone call.

Older, cheaper cards support only half-duplex sound. When you're conferencing through a half-duplex sound card, you and your partner must take turns speaking and listening, just as if you were using cheesy speaker phones or walkie-talkies. ("How are you? Over!")

The speed of your Internet connection also plays a role. The faster your connection, the clearer the conversation. Connections at 28.8KB provide acceptable sound, although you may hear heavy static and occasional interruptions. A 56KB or faster connection is best for clear voice conversations and a must for videoconferencing.

Setting Up Conferencing

Before you can use a conferencing program, you must supply it with a little information. The first time you start NetMeeting, it launches a setup wizard to collect this information from you. Just work your way through the steps to configure NetMeeting, as shown in the following To Do.

To Do: Set Up NetMeeting

1. Open NetMeeting by choosing Programs, Internet Explorer, NetMeeting or Programs, NetMeeting, depending on your system and your version of NetMeeting (Figure 17.2).

17

FIGURE 17.2

Step 1: Open up NetMeeting.

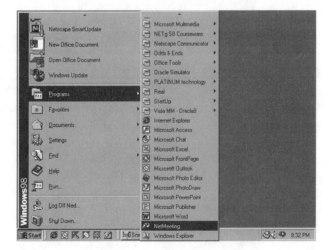

2. Click Next (Figure 17.3).

3. Leave the check box labeled Log on to a directory server when NetMeeting starts checked, and leave the list labeled What directory server you would like to use? set to uls.microsoft.com. (You can change both options later if you need to.) Then click Next (Figure 17.4).

FIGURE 17.3

Step 2: Click Next.

FIGURE 17.4

Step 3: Leave the default entries and click Next.

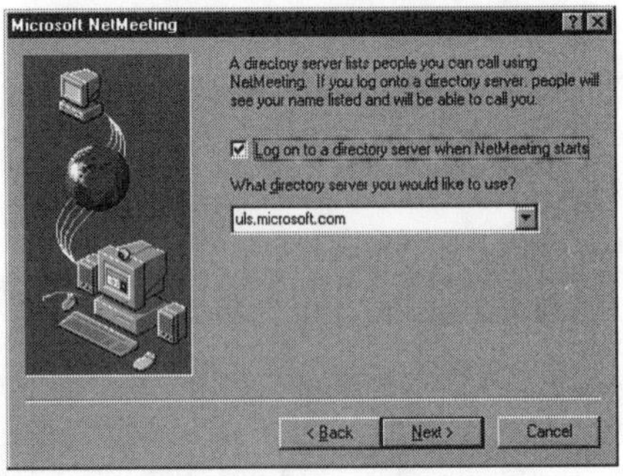

4. Type the information that you want to have listed in the directory (where others can look you up to contact you), and then click Next (Figure 17.5).

FIGURE 17.5

Step 4: Type in your information and click Next.

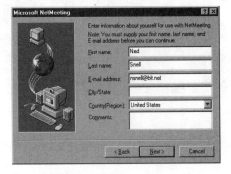

Before the setup wizard will let you continue to step 5, you have to enter at least your first and last name and your email address in the dialog shown in step 4.

As with chat (see Hour 18, "Chatting Live!"), it pays to be discreet and cautious with personal information in NetMeeting. Directory servers, like some chat servers, are cruised by some lonely, creepy people, and you may not want to reveal too much about yourself. Consider using a phony name and email address (or business, rather than personal, contact info), just to preserve your privacy.

5. Decide which category in the directory to list yourself in: personal use, business use, or adults-only use. (Use the last one at your own risk!) Then click Next (Figure 17.6).

FIGURE 17.6

Step 5: Decide how to list yourself in the directory.

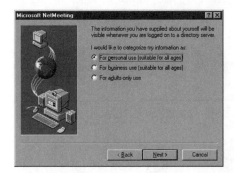

6. Make sure the type of connection you use is the one selected, and then click Next (Figure 17.7).

FIGURE 17.7

Step 6: Specify your type of connection.

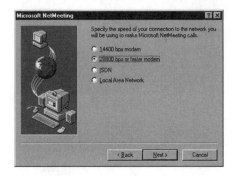

17

▼   7. Click Next (Figure 17.8).

FIGURE 17.8

Step 7: Click Next.

8. Click the Test button, and listen to your speakers and headphones to judge whether the volume is set properly. If necessary, use the slider control to raise or lower the volume, and click Test to test it. When the volume suits you, click Next (Figure 17.9).

FIGURE 17.9

Step 8: Test your speakers and the playback volume.

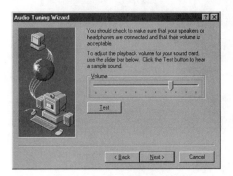

9. Read the paragraph that begins "I am using...", speaking as clearly and loudly as you would speak during a call in NetMeeting. NetMeeting uses your voice's volume to set a recording level for future NetMeeting sessions. When you're done, click Next (Figure 17.10).

▼   10. Click Finish (Figure 17.11).

FIGURE 17.10

Step 9: Set your micro-phone's recording level.

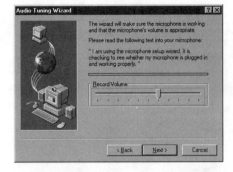

FIGURE 17.11.

Step 10: Finish up.

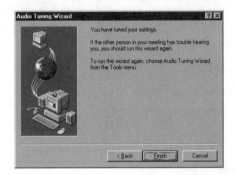

NetMeeting starts and logs on to the directory server you chose. After you're logged on, you see a list of other users who are logged on to the same server. You can scroll through the list and find your name in there. Now anyone who wants to talk to you can find your name on the list and call you up. ▲

Getting Around in NetMeeting

NetMeeting has a simple interface that's easy to figure out. In the main window—the Directory window (see Figure 17.12)—the biggest section contains the list of people logged on to the directory server that you've chosen. To its left are buttons that enable you to change what you see in the main view.

Above the directory listing are the Category and Server drop-down lists. Above those lists is the audio level adjustment toolbar. Finally, the toolbar and menus are at the top of the window, as with most Windows applications.

FIGURE 17.12

NetMeeting divides conferencing activities into a family of windows.

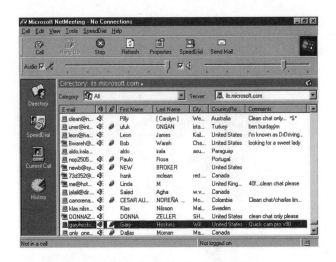

The Directory Listing

When you first start NetMeeting, you see a list of people. These are the people in the category you selected and on the server you selected when you ran the NetMeeting setup wizard. Because I chose ils.microsoft.com as my server and put myself in the For Personal Use category, I can see the list of everyone who made the same choices.

In this list, you see eight columns:

E-mail	The person's email address.
Audio	A small yellow speaker in this column means that this person can talk to you.
Video	A small gray video camera in this column means that this person can send live video over the Internet.
First Name	The person's first name.
Last Name	The person's last name.
City/State	The city and state that this person is currently in.
Country	The country that this person is in.
Comments	Comments that this person entered in the comments field, if any.

Keep in mind that all this information is entered by the person using NetMeeting, other than that in the Audio and Video columns. Some people choose not to reveal their true identities or locations. You shouldn't accept the information listed here as 100% accurate.

By default, the listing is sorted by email address, but you can sort it by any information you like. To sort the entries by a different column, just click on the column header. For example, if you want the entries to be sorted by country, you can click on the Country heading above the listings.

The Category and Server Lists

Above the directory listing are the Category and Server drop-down lists. These control who shows up in the directory listing. When you start NetMeeting, by default it logs you on to the server you chose in the NetMeeting setup wizard and displays the category you chose for your entry.

If you want to see the entries on a different server, just click the down-arrow to the right of the Server drop-down list and choose the server that you want to use.

Similarly, to see the list of people in a different category than yours, just choose the category you want to see from the Category drop-down list. Setting the Category field to Business, for example, will let you see the list of people who have designated that their information is for business use.

The Button Bar

To the left of the directory listing is a bar with four buttons you can use to switch between four different windows:

- **Directory:** Opens the Directory window (look back at Figure 17.12).
- **SpeedDial:** Opens your SpeedDial list.
- **Current Call:** Shows activity in the current conference.
- **History:** Shows where you've been.

The Directory window contains the Category and Server fields and the directory listing. The first time you start NetMeeting, the Directory window is the one you see. Clicking on the other tabs enables you to see different information pertaining to calls you can make, the current call, or calls you've received.

NEW TERM **Current call.** This is how NetMeeting describes the conference in which you are currently engaged.

You can use the SpeedDial window the same way you would use a SpeedDial button on your telephone. This window keeps a short list of people you call regularly so you don't have to search for their names in the main directory listing. You can also include people who frequent different servers on the same list so that you don't have to keep changing servers to find the person you want to call.

After you've added someone to your SpeedDial list, NetMeeting starts on this screen instead of the Directory screen because you're more likely to want to call the person whose number you've saved than someone you haven't talked to before.

The Current Call window shows a list of the people in on the current call. You will always find at least two names in this list if you're in on a call, or none if you're not. Also, if you or another person is sending video, you'll see it in the video boxes on the right side of the screen on this window.

Finally, the History window holds a list of all the calls you've received from other people. This window also lists the caller's name, the date and time of the call, and whether you accepted, rejected, or ignored the call.

The Audio Level Controls

Using the audio level controls, you can change the level of your voice and the voice of the other person in on the call (see Figure 17.13).

FIGURE 17.13

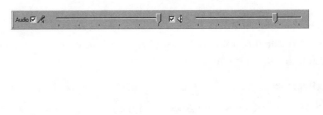

The audio level controls enable you to adjust the volume of your voice and the voice of the person you're talking to.

Just drag the slider for either the microphone (your voice) or the speaker (the other person's voice) to the left to lower the volume, or to the right to increase it. In most cases, you won't need to adjust the microphone level because that should have been set automatically by the NetMeeting setup wizard. You can change the speaker volume to suit your taste for each individual call, however. You can also use the check boxes on the audio level controls to temporarily mute yourself or your conversation partner.

Answering a Call

To talk to someone on the Internet with NetMeeting, you have to call someone or someone has to call you. This section covers answering a call; the next section covers making a call.

When someone calls you, the first thing that happens is that you hear the phone ring. It's not really the phone ringing, though; the sound is coming out of the speakers on your computer. Next, at the bottom right side of your screen, there's a NetMeeting dialog that says who is calling. It also has two buttons: Accept and Ignore. If you don't want to talk to the caller, click the Ignore button. To answer the call, click the Accept button.

After you accept a call, the NetMeeting window switches automatically to the Current Call window. Here you'll see the name of the caller and your name, along with a little information. To the right of each name are several columns:

17

Audio	A little yellow speaker in this column means that this person can talk over the Internet.
Video	A small gray video camera in this column means that you should also see live video in the Remote Video frame to the right (see "Advanced Conferencing Techniques" later in this hour).
Chat	A small white and blue rectangle in this column means that the chat window is open (see "Advanced Conferencing Techniques" later in this hour).

It may take a few seconds for NetMeeting to complete the connection between your computer and the caller's. After it has finished, though, start gabbing—your conference is under way.

When you finish talking to the caller, one of you has to hang up. In NetMeeting, this means clicking the Hang Up button on the toolbar. You can hang up at any time, just like you can with the telephone.

Placing a Call

Calling someone with NetMeeting is actually easier than using the White Pages and a telephone. You don't need to remember or dial anyone's phone number; you just have to double-click a name in the directory list. After you've connected with someone, you can have NetMeeting automatically save the listing for you.

When your partner answers, NetMeeting switches over to the Current Call window and you may proceed with your conversation.

Advanced Conferencing Techniques

Most folks use their conferencing software for voice calls and nothing else. However, you may want to know about the three other forms of conferencing and collaboration that are enabled by Internet conferencing software: videoconferencing, text chatting, and whiteboard drawing.

Videoconferencing

Few conferencing programs today support videoconferencing, and for good reason: It doesn't work very well yet. Making live video look good requires moving and processing tons of data very quickly, and even the fastest modems and computers are not quite up to the task. The video image you'll see of your conference partner (and the one they'll see of you) is small, fuzzy, and jerky, like watching a faraway station on a two-inch TV in a thunderstorm.

Besides not always looking too good, videoconferencing often degrades the audio quality of the call. You and your partner may find it preferable to shut off the video so you can hear each other more clearly.

That said, setting up and using video in NetMeeting—one of the few programs that supports it—is a breeze. All you really need to do is install a computer video camera on your PC or Mac. These cameras—usually designed to sit on your desk or mount on top of your monitor—come in color and black-and-white models, and they can cost less than $100. Some notebook PCs from Sony and other companies also come with built-in cameras for conferencing.

Once a video camera has been installed and configured in Windows or Mac OS, NetMeeting automatically senses and takes advantage of it. If your partner has a video camera installed, the image from that camera automatically appears in the Remote Video Frame, a small square on the right side of the Current Call window. If you have a camera installed, your partner also sees you.

Text Chatting

Text chatting means using your conferencing software to conduct a conversation through a series of typed messages, just like using chat.

It's important to remember that a text conference is not the same thing as IRC Chat, which you'll learn about in Hour 18. A text chat in a conference program is a private conversation between users of a conferencing program, while bona fide IRC sessions take place on a public chat server between users of any IRC program.

Why would anybody have a text chat instead of a voice chat? Well, several reasons come to mind:

- One or more of the participants is speech- or hearing-impaired.

- One or more of the participants has insufficient hardware, or too slow a connection, to support a voice conference. Text conferences require no sound card and work fine over slow connections.

- The conference requires the input of more than two participants. Voice conferences and videoconferences are limited to two parties, while a text chat can include three, four, or more participants.

To hold a text chat in NetMeeting, you establish the call just as you would for a voice conference. All participants then switch to text chat mode by clicking the Chat button. Everyone types whatever they have to say, and all statements typed by all participants appear in a scrolling display in the conference program. Each statement is labeled with the name of the speaker, so everybody knows who said what.

Whiteboard

Ever been in a meeting where someone feels the need to present his idea visually, so he jumps up and starts drawing on a blackboard, or the more modern office "whiteboard"?

In NetMeeting, you can do the same thing. Click the Whiteboard button while you're in a call, and a separate window opens. This is the *whiteboard,* a space in which you can draw and jot notes (see Figure 17.14). Anything that anyone in the call draws on the whiteboard appears to all participants, so partners can even add to one another's drawings.

Using a whiteboard is just like using any drawing program. You select a drawing tool from a panel of buttons and then use your mouse to draw lines or shapes in the drawing area. You can also click a colored square to choose the color the tool produces, and even click a text tool (the A button in the drawing tools) to type notes on the whiteboard.

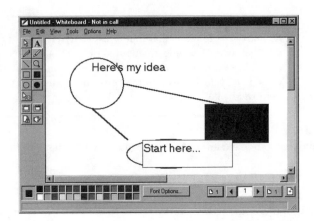

Figure 17.14

A whiteboard lets you present your ideas in a conference visually.

Summary

As you can see, using a conferencing program through the Internet is terrifically useful, as long as everyone uses the same program you do or one that's compatible. This capability of the Internet has yet to grow up, but when it does, we'll all be using it in one way or another.

Q&A

Q I don't like using my mic and speakers or a headset to have a conference; I feel like a taxi dispatcher. Is there any way I can make voice conferencing more like a phone call?

A Several companies have been working on that. You may have seen ads for devices that look just like telephones, but are really just cleverly designed mics and speakers. You plug these "phones" into your sound card so you can have a more phone-like experience.

Although these devices can be handy or fun, they still can't fix the fact that an Internet conference is not as clear as a regular telephone call. That problem has more to do with the Internet's limitations than with the device you speak into.

HOUR 18

Chatting Live!

Feel the need to reach out and touch someone, live and (almost) in person? Chat puts you online in a live conversation with other Internet users anywhere in the world.

There are lots of chat programs, but the one Microsoft offers for free, Microsoft Chat, does everything most other chat programs do. Also, Microsoft Chat displays the chat in kind of a cool way, as you'll soon see. For that reason, you'll explore Internet chatting in this hour principally through Microsoft Chat (although there are plenty of different chat programs to choose from).

At the end of the hour, you'll be able to answer the following questions:

- What is Internet chatting, also known as Internet Relay Chat (IRC)?
- How is Microsoft Chat different from a typical chat program?
- How do I join in an online chat session?
- How do I choose the identity by which I will be known in the chat?
- How do I enhance my contributions to the chat with expressions, gestures, and other touches?
- How do I exit one chat and enter another?

You may as well know that a substantial amount of chat traffic on the Internet is dedicated to sex chats of various persuasions and fetishes. There are many sex chat rooms, and sex-chat-oriented chatters often wander into non-sex-oriented rooms looking for new friends.

If that's okay with you, have fun. Live and let live, I always say, especially between consenting adults. But if you have an aversion to such stuff, tread carefully in chat. If you have a *severe* aversion to it, it's best to stay out of chat altogether.

And regardless of your own interests, I strongly advise against permitting children to use chat, especially unsupervised. My warning isn't about sex, but about safety. You'll find more about kids and chat in Hour 21, "Enjoying Safe Family Fun."

Understanding Internet Chatting

When you're in an Internet chat, everything you type appears on the screens of everybody else participating in that particular chat. Thousands of different chats are under way at once, each in its own chat room. When you join a chat you enter a room, and from then on you see only the conversation that's taking place in that room.

NEW TERM   **Chat room.** This is a space where a single conversation is taking place. In Internet chat parlance, a chat room is sometimes known as a *channel*. This can be a confusing term, however, because it has several other meanings on the Internet. Stick with *chat room*.

In most chat rooms, the conversation is focused on a given subject area. In a singles chat room, participants chat about stuff singles like to talk about. In a geology chat, people generally talk about rocks and earthquakes.

When you're in a chat room, everything that everyone else in the same room types appears on your screen, as shown in Figure 18.1. Each participant's statements are labeled with a nickname to identify who's talking. Those participating in a chat (known as *members*) choose their own nicknames and rarely share their real names. In a chat, you can be whoever you want to be, and so can everyone else.

NEW TERM   **Nickname.** Your *nickname*, which you choose yourself, is how you're known to others in a chat. Your nickname appears on every statement you make so everyone knows who's talking.

FIGURE 18.1

An Internet chat is conducted as an ongoing volley of typed statements between participants sharing a chat room.

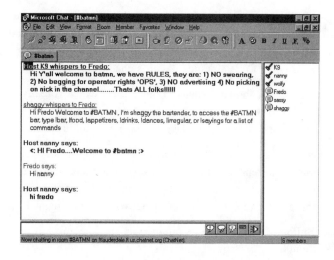

Besides IRC-type chatting, there's another type: Web chatting. A Web chat takes place within a Web page and is generally hosted as a discussion related to the Web page's topic.

To join a Web chat with your browser, you need the right plug-in for the type of Web chat that's under way. There are several types, but most Web chats are supported by the ichat plug-in. You'll usually find a link for downloading ichat on any Web page where a chat takes place. But you can also get ichat right from the source:

www.ichat.com

18

About Microsoft Chat

To chat, you must have a program called a *chat client*. Microsoft Chat is an example. If you don't have Microsoft Chat, you can download it from

www.microsoft.com/windows/ie/chat/

To learn about or download other chat clients, apply the file-searching techniques from Hour 11, "Finding Programs and Files," or check out the Tucows Internet software directory at www.tucows.com.

Like any chat program, Microsoft Chat—henceforth to be known simply as *Chat* with a capital *C*—lets you communicate with chat servers. You can view the list of chat rooms, join a chat room, read what everyone says in the chat room, and make your own contributions to the discussion. What's different about Chat is the way it displays the conversation.

NEW TERM **Chat server.** This is where a chat takes place and is more properly called an *IRC server*. (*IRC* stands for *Internet Relay Chat*, the full formal name for Chat.) Just as you need a Web browser to communicate with a Web server, you need a program called a *chat client* to communicate with a chat server.

Like the chat client shown earlier in Figure 18.1 (which is really just Chat in its text mode, which you'll learn more about later), most chat clients show the text of the conversation a line at a time and label each line with the speaker's nickname.

Chat, however, can display the conversation as text or as a comic strip, using little cartoon characters to represent members and showing their words in cartoon word balloons (see Figure 18.2). The folks at Microsoft think this approach makes chatting feel more human, more fun. In its first versions, Chat was actually named Microsoft Comic Chat.

NEW TERM **Balloon.** This is the little bubble you see in comics in which the words or thoughts of a character appears.

FIGURE 18.2

Microsoft Chat can make a chat session look like a comic strip, with a different cartoon character for each participant.

It's important to understand that chat servers support any IRC client, so most folks you'll end up chatting with probably won't use Microsoft Chat. Many will use ordinary text IRC clients; they'll see your statements labeled with your nickname but won't see your comic character.

On your display, Chat converts all statements in a chat—even those made by users of text-only clients—into comics. Other Chat users in the same room appear as their chosen cartoon characters. For users of other chat clients, Chat automatically assigns and shows unused characters.

Joining a Chat Room

Now that you understand what chatting is all about, it's time to hit a server and see it for real. On the way, though, you'll perform some automatic configuration that Chat needs to operate properly.

Before you open Chat, you can be online or off. If you're offline when you begin, Chat connects to the Internet automatically. Also, your browser need not be open for you to use Chat, although it won't hurt anything if it is open.

To Do: Start Chat and Display the Chat Rooms List

1. Open Microsoft Chat. In Windows 95/98/NT, you do so by choosing Programs, Microsoft Chat.

2. Select the Show All Available Chat Rooms option, and then click OK to connect to the chat server listed in the dialog (Figure 18.3).

FIGURE 18.3

Step 2: *Select Show All Available Chat Rooms and then click OK.*

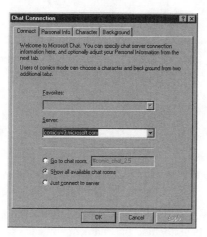

18

3. A message appears. This message differs by server, but typically it contains any special rules or instructions for the server, plus (as shown here) any disclaimers in which the server operator reminds you that he's not responsible for what people say there (Figure 18.4).

FIGURE 18.4

Step 3: Read the chat server's message.

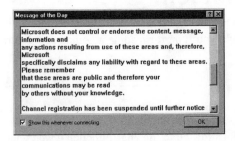

4. A list of all chat rooms available on the server appears (Figure 18.5). You are now connected to a chat server and are ready to chat—except that, as a new user, you have not yet selected a nickname and a comic character, as described next.

FIGURE 18.5

Step 4: A list of available chat rooms appears.

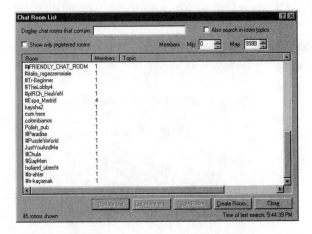

Choosing an Identity

Before you can join in a chat, you must create a nickname. And because of Chat's unique presentation style, you must choose a comic character too. In addition, you can select a background that appears behind the characters in each panel of the comic, as you see it on your screen.

After you choose a nickname, character, and background, Chat remembers them for future sessions. You do not need to choose them again unless you want to change them.

To Do: Choose Your Chat Identity

1. Choose View, Options to open the Options dialog box, and choose the Personal Info tab if it is not already selected (Figure 18.6).

FIGURE 18.6

Step 1: Choose View, Options to open the Personal Info tab.

2. Click in the Nickname box and type a nickname for yourself (Figure 18.7). Your nickname should be one word with no spaces or punctuation, and it should also be unusual enough that another member hasn't chosen the same nickname. (If you attempt to enter a room where someone is already using the same nickname as you, Chat prompts you to change your nickname before entering.)

18

FIGURE 18.7

Step 2: Type in a nick-name.

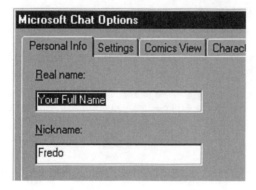

▼

On the Personal Info tab, you can enter other information besides your nick-name, such as your real name and email address. Think carefully before doing so, however. Any information you supply here can be seen by other members whose clients (like Chat) can display member profiles. If you want to keep your anonymity, enter your nickname and *nothing else*.

3. Click the Character tab and select the character you want to play by clicking a name in the Character column (Figure 18.8). The Preview column shows what the selected character looks like—what *you* will look like to other Chat users if you stick with that character.

FIGURE 18.8

Step 3: *Select a character.*

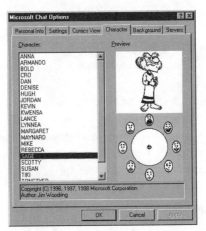

When you're choosing a character in the Character tab, you can click the faces in the emotion wheel (beneath the character preview) to see what the character will look like when you apply a given emotion to it when making a statement. You'll learn about choosing emotions later in this hour.

4. Click the Background tab and choose a background to use when chatting (Figure 18.9).

▼

FIGURE 18.9

Step 4: Choose a background.

Entering a Room

To enter a chat room, you select a room from the chat room list. Figure 18.10 shows the list of chats available on the server. Each server has its own list, and the lists change often.

18

FIGURE 18.10

To enter any room in the list, double-click its name.

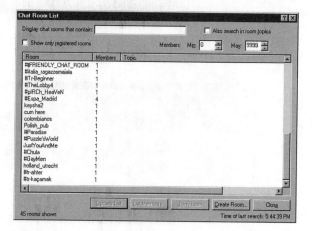

The chat room list reappears after you finish selecting your identity, but you can open the chat room list anytime you're connected to the server by clicking the Chat Room List button on Chat's toolbar.

In the list, the name of each room begins with a pound sign (#). The name of the room is followed by the number of members currently in the room, and sometimes also by a description of the conversation that usually takes place there.

You can switch between Chat's text view and comics view anytime. Just click the Comics View button or Text View button on the toolbar.

Understanding What You See

Observe that the Chat window (see Figure 18.11) is broken up into five sections, or *panes*, covered clockwise from the upper left:

- The biggest pane is the viewing pane, where you see the chat session as it progresses.
- The small pane in the upper right is the member list pane, which lists all members in the current chat room.
- The pane showing your character is the self-view pane, which reminds you of who you are.
- The ring of faces is the emotion wheel, from which you can select your character's facial expression.
- The small text box at the very bottom of the window is the compose pane, where you type your statements.

FIGURE 18.11

Chats happen in the chat window.

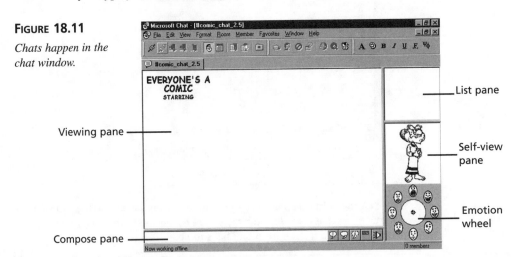

When you first arrive in a room, you may not see any comic panels right away. The server shows you only what's been said since you entered the room. After you enter, statements begin appearing one by one as members make them.

Contributing to the Conversation

Now that you're in a room, you can just *lurk* or listen in on the conversation, or you can contribute to it by sending your statements for all the others to see. Note that you are not obligated to add anything to the conversation. In fact, just lurking in a chat room is a great way to learn more about chats before diving in.

Making Statements

When you're ready to contribute your comments to the chat, just type them so that they appear in the compose pane. As you type, you can use the Backspace, Delete, Insert, and arrow keys to edit your statement and correct mistakes. When your statement is worded the way you want, press Enter.

While you're typing and editing your statements in the compose pane, no one sees them but you. A statement is sent to the chat only when you press Enter. This gives you a chance to choose your words carefully and correct typos before committing your statement to the chat.

18

After you press Enter, those in the room who are using regular chat clients see your statement labeled with your nickname, so they know you said it. Those in the room who are using Microsoft Chat see your chosen comic character speaking the words in a *say balloon,* the type that surrounds words that comic characters say aloud.

Choosing Balloons

When you contribute, you can choose the style of the comic word balloon in which your words will appear to you and to other Chat users. You choose the style of the word balloon by clicking a button next to the compose pane (see Figure 18.12).

FIGURE 18.12

To choose the style of balloon in which your words appear, click a button to the right of the compose pane.

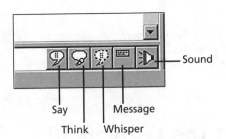

— Sound

Say   Message
Think   Whisper

For example, for a particular statement, you can choose a thought balloon so that the words appear in the balloon style generally used in comics to represent what the character is thinking. (For example, Snoopy can't actually speak, so all of his words appear in thought balloons.) The balloons you can use are as follows:

- **Say:** For normal statements.
- **Think:** For thoughts.
- **Whisper:** To sound secretive when commenting.

To choose a balloon, just type your statement in the compose pane as always and then click one of the balloon buttons *before* pressing Enter.

> The row to the right of the compose pane contains two more buttons you can use: Message and Sound.
>
> The Message button contains the statement in a box (not a balloon) to indicate that it's a message and not a part of the conversation per se. The Sound button opens a dialog in which you can select a sound file to play to all those in the chat room (or at least those whose computer and chat program can play sounds).

Showing Emotions

The emotion wheel in the lower-right corner of the chat window (see Figure 18.13) lets you change the expression of your character's face when making a statement.

Figure 18.13

Use the emotion wheel to choose your character's expression.

 Because some members in the room may not be using Chat and therefore can't see expressions, be sure your words alone carry your meaning.

To show emotions, type your statement (and choose a balloon, if desired) and then select a face from the emotion wheel. The character in the self-view pane changes to show how your character will appear if you commit to using the selected expression. As long as you don't press Enter, you can choose a different expression until you find one you like.

When the self-view pane appears the way you want it to, press Enter to submit your statement.

18

 To choose your character's normal, *neutral* expression, click the + at the center of the emotion wheel.

Gesturing

If you watch a chat for awhile, you'll notice that the characters are not static. They change body positions and make gestures from panel to panel. The gesturing is selected automatically by Chat, based on words you use in your statements. For example, if a statement contains the word *I,* your character will point to himself or herself.

You can use other member's nicknames to control to whom the gesture is made. For example, if you say "Hi," your character waves to the group. If you say "Hi, Eloise," your character waves to the member using the nickname Eloise.

Table 18.1 describes the gestures that Chat applies. Observe that some gestures are based on words used to *begin* a statement, and others are based on words *within* the statement.

When a statement both begins with a gesture word and contains a gesture word, Chat applies the gesture for the beginning word.

TABLE 18.1   GESTURES USED AUTOMATICALLY BY CHAT CHARACTERS

Statement Begins With	Character's Action
I	Points to itself
You	Points to another member
Hello or Hi	Waves
Bye	Waves
Welcome	Waves
Howdy	Waves
Statement Contains	**Character's Action**
are you	Points to another member
will you	Points to another member
did you	Points to another member
aren't you	Points to another member
don't you	Points to another member
I'm	Points to itself
I am	Points to itself
I'll	Points to itself
I will	Points to itself

Summary

Chat's fun, as long as you stay among people whose reasons for chatting are the same as yours. Like a carnival or circus, Chat is an entertaining place with a seedy underbelly and should be enjoyed with caution. But if you're careful, you can have safe, interactive fun with Chat.

Q&A

Q Sometimes the sequence of statements in a chat looks all jumbly to me. Like, somebody asks a question, and then three unrelated statements appear, and then someone answers the question a few panels later. What's the deal?

A In a chat with three or more members, the conversation often appears out of order. This jumbling happens because each member's words take a different amount of time to reach the server, and some members take more time composing their statements than others.

Once you've used Chat for a while, you'll get used to the jumbling and your brain will develop the ability to sort out the conversation intuitively.

18

HOUR 19

Tools for the Serious User: FTP and Telnet

People surfed the Net for over a decade before there was a World Wide Web. During those years, the principal tools for using the Net—other than email and newsgroups—were good old Telnet, FTP, and, in the final pre-Web years, Gopher. Once you get the hang of them, these tools aren't really any more difficult to use than the Web or email. But because they take you beyond the familiar confines of the more popular Internet tools, you might lump FTP, Telnet, and Gopher together as "serious" tools—after all, you won't use them unless you're serious enough about what you're doing to go beyond the Web.

There's so much available on the Web these days that most newcomers to the Net never bother with FTP, Gopher, or Telnet. Much of what used to be accessible only through these tools now resides on Web pages. But not *everything* in the serious tools' domain has made it to the Web yet, so these tools remain an important part of your Net toolset. In order to use *all* of the Internet, you must be familiar with these powerful tools, which are easier to use than you might expect. (You don't have to be all *that* serious!)

At the end of this hour, you'll be able to answer the following questions:

- What's FTP, and how can I use it to download files?
- What's Gopher, and how can I use it to browse for information?
- What's Telnet, and how can I use it to explore and operate other people's computer systems?
- How can I use these tools from within their own client programs *and* from my Web browser?

Downloading Files with FTP

You already know how to download files from the Web (unless you skipped Hour 11, "Finding Programs and Files," and if so, you're in big trouble!). But some files you may want are stored not on Web servers, but on *FTP servers*.

FTP stands for *File Transfer Protocol*, but you really don't need to know that. Everybody uses just the abbreviation, like NBC or VCR. Still, the name says it all: FTP is used for transferring files between computers. The files stored on FTP servers are waiting to be downloaded by an *FTP client*, a program on your computer that communicates with FTP servers through the Internet.

Many FTP servers are *password-protected* to limit access to only authorized users. When you try to access a password-protected FTP server, you're prompted to enter a username and password. If you don't have a correct username and password for using that particular server, you're locked out.

However, many FTP servers are called *anonymous* FTP servers because they require no username and password at all, or they display instructions that allow you to enter a "guest" username and password (usually your email address) to use the server. When you access an anonymous FTP server through your Web browser, you often do not have to log on (even with a guest password) because your browser automatically completes the logon with your email address, if required.

The kinds of files you can download from FTP servers are the same as those you download from Web pages (`.exe`, `.doc`, `.zip`, and so on) and are subject to the same issues and considerations (such as whether a particular file can run on your type of computer). If you're not sure about file types, review Hour 11.

Understanding FTP Addresses

As with any server, you access an FTP server by entering its address. FTP server addresses are made up of sections separated by periods, just like Web addresses, and often—but not always—begin with ftp. For example, the following are FTP server addresses:

ftp.microsoft.com

ftp.mcp.com

Files for downloading are stored in particular directories on FTP servers, just as Web page files are stored in particular Web server directories (see Figure 19.1). The FTP address can point directly to a file or directory. For example, the address

ftp.mcp.com/samples/doc.txt

points directly to a file called doc.txt in a directory called samples on a server called ftp.mcp.com.

FIGURE 19.1

FTP servers organize files into directories.

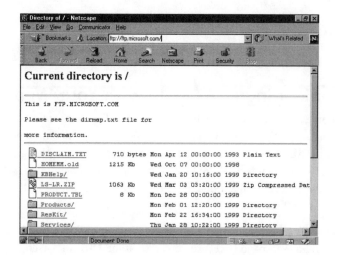

When you view an FTP directory through some Web browsers, some links in the directory may be preceded by folder icons, indicating that they lead to further listings (*subdirectories*), while other links show icons that represent the types of files found there (such as a printed page for a document file).

When you look at an FTP directory through Internet Explorer 5 in Windows (see Figure 19.2), it looks exactly like an ordinary folder on your PC. The browser window looks like a folder window, files appear as icons, and FTP subdirectories appear as folders. You can open and close FTP folders and files in this window exactly as you would if the folders and files were on your hard disk.

FIGURE 19.2

Through Internet Explorer 5 in Windows, an FTP directory looks just like another folder on your PC.

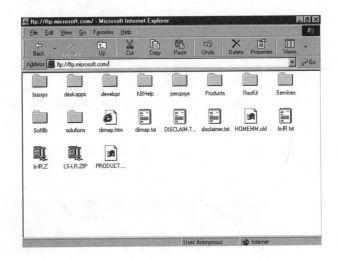

Downloading an FTP File with Your Web Browser

As I pointed out earlier in this book, many Web browsers are multipurpose clients. At the very least, any Web browser can act as a Web client and communicate with Web servers. But many Web clients—including all versions of Netscape Navigator and Internet Explorer—can double as FTP clients (and triple as Gopher clients—but more about that later). If you have such a browser, you don't need a separate FTP client for downloading files from FTP servers.

From a browser, you may use FTP by entering an FTP URL in the address box, just as you would a Web page URL. Remember that the URL of a Web page begins with `http://` (even though you don't have to type that part in many browsers). An FTP URL is made up of `ftp://` followed by the FTP server address. For example, the URLs for the FTP addresses shown in the preceding section are

`ftp://ftp.microsoft.com`

`ftp://ftp.mcp.com`

`ftp://ftp.mcp.com/samples/doc.txt`

If your Web browser allows you to omit the `http://` prefix when entering a Web page URL, it probably also lets you omit the `ftp://` prefix in an FTP URL.

However, this feature does not work as reliably with FTP URLs as it does with Web URLs. When you're entering an FTP URL in any Web browser, always include the complete `ftp://` prefix.

You can download a file either by entering the complete FTP address of the file or by entering the address of the FTP server and then browsing through its directories to locate and select the file. When you view FTP directories through a browser, every directory name is a link. Click a directory name and the contents of that directory appear.

Whichever way you get to an FTP file, once you select it, the download proceeds exactly like a regular Web download (see Hour 11).

Because most Web browsers do FTP, you'll often come across links in Web pages that are *FTP links*—they point either to an FTP server or directory, or to a specific file on the server. In particular, the hits turned up by file searches (see Hour 11) often include links to files that reside on FTP servers.

If the link points to a file, clicking the link starts the download, just like any other download. You may not even know you're doing an FTP download unless you look closely at the download status message.

If the link points to an FTP server or directory, you'll need to browse through the directory listings to find and select a file. That's when knowing FTP comes in handy.

19

To Do: Use Your Browser to Get an FTP File

1. Begin in your browser, online and on any page. In your address box, enter the following URL to display the top-level directory on Microsoft's anonymous FTP server (Figure 19.3):

   `ftp://ftp.microsoft.com`

2. Click any link preceded by a folder icon or labeled "Directory" (Figure 19.4). A new directory listing appears.

▼

FIGURE 19.3

Step 1: Enter an FTP URL into a Web browser's address box.

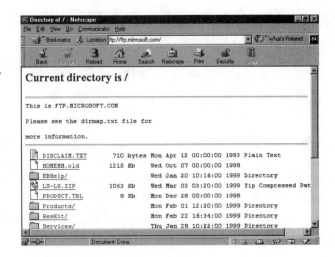

FIGURE 19.4

Step 2: Click on a folder icon link.

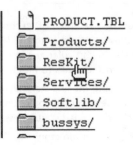

3. Click the Back button to return to the top directory (Figure 19.5). In a browser, you move down through the FTP directory structure by clicking links and back up by clicking your Back button.

▼

FIGURE 19.5

Step 3: Click the Back button to return to the top directory.

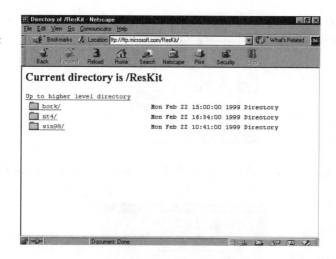

4. Find the link for LS-LR.ZIP (Figure 19.6). This file contains a complete index to the Microsoft FTP server in a compressed Zip file (see Hour 11).

FIGURE 19.6

Step 4: Find the link for LS-LR.ZIP.

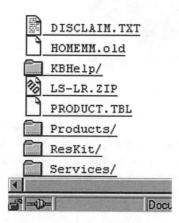

19

5. Click the link to start the download (Figure 19.7).

FIGURE 19.7

Step 5: Click the link.

6. Continue downloading the file if you wish, or cancel the download.

FIGURE 19.8

Step 6: Choose whether to run the file after it's downloaded ("Open it") or save it to your hard disk.

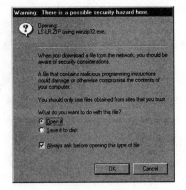

For a variety of technical reasons, downloading a file from an FTP server often takes less time than downloading a file of the same size from a Web server—even when you run the FTP download from a Web browser.

If you know you can acquire the same file from both a Web server and an FTP server, you may be able to cut the download time by choosing the FTP server, especially if it's a big file (larger than 1MB).

Using an FTP Client

For most people, the FTP capabilities of a Web browser are all the FTP power they need. But you should know that FTP can do more than download a file. Using FTP, you can send (or *upload*) files to an FTP server so others can download them, and you can control your uploading and downloading to a very fine degree—such as downloading a whole family of files in one operation. Such advanced FTPing typically requires a real FTP client, not a Web browser posing as one.

Why would you ever upload a file? Well, one common case is if you're publishing a Web page. After you create a Web page on your computer, you
must upload it to a Web server to make it accessible to others. See Hour 23,
"Creating Web Pages and Multimedia Messages."

Windows 95/98/NT and the Mac have their own built-in FTP clients (see Figure 19.9),
but they're rather old-fashioned, requiring you to learn and use a family of FTP commands. Most casual Net users don't use FTP often enough to justify learning to use these
utilitarian FTP clients.

FIGURE 19.9

*The FTP client built
into Windows
95/98/NT is a little too
complex for beginners.*

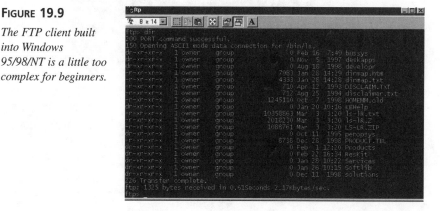

A better choice is an easy-to-use FTP client, which combines the simplicity of a Web
browser with the full power of FTP. You can find many such clients online by using the
search techniques from Hour 11 or by looking in the Tucows Internet software directory
at www.tucows.com.

A popular choice for Windows is WS_FTP, which you can get from www.ipswitch.com.
Another similar program is FTP Commander (see Figure 19.10), a freeware program you
can download from www.vista.ru. Like most easy FTP clients, these programs display
the directory of the FTP site you've accessed on the right side of the window and your
PC's hard disk directory on the left. To download a file, you simply move it from one
side to the other. In FTP Commander, you do this by highlighting the files you want to
transfer and then clicking the Copy button that points to the other side of the window. In
a graphical FTP client like WS_FTP, you can do it the same way, or you can actually
drag files from one side to the other.

19

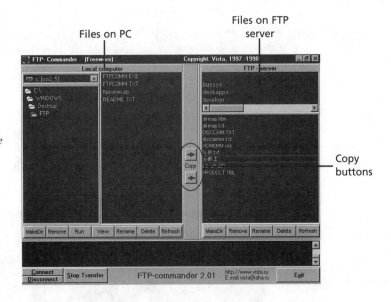

FIGURE 19.10

In easier-to-use FTP clients such as FTP Commander, you transfer files by moving them from one side of the screen to the other.

Files on PC

Files on FTP server

Copy buttons

Remember that URLs are used only in Web browsers. When you're accessing an FTP server through a real FTP client, you do not enter an FTP URL—such as `ftp://ftp.microsoft.com`—but only the FTP address itself—such as `ftp.microsoft.com`.

Burrowing Through the Net with Gopher

Gopher was the first real attempt to make the Net easier to use, and it worked—but not as well as the Web, which was developed hot on Gopher's heels.

Gopher introduced the idea that you can explore online information by navigating through an organized index of menu items—*links*, in effect (see Figure 19.11). You can explore all of the information stored on Gopher servers the world over (most of which are in colleges and universities) by clicking your way through the menus and links in Gopherspace.

NEW TERM **Gopherspace.** This term describes all of the Gopher servers in the world and the information they contain. All of the Gopher servers are interconnected, so clicking a menu item on a menu displayed by one Gopher server may display a new menu or file that's stored on another Gopher server.

As on an FTP server, all of the online information accessible through Gopher is organized like a table of contents or index. You generally begin at a high-level directory.
When you click an item in that directory, a more specific subdirectory of choices
appears. You continue clicking down through the menu structure until you reach your
goal—usually a document that shows you the information to which your choices
have led .

Also like FTP, when each item in a Gopher menu is viewed through a Web browser (or
graphical Gopher client), it's preceded by an icon that indicates what the link leads to.
Items flagged by folder icons lead to other Gopher menus, items flagged by page icons
lead to documents, and so on.

FIGURE 19.11

*Gopher provides a
system of menus you
can browse.*

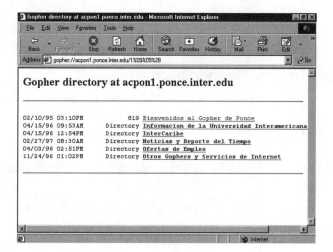

Browsing Gopherspace Through a Web Browser

Just as most Web browsers can act as FTP clients, most of them—including, yet again,
all versions of Netscape Navigator and Internet Explorer—can also be used as Gopher
clients. So you probably already have your Gopher client, ready to go.

In case you hadn't already guessed, you access Gopherspace through a Web browser by
entering a Gopher URL in the address box. A Gopher URL begins with the prefix
gopher:// followed by a server address. (This URL stuff gets pretty obvious after
awhile, doesn't it?)

19

Unlike a real FTP client, a real Gopher client offers no advantage over using your Web browser for Gopher. But just in case you use a browser that doesn't do Gopher, note that there are Gopher client programs available for just about any system.

Your ISP can probably set you up with a Gopher client from among the programs it offers to subscribers. You can also find a Gopher client by using the search techniques from Hour 11 or by looking in the Tucows Internet software directory at www.tucows.com.

Gopher was developed at the University of Minnesota. In fact, Gopher borrows its name from U Minn.'s mascot, although the name also implies that you use it to "burrow" or "go for" information. The U Minn. Gopher—sometimes known affectionately as "Mother Gopher"—is a great place to begin exploring, as shown in the following To Do.

To Do: Explore Gopherspace

1. Begin in your browser, online and on any page. In your address box, enter `gopher://gopher.micro.umn.edu/` to display the top-level directory on Mother Gopher (Figure 19.12).

FIGURE 19.12

Step 1: Go to the University of Minnesota Gopher site from within Netscape.

2. Click the top choice, Information About Gopher (Figure 19.13).

FIGURE 19.13

Step 2: Click Information About Gopher.

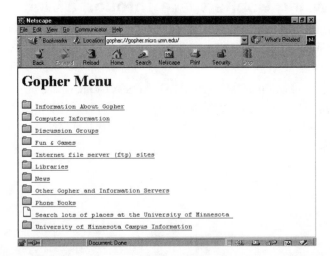

▼ 3. Click About Gopher (Figure 19.14).

FIGURE 19.14

Step 3: Click About Gopher.

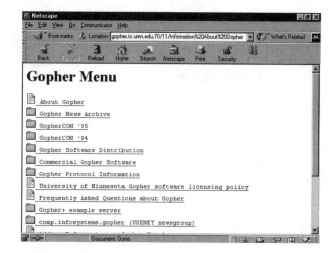

4. Click the Back button once to close the document and return to the menu (Figure 19.15).

FIGURE 19.15

Step 4: Click the Back button to close the document.

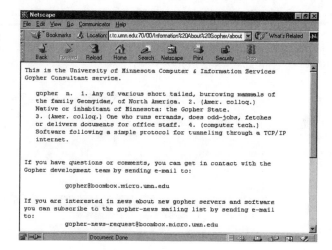

19

▼

▼   5. Burrow away! (Figure 19.16)

FIGURE 19.16

Step 5: Explore at will.

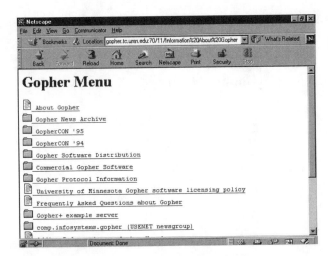

▲

Using Remote Computers Through Telnet

Using one Web server is like using any other. The same goes for FTP servers, news servers, and Gopher servers. Telnet, however, is the exception to the rule. Using Telnet, you access another computer out there on the Internet—known to Telnet as a *remote computer*—and use that computer as if you were using a terminal that was connected directly to that computer. (See Figure 19.17.)

FIGURE 19.17.

Telnet lets you access a remote computer and use it as if you were there.

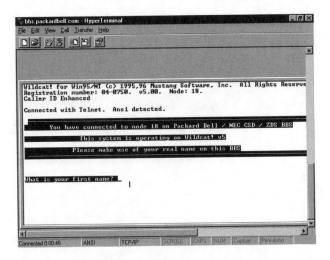

Understanding Telnet

Many libraries have a computerized card catalog system, which visitors to the library use from terminals or PCs located at the library. If the library has configured the card catalog to support access via Telnet, you can use your Internet connection to access the card catalog system from thousands of miles away. What you'll see on your screen is exactly what you'd see if you went to the library in person and used one of the card catalog terminals.

The trick with Telnet is that all of the computers you're accessing work differently. Each has its own procedures for logging on, navigating menus, and more. In fact, accessing a remote computer through Telnet is the easy part. Getting logged on to that computer, and then figuring out how to operate it, is the challenge.

NEW TERM **Log on.** Actually, this term isn't so new; you've been logging on to the Internet—entering your username and password—since Hour 4, "Connecting to the Internet." You must also log on (or log in, or sign in, or sign on—it's all the same thing) to most remote computers you access through Telnet, either by using a private name and password you've been given for using that system or by entering a guest or visitor username and password.

When you start a Telnet session from a Web link, you'll often find instructions on the same page the link is on, describing how to log on after you click the link. Some helpful Telnet systems actually tell you the guest username and password when you arrive. Some Web pages even serve as handy directories to computers accessible through Telnet. For example, check out `www.internetdatabase.com/telnet.htm` (see Figure 19.18).

19

FIGURE 19.18

Typically, you'll initiate Telnet sessions from Web pages, where you can also learn how to log on to the Telnet session you're about to access.

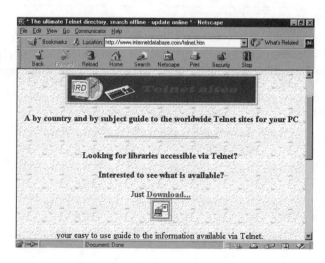

If you are a student or faculty member at a university, the computer services department may be able to give you a password and instructions for Telnetting into the school's library catalog. You can choose your books from home without waiting to use a terminal at the library, and you can make sure the library actually has the book you want before you go trudging over there in the snow/rain/heat/traffic/pollen.

Getting a Telnet Client

Now, I know what you're expecting. You're expecting me to tell you that your Web browser doubles as a Telnet client. You lose. (*Psych!*). You can use Telnet only through a real Telnet client.

Fortunately, Windows 95/98/NT and the Mac have built-in Telnet clients. Even more fortunately, most Windows and Mac Web browsers know how to open the Telnet client automatically, as a *helper program* (see Hour 7, "Playing Online Video, Music, and Broadcasts"), when you click a link leading to a Telnet server. So although you must operate the remote computer through your Telnet client, you can navigate to the server and begin your Telnet session from within your browser.

 If you use Windows 3.1 or another system that lacks a built-in Telnet client, ask your ISP for one, or find your own using the search techniques from Hour 11 or the Tucows directory at www.tucows.com.

The U.S. Library of Congress has a great Web page. But the whole card catalog (LOCIS—Library Of Congress Information System) has not yet been put on the Web. It remains accessible only through Telnet. Give it a try in the following To Do.

To Do: Visit the Library of Congress Through Telnet

1. Go to the Library of Congress Web page (Figure 19.19) at www.loc.gov.

FIGURE 19.19

Step 1: Go to the Library of Congress Web page using your Web browser.

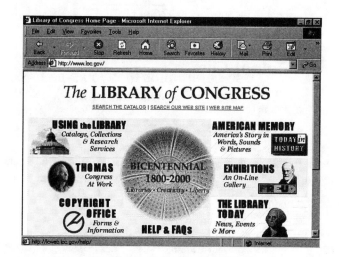

2. Click the SEARCH THE CATALOG link (Figure 19.20).

FIGURE 19.20

Step 2: Click the SEARCH THE CATALOG link.

The **LIBRARY**

19

▼ 3. Click the TELNET to LOCIS link (Figure 19.21).

FIGURE 19.21

Step 3: Click the TELNET to LOCIS link.

4. Your Telnet client opens and the main menu of the LOCIS catalog appears (Figure 19.22). Observe that each menu item is preceded by a number. To choose an item, you type its number and then press Enter. Press 1 and then Enter to open the Catalog menu.

FIGURE 19.22

Step 4: In your Telnet client, press 1 and then Enter.

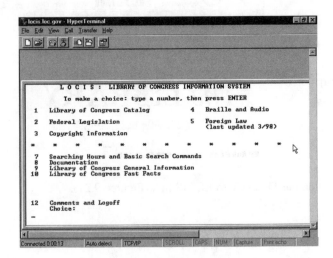

Note that Telnet systems don't support your mouse, trackball, or any other pointing device. You do everything in a Telnet session with your keyboard.

▼ 5. In the Catalog menu, type 12 (for Return to LOCIS MENU Screen) and press
Enter (Figure 19.23).

FIGURE 19.23

Step 5: Type 12 and press Enter to return to the main screen.

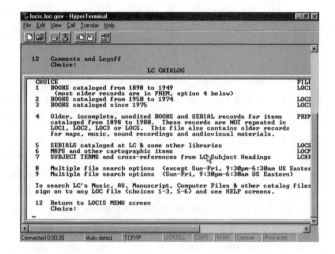

6. Type 12 and press Enter again to log off LOCIS. Then close your Telnet client
(Figure 19.24).

FIGURE 19.24

Step 6: Type 12 and press Enter again to log off.

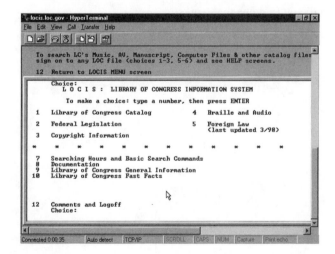

19

Many Gopher links lead to Telnet sessions. A link that leads to Telnet is preceded by an icon that looks like a computer terminal. If you're browsing Gopher from within your Web browser, clicking this link generally opens the Telnet client that your Web browser is configured to open.

▲

Summary

Serious, *schmerious!* FTP, Gopher, and Telnet are a little more difficult than Web browsing, but you'll only use them when no Web page offers what you need. It's nice to have the keys to several different doors, so you'll always have a place to go.

Q&A

Q **I noticed that the Library of Congress gave me two choices for accessing LOCIS—TELNET to LOCIS and TN3270 to LOCIS. What's that all about?**

A When you use Telnet, you're making your computer perform something called *terminal emulation*. That is, it's pretending to be the kind of computer terminal that the remote system is designed to interact with. TN3270 is a common type of terminal. LOCIS lets you choose the type of terminal access (generic Telnet or TN3270), depending upon the kind of terminal your Telnet program emulates.

If you start your Telnet sessions from Web links and use the Telnet program your browser is configured to open, you can usually forget about terminal issues. But if you find that the screen images displayed by a Telnet session seem scrambled, it's likely that the remote computer wants your Telnet program to emulate a different terminal. Try changing the terminal emulation from the menus in your Telnet client until you find one that works.

HOUR 20

Working Smarter by Working Offline

"Are you *still* online? I need the *phone!!!*" Sound familiar?

There's no law that says you have to do anything at all offline—stay online all you want, see if I care. These days most of us have unlimited Internet accounts, so it costs us nothing extra to stay online as long as we need to. Still, many of us have only one phone line, and often it's hard to do what you want to do online while still keeping the phone line free for other uses. This hour shows you how you can spend less time online while doing more.

Personally, I find there's a psychological benefit to working offline. When I write email offline, I take my time and express myself more effectively. I often open messages waiting in my Outbox to make final fixes and other edits before sending them. Similarly, when I'm offline I read Web pages and newsgroup messages more carefully and thoughtfully. Something about being online makes me feel like the sand is running out of the hourglass, and I hurry too much. You too may find that the more you do offline, the better your overall Internet experience is.

At the end of this hour, you'll be able to answer the following questions:

- How can I conveniently round up the latest online info and store it on my computer so I can view it offline?
- How can I make composing email offline more convenient in Outlook Express and Messenger?
- How can I download entire newsgroups so I can read their messages offline?

In addition to the offline techniques you pick up here, you may have heard of two others: Channels and Netcasting. These are two different approaches to a technology called *push*, wherein info is "pushed" from the Net to you. Channels were introduced in Internet Explorer 4 and included in Windows 98, and Netcasting was supported by an optional component of Communicator 4 called Netcaster.

You will see traces of these technologies, especially if you have an outdated browser. Online, you may see buttons here and there labeled "Add Active Channel," which are leftovers from the Channel days. But in practice, these technologies are orphans. IE5 still supports channels but offers no tools for dealing with them, and Netcaster has disappeared altogether in Netscape Communicator version 4.5 and higher.

So although it remains possible to do some offline work through Channels and Netcasting using old tools, I do not recommend it. You will find that the offline browsing techniques you learn in this hour work for virtually all Web pages, newsgroups, and email (unlike Channels and Netcasting), are easy to use, and are not already on the closeout shelf of Internet innovations.

Reading Web Pages Offline, Anytime

In Hour 6, "Revisiting Places You Like," you learned how to print or save Web pages for use offline. That's great in a pinch, or for information you find online that will never change, such as the text of the Declaration of Independence.

But pretty quickly, most saved or printed Web pages fall out of date—the real page that's online changes, but your saved or printed version can't. In order to take advantage of up-to-date content while still working offline, you need a convenient way to quickly download the current versions of sites you like to keep up with. You can then go offline and peruse them at your leisure.

Exactly how you do this depends upon what browser you use. Over the next several pages, you'll learn how to do this in Internet Explorer 5 (the easiest browser to use for offline work).

> Netscape Communicator includes facilities for working with email and newsgroups offline, just as IE5 does. But unlike IE5, the current version of Communicator at this writing (4.6) does not include a facility for working offline with Web pages.
>
> You may find that, using Communicator's History file (see Hour 6), you can still open many of the pages you've visited recently while you're offline. Copies of those pages are stored in the cache file that Communicator saves to speed up the display of pages you visit often. Unfortunately, cached pages come and go.
>
> If Communicator has come out in a newer version by the time you read this, that version may include offline Web browsing. If it doesn't, and offline browsing is important to you, give IE5 a try.

Making Web Sites Available Offline in Internet Explorer 5

If you want to get into offline work, IE5 is the easiest and most effective tool for doing so, as of this writing. Not only does it make it easy to capture Web sites for offline use, but it also makes working with offline email and newsgroup a snap (see the sections on offline email and newsgroups later in this hour).

The following To Do shows how to set up a page for offline browsing.

To Do: Select a Page for Offline Browsing in IE5

1. Online in IE5, go to the page you want to browse offline (Figure 20.1).

2. Choose Favorites, Add to Favorites, just as you would for any new favorite you wanted to create (Figure 20.2).

3. In the Add Favorite dialog box, check the check box labeled Make Available Offline, and then click OK (Figure 20.3).

4. IE5 immediately informs you that it is *synchronizing*—downloading the page to your computer for offline use (Figure 20.4). (To learn more about synchronizing, see "Updating Offline Pages" later in this hour.)

▲ To Do

20

▼

▼

FIGURE 20.1

Step 1: Go to your target page in Internet Explorer 5.

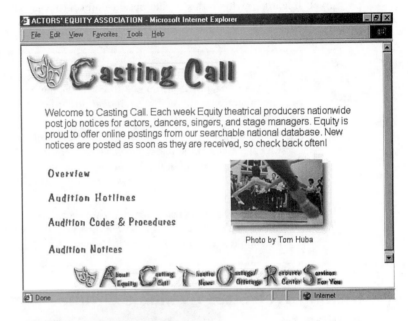

FIGURE 20.2

Step 2: Choose Favorites, Add to Favorites.

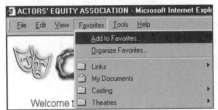

FIGURE 20.3

Step 3: Check Make Available Offline, and then click OK.

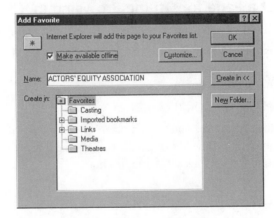

▼

After synchronization finishes, you can disconnect and then read the pages offline, as described in the next section.

FIGURE 20.4

Step 4: Internet Explorer 5 starts to synchronize.

Reading Pages Offline

To read a page offline, you must first shift Internet Explorer 5 into its offline mode:

- If you're not online already, open IE5 and then click Cancel in your connection dialog so you don't connect to the Internet. Click the Work Offline button that appears.

- If you're online, don't close IE5. Close your Internet connection and then, in IE5, choose File, Work Offline.

Once you're in offline mode, just open your Favorites menu. The pages available to be read offline appear in bold type (see Figure 20.5). The others are grayed out to show that you must connect to the Internet to view them.

FIGURE 20.5

When you're in offline mode, the pages available for offline viewing appear in bold type.

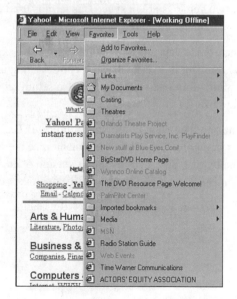

20

Some favorites may appear in bold even though you did not check the Make Available Offline check box for them. These are sites you've visited recently enough that copies of them are still stored in the cache file, which IE5 saves to speed up the display of pages you visit often.

Only the most recently visited pages are in the cache file, so you can't count on it to always hold the pages you want to see offline. Be sure to check the Make Available Offline check box, making the page available no matter how long it's been since you last visited it online.

Choose any favorite in bold and read away. You can even click the links on the page. If you click a link that leads to a page that's not available offline, a dialog asks whether you want to connect to the Internet to see that page.

When you're finished working offline, return IE5 to online mode by choosing File, Work Offline again.

Updating Offline Pages

From time to time, you'll want to update the offline pages stored on your computer so that their contents match the latest versions that are online. To do that, you must *synchronize*.

NEW TERM **Synchronize.** To download the latest online content (Web pages, email, or newsgroup messages) so that the offline version on your computer matches the current version online—the two versions are in sync. This term is used the same way in IE5, Outlook Express, and Communicator.

How often you must synchronize depends on how frequently you expect the online content to change. But synchronizing is so easy that you can simply sync up all your offline content as often as you want, all in one step. You can also set up schedules by which IE5 will automatically synchronize for you.

To synchronize, go online and then choose Tools, Synchronize. The Items to Synchronize dialog appears, as shown in Figure 20.6. Click the Synchronize button. IE5 contacts every page in the list, one by one, and saves the latest version of each on your computer. When the synchronization is finished, you can go offline and take your time reading the updated content.

FIGURE 20.6

Choose Tools, Synchronize to open this dialog, from which you can synchronize or change your sync settings.

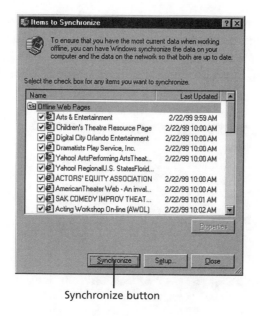

Synchronize button

 In Figure 20.6, note that a check mark appears next to each page. If you want to skip synchronization for any page, remove its check mark before clicking the Synchronize button.

In Figure 20.6, observe that there are some other buttons you may use to customize your synchronizations:

- Click the Setup button to open a dialog where you can choose from among general options for synchronization, such as configuring IE5 to sync automatically every day, week, or month.
- Click a page in the list to select it and then click the Properties button. This opens a dialog where you can choose from among options for that page alone, such as a daily, weekly, or monthly automatic sync.

One handy feature of the dialog for changing the sync properties of individual pages is on the Download tab, shown in Figure 20.7. By default, when you sync a page you get only the content on *that* page, and not the content on any of the *other* pages to which that page may link. By increasing the number in the blank following the words "Download pages," you can sync not only the page, but also others it links to.

20

For example, if you put a 2 in that box, synchronization would download the specified page *plus* all the pages it linked to. A 3 would download the page, all pages it linked to, and all pages *those* pages linked to. (Although this option expands your ability to work offline, use it sparingly because it may dramatically increase the time required for synchronization.)

FIGURE 20.7

You can customize properties for each page you designate for offline viewing.

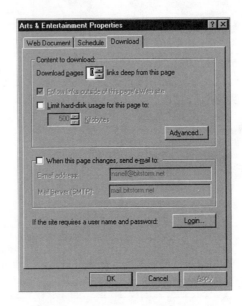

Offline Email and Newsgroups

The Web has no monopoly on letting you work offline. In some ways, you may have even more to gain from doing email and newsgroup tasks offline. Both IE5 and Netscape Communicator feature great tools for making the most of offline mail and news, as you'll learn in the next few pages.

Setting Up Offline Email in Outlook Express

To make Outlook Express a better offline email program, all you need to do is change a few settings...

First, you need to tell Outlook Express to save new messages you write in the Outbox folder until you decide to send them. In Outlook Express, choose Tools, Options, and then click the Send tab (see Figure 20.8). Clear the check box labeled Send Messages Immediately. This prevents the program from trying to connect to the Internet each time you send a message. Instead, you can do all your composing offline and click the Send button on each message when you finish writing it. The messages wait in the Outbox until you click the Send/Recv button. Then Outlook Express connects to the Internet, sends all the messages waiting in the Outbox, and retrieves all new email for you, all in one shot.

FIGURE 20.8

Clear the Send Messages Immediately check box to make Outlook Express save messages in the Outbox folder, to be sent later.

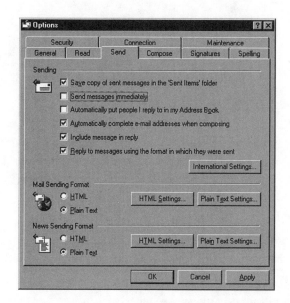

Another change that makes offline work more convenient for some folks is telling Outlook Express to disconnect as soon as it finishes sending and receiving messages. This enables you to click Send/Recv and then forget about the rest. Outlook Express connects (if necessary), sends all Outbox messages, retrieves any new messages, and then disconnects, all without any further input from you (unless you're required to enter your password to connect). If you routinely go online just to check email and then get right off again instead of moving on to Web browsing or another activity, this change is for you.

Choose Tools, Options, and then click the Connection tab (see Figure 20.9). Check the check box labeled Hang Up After Sending and Receiving.

20

FIGURE 20.9

Check the Hang Up After Sending and Receiving check box to make Outlook Express disconnect automatically after sending all waiting messages and receiving any new ones.

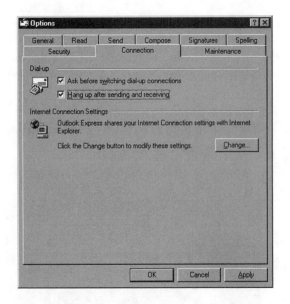

Synchronizing News in Outlook Express

If you use newsgroups regularly (see Hour 15, "Reading and Posting to Newsgroups"), you may find that offline news browsing is the most valuable of all offline techniques.

Ordinarily, when you open a newsgroup online, only the messages' headers are copied to your computer to appear in the message list. No actual message is copied to your computer until you open it online. But by synchronizing newsgroups in Outlook Express, you can download entire newsgroups—messages and all—to your computer. Then you can disconnect and browse them offline at your leisure.

To set up offline newsgroups, first be sure you have already subscribed to any newsgroup you'll want to use offline (see Hour 15). Then follow the steps in the following To Do.

To Do: Set Up Newsgroups for Offline Browsing in Outlook Express

1. Click the name of a subscribed newsgroup you will want to browse offline. Then click the Settings button (Figure 20.10).

FIGURE 20.10

Step 1: Select a newsgroup and then click Settings.

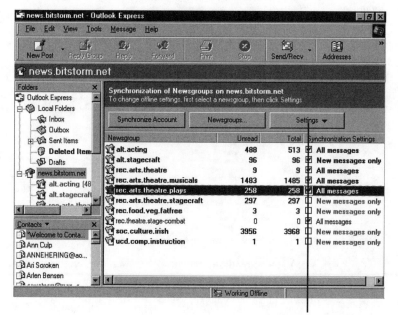

Settings button

2. Choose the sync settings for this newsgroup (Figure 20.11):

   All Messages: Synchronization will download all messages in the newsgroup to your computer for offline browsing.

   New Messages Only: Synchronization will download only the new messages (those posted since the last time you synchronized) to your computer. This is the recommended choice because it gets you up-to-date the quickest.

20

▼

FIGURE 20.11

Step 2: Choose the synchronization settings for the news-group.

3. Repeat steps 1 and 2 for all newsgroups you want to use offline (Figure 20.12).

FIGURE 20.12

Step 3: Repeat for each newsgroup.

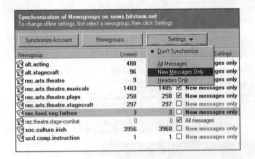

4. When you're ready to synchronize, click the Synchronize Account button (Figure 20.13). After synchronization is complete, you may disconnect from the Internet and read your newsgroups offline.

FIGURE 20.13

Step 4: Click the Synchronize Account button.

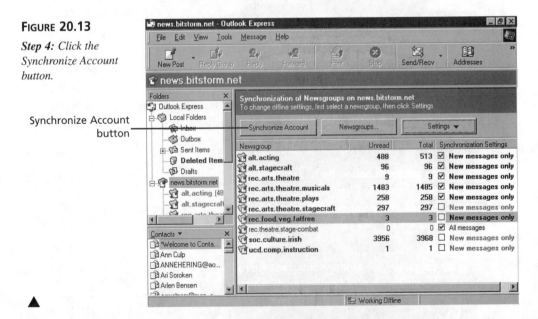

Synchronize Account button

The next time you synchronize, all you have to do is step 4. Steps 1 through 3 are necessary only when you want to change the synchronization settings.

Here are a few handy tips for offline newsgroups:

- If you've set up Outlook Express so that it saves new messages in your Outbox folder (as described earlier in this hour), any newsgroup replies or new postings you send *also* go to the Outbox, so you can continue working offline.

- Choosing Tools, Synchronize All does three things: 1) Sends any messages waiting in Outbox; 2) Retrieves any new messages; and 3) Synchronizes newsgroups. One-step sync!

- If you find that your newsgroup sync takes too long, sync fewer newsgroups. Or reduce the number of messages downloaded for each group by choosing Tools, Options, clicking the Read tab, and then lowering the number shown in the box in the tab's News section.

Synchronizing Mail and News in Netscape Messenger

In Netscape Messenger, you set up your mail and news synchronization all in one place. Isn't that nice? To learn how, see the following To Do. Before you begin, be sure you have already subscribed to any newsgroups you'll want to use offline (see Hour 15).

To compose email offline in Messenger, you don't have to reconfigure anything. Just compose your message as usual, offline. When you're done, *don't* click the Send button on the message window. Instead, choose File, Send Message Later. All messages you send this way are held in the Unsent Messages folder until you click the Get Msg button, or until you synchronize (as described next).

20

To Do: Set Up Netscape Messenger 4.6 for Offline Mail and News

1. In Messenger, choose File, Offline, Synchronize (Figure 20.14).

FIGURE 20.14

Step 1: Choose File, Offline, Synchronize.

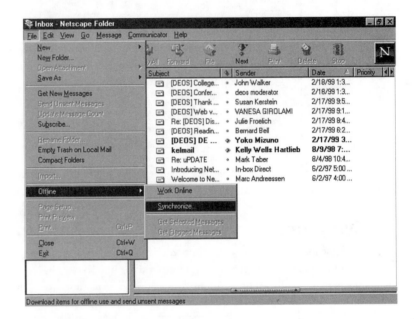

2. Click the Select Items button (Figure 20.15).

FIGURE 20.15

Step 2: Click Select Items.

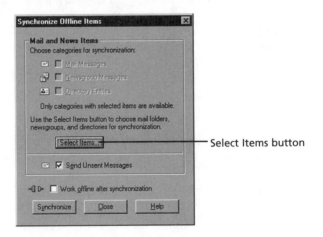

Select Items button

▼ 3. Select a newsgroup or mail folder you want to include in synchronization (Figure 20.16).

FIGURE 20.16

Step 3: Select folders to synchronize.

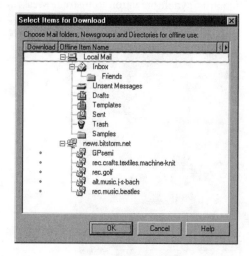

4. Press and hold the Ctrl key, and then select any *other* mail folders or newsgroups you want to include. Then click OK (Figure 20.17).

FIGURE 20.17

Step 4: Click OK.

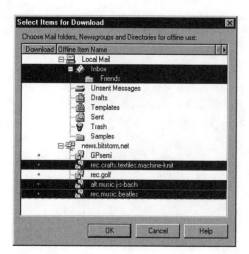

20

▼

▼   5. Next, choose options. Check the Send Unsent Messages check box to send any
         messages waiting in the Unsent Messages folder whenever you synchronize.
         Check Work offline after synchronization to instruct Messenger to disconnect
         automatically as soon as synchronization is complete (Figure 20.18).

FIGURE 20.18

*Step 5: Choose
options.*

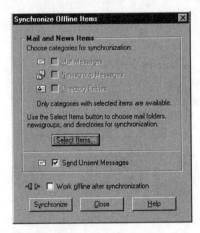

      6. Click the Synchronize button (Figure 20.19).

FIGURE 20.19

*Step 6: Click the
Synchronize button.*

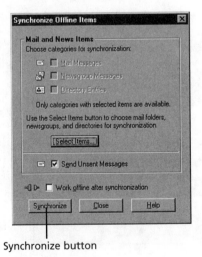

Synchronize button

         The next time you want to synchronize, you only need to do step 1 and step 6 unless you
▲   want to change your settings.

Summary

Working offline is a relatively new idea, and a surprising number of Internet users do not use—or even really know about—the offline features in their Internet programs. More importantly, the availability of faster, cheaper connections, two-phone-line homes, and content that can't be used offline (such as live stock tickers or streaming audio and video) is inclining lots of folks to spend *more* time online, not less. But everybody's needs are different, and when you know how to work offline, the Internet does not control your schedule—*you* do.

Q&A

Q I try to use offline techniques, but I'm still tying up my phone line. Is there anything else I can try, short of putting in a second phone line?

A In a rapidly growing number of areas, homeowners can get *Integrated Services Digital Network (ISDN)* service from their local phone companies. ISDN provides a single digital phone line to your home that can carry multiple simultaneous connections. So you can talk on the phone while you surf the Net and receive a fax, all through one line.

ISDN costs more than regular phone service. You'll also pay more to your Internet provider for ISDN service, and you'll have to buy a new ISDN modem. Is all that cheaper or more expensive than adding a second line? Dunno—ask your local phone company. And keep in mind that ISDN offers one benefit that a second line can't: dramatically faster Internet connection speeds at either 64KB or 128KB (depending upon what you pay to your phone company and ISP).

Less common now than ISDN is a newer technology called ADSL (Asymmetric Digital Subscriber Line), which offers many of the same capabilities as ISDN (including high-speed Internet and the ability to use the phone and the Net at the same time), but may work over existing copper phone lines that cannot support ISDN. ADSL (for which you do have to buy a new modem, as you would for ISDN) is just coming online now in a very few locations, so it's hard to tell where ADSL is headed, or whether it will become available in your area (ask your local phone company).

As if you don't already have enough options, note that in a growing number of cities, Internet service is offered through cable TV lines by the cable providers. If you use cable Internet, you'll never tie up your phone line while online.

20

Q **I don't mind tying up my phone line, except that people can't leave me messages on my answering machine while I'm online. What can I do?**

A Chuck the answering machine and get voice mail from your phone company or another reliable provider. Make sure the company you choose understands that when your line is busy, you want callers to be directed straight to voice mail instead of hearing a busy signal. If you use call waiting, you may have to have your voice mail configured so that it rings once or twice first (so you'll know you have a call if you're talking on the phone) and then jumps to voice mail (in case you're online). Get into the habit of checking for voice messages as soon as you go offline.

Note that many voice mail systems indicate that you have messages by making the dial tone on your phone line stutter a little. In some cases, that stuttering causes modems to think there's no dial tone, so they refuse to connect. If you do get voice mail, you may find that if you have messages waiting, you can't go online until you've listened to the messages so the dial tone can revert to normal.

PART VI

Getting the Most Out of the Internet

Hour

HOUR **21**

Enjoying Safe Family Fun

Is cyberspace a family place? If you have kids, you may be wondering. One day the media touts the Net as the greatest thing since Gutenberg, and the next it's the harbinger of the Apocalypse, an instrument of pornographers, pedophiles, and disgruntled loners.

Actually, it's neither. It's a tool, and like any tool, it can be put to good uses and bad. A hammer can build shelter or bash a finger. I think an adult has a right to use the Internet any way he or she wants to—within the law and without bothering anybody. But if you have kids who will use the Net (and they should!), you need to know how to insulate them from the Net's racier regions.

More importantly, there have been cases of pedophiles and other such creeps starting online relationships with kids (and gullible grownups!) that eventually lead to face-to-face meetings, and then to tragedy. In this hour, you learn commonsense rules for creep-proofing your kids.

At the end of the hour, you'll be able to answer the following questions:

- How can I get my family's surfing off to a fun, safe start?
- What steps can I take and teach to my kids to keep them safe online?
- How can I use a utility or Internet Explorer's built-in censor to block out the smutty stuff?

Choosing a Family Starting Point

A good first step for family Web surfing is to choose a good starting point, a "family home page" of sorts. A good general-purpose family page provides a jumping-off point from which all of the links are family-friendly. Kids starting out should be taught to begin at that page, use only the links on that page, and use the Back button to return to that page after visiting any of its links. These habits corral a kid's surfing to a limited, appropriate range of sites.

You'll probably want to browse and search for a family page that best fits your family (some good choices appear in Appendix A, "Fun Web Sites to Visit"), but here are a few suggestions:

- Yahooligans! at www.yahooligans.com. A kid's offshoot of the Yahoo! search tool with links and a search engine that both lead only to good kid stuff (see Figure 21.1).
- 4Kids Treehouse at www.4kids.com. A colorful site with great links and activities for kids, plus resources for parents.
- Family.com at www.family.com. An online family magazine.
- Kids Avenue at kidsavenue.home.mindspring.com. A fun collection of kids' links and activities.
- The American Library Association's Cool Sites for Kids page at www.ala.org/alsc/children.links.html.

Once you've picked a page, you may choose to make it your regular home page (see Hour 6, "Revisiting Places You Like"), or you may simply open that page at the beginning of any online session with your kids.

Once you've learned how to create Web pages (Hour 23, "Creating Web Pages and Multimedia Messages"), you can create your own family home page and fill it with links you'd like your kids to have easy access to.

FIGURE 21.1

Yahooligans! makes a good starting point for family Web surfing.

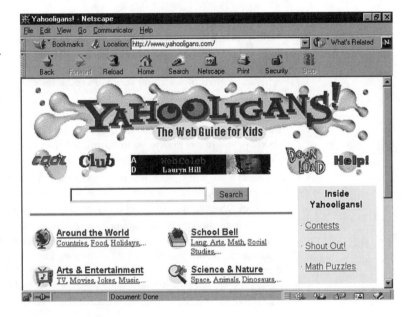

Important Family Safety Steps

Everybody's different, and so is every family. It's not my place to say what's best for you or your kids, but if you want some guidance about keeping your kids safe online, permit me to offer a few suggestions here. Then follow your own judgment.

Supervise!

This one's so obvious, and yet so difficult. As a parent, I know that it simply isn't practical to supervise our kids every second of the day. And if you're a tired parent of a preteen, the idea of the kid going off to his room for an hour to surf the Net is appealing.

You must make your own choice about when to cut the cord, based not on what's convenient but on your kid. Some kids are mature enough to surf responsibly at seven, but others can't be trusted at seventeen. Only you know your kids well enough to decide.

If you're not sure whether your kid is ready to go solo but you don't have time to supervise, keep him offline until either he's ready or you have the time. The Internet has lots to offer a kid, but your kid can live without it until the time is right for both of you.

21

I know some experts say it's not good to spy on your kids. But if your kid surfs unsupervised and you want to know what he's been up to, open the browser's history file (see Hour 6) to see exactly where he's been. It's the cyber-equivalent of searching your kid's room for drugs or weapons.

If your kid is visiting the Web sites of hate groups or providers of unsavory content, he may be picking up dangerous reinforcement of feelings or ideas that endanger both your kid and others around him. At the very least, your child's online habits may serve to tip you off that your kid is in trouble, in the same way that radical changes in appearance or mood might.

If you, as a diligent parent, notice signals that your kid may be at risk, it's important for you to find a way to supervise or control that kid's online activities, OR keep tabs on what he's been doing online, OR pull the plug.

Beyond that, though, it may be important to recognize that if you kid is in trouble online, that's probably a symptom of a larger problem that has nothing to do with the Internet. In such cases, controlling what your kid does online is only Step 1. After that, you need to identify and address the REAL problem, and maybe find some help for your child.

Don't Defeat Passwords

Your Internet connection, email account, and a few other activities require you to enter a username and password to prevent unauthorized access. Some software, particularly Internet connection software, enables you to enter the password in a dialog once so that you never have to type it again. That's a convenient feature, but it enables anyone who can flip a switch to get online using your computer.

My advice is that you leave your computer configured so that a password is required for both connecting to the Internet and retrieving email. Never tell your kids the passwords, and never log on or retrieve email in their sight.

This will ensure that you always know when your kids are online, and that they cannot receive email from anyone without your knowledge.

Resist Chat

It's a shame, because there's plenty of good clean fun to be had in chat rooms. It must be said: Chat rooms are the most dangerous places on the Internet. This is not because of all the sex-related chat rooms, although it's related to those.

On the Web, the worst thing that can happen to a kid is that he or she will be exposed to *ideas*—words and pictures—that you don't approve of. In chat, your kids can easily meet up with *people* who may hurt them. People are much more dangerous than ideas.

It works like this: A pedophile or some other dangerous character—often posing as a kid—frequents chat rooms where kids hang out and establishes friendships, especially with lonely kids who are easy prey. As the friendship grows, the creep manipulates the kid into dropping the anonymous chat nicknames and exchanging email addresses for private correspondence. Eventually, a private, face-to-face meeting is arranged.

There already have been numerous cases of kids abused this way. And the initial contact is almost always made in a chat room.

> Most chat clients (including Microsoft Chat) include a dialog on which you can not only create your chat nickname, but also enter personal information such as your name or email address. (I pointed this out in Hour 18, "Chatting Live!", but it bears repeating.)
>
> Because this information is accessible to others online with whom you chat, I strongly recommend entering nothing on such dialogs except your nickname.
>
> It's also a good idea to change your nickname from time to time, to keep chat friendships from getting too close.

Obviously, I recommend never allowing a child to use chat unsupervised, even if that child is trusted to surf the Web unsupervised. Even supervised chatting is risky—by teaching a child how to chat, you increase the chances that the child may sneak into a chat session unsupervised.

In fact, if you don't use chat yourself, I'd recommend simply not installing a chat client on your computer so you needn't worry.

Online Rules for Kids

I know, I know, my kids hate rules too. But these rules are pretty easy, and it's essential that you teach them to your kids even if you can't always be sure they will be followed. In particular, if you have older kids who you permit to use the Net unsupervised, it's important that they know the rules for safe surfing. (Some folks suggest writing these rules up, having the kids sign them as a contract, and then posting the contract on the wall behind the computer.)

Tell your kids the following:

21

- Never reveal to anyone online your real name, email address, phone number, mailing address, school name, or username/password without a parent's involvement and consent. Any other personal information, such as birthday or Social Security number, is also best kept secret. And never, ever, ever send anyone a picture of yourself.

- Never reveal anything about your parents, siblings, teachers, or friends. Any such information can help a creep find you, and it exposes family and friends to risks, too.

- Never arrange to meet in person any online friend unless a parent consents before the meeting is arranged, the parent will be present at that meeting, and that meeting will take place in a public setting, such as a restaurant or mall.

- Anytime you come across anything online that makes you uneasy, go elsewhere or get offline. There's too much good stuff online to waste time looking at the bad.

- Never download or upload a file, or install any software on the computer, without a parent's consent.

Resources for Parents

Want to know more about protecting your kids online, teaching them to use the Net smartly, finding great family sites, or just plain old parenting advice? You'll find all of this and more online:

- Parent Soup at www.parentsoup.com (see Figure 21.2).

- The Parents Place at www.parentsplace.com.

- Parent Time at www.pathfinder.com/ParentTime/homepage/homepage.all.html.

- Kids Health at www.kidshealth.org.

- *All About Kids* magazine at www.aak.com.

FIGURE 21.2

Parent Soup, one of the best online resources for moms and dads.

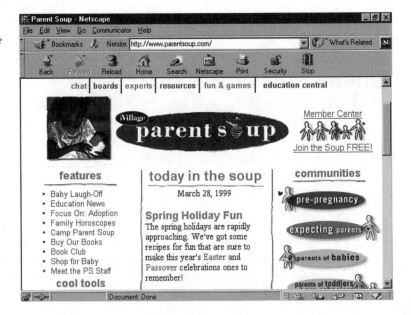

Censoring Web Content

You've probably heard that there are programs that can control what your kids see online. So why didn't I just mention them in the first place and save you all this "online rules" crud?

Well, it's debatable how effective these programs are. First, most are really focused on the Web and aren't much protection elsewhere, such as in chat or email. And most censoring programs—erring properly on the cautious side, I suppose—inevitably censor out totally benign stuff that you or your kids may find valuable. (You'll see an example of this later, with Content Advisor.)

Also, these programs may filter out sexual content, depictions of violence, and profanity, but what about ugly ideas? For example, these programs generally do not block out racist, sexist, or nationalist hatemongering as long as those views are expressed without the use of profanity or epithets.

So even though these self-censoring tools are available, they're no replacement for adult supervision and safe-surfing practices. And if you really do supervise your kids, you probably don't *need* a censoring program. Still, you may find one or more of these programs useful, and they are getting better.

Getting a Safe-Surfing Program

Microsoft Internet Explorer has its own censoring program, which you'll learn about next. If you don't use Internet Explorer or don't like its Content Advisor, you'll want to check out the Web pages of other popular self-censoring utilities.

From these pages, you can learn more about each product and, in most cases, download a copy for your system:

- Net Nanny: www.netnanny.com
- SurfWatch: www.surfwatch.com
- Cybersitter: www.solidoak.com/cysitter.htm
- The Internet Filter: turnercom.com/if
- Cyber Patrol: www.cyberpatrol.com

 If you use WebTV as your Internet window, note that it supplies its own censoring system that you can apply to restrict what your kids can see.

21

Using Internet Explorer's Built-In Content Advisor

Internet Explorer, versions 3 through 5, has its own built-in system called Content Advisor for controlling access to Web sites. Content Advisor works very much like the other safe-surfing programs, except it's a little harder to use than some, and it possesses many of the same strengths and drawbacks.

Understanding Content Advisor

Content Advisor relies on a rating system from the Recreational Software Advisory Council (RSAC), which also rates entertainment software and video games.

The RSAC ratings system assigns a score (0 to 4) to a Web site for each of four criteria: Language, Nudity, Sex, and Violence. The higher the score in each category, the more intense the content that page contains.

For example, if a site has a score of 0 in the Language category, it contains nothing worse than "inoffensive slang." A Language score of 4, however, indicates "explicit or crude language" on the site. Once a Web site has been rated, the rating is built into the site so that Content Advisor can read the site's score before displaying anything.

Using the Content tab, you choose your own limit in each RSAC category. For example, suppose you are okay with violence up to level 3 but want to screen out all sexual content above a 2. After you set your limits and enable Content Advisor, Internet Explorer refuses to show you any page whose RSAC rating exceeds your limits in any category (see Figure 21.3).

FIGURE 21.3

Once you've enabled it, Content Advisor blocks Internet Explorer from displaying Web pages whose RSAC ratings exceed your limits.

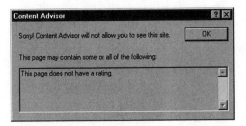

There's one problem: Only a tiny portion of sites online have been rated. Enabling Content Advisor therefore blocks not only rated pages you might find offensive, but also *all* pages—offensive or not—that have not been rated, which includes most of the Web. For example, Content Advisor displayed the warning shown in Figure 21.3 when I was merely trying to access the Yahoo! search engine, which—like all search engines—is not rated.

As you may guess, blocking unrated pages severely cramps your surfing and has little to do with protecting you from offensive content. As you'll see in the upcoming To Do, you can choose an optional setting to allow unrated pages, but doing so defeats the purpose of Content Advisor because those pages will be permitted regardless of their content. You can also create a special list of pages that are always accessible (or never accessible) regardless of the Content Advisor's settings, but obviously that list would be pretty short relative to the wealth of sites available online.

> Content Advisor works for both Web browsing and Microsoft's Chat program (see Hour 18), blocking entrance to unsavory or unrated chat rooms.
>
> To use Content Advisor for Chat, replace step 1 of the following To Do by opening Chat and choosing View, Options, and then choosing the Settings tab. Proceed with the remaining steps of the To Do.
>
> However, note that although Content Advisor may keep kids out of X-rated chats, it does nothing to protect them from the pervs who wander into G-rated chats. My advice, no matter what censorship tools you may deploy: Kids don't belong in chat. Period.

To Do: Enable and Configure Content Advisor

1. In Internet Explorer, open the Internet Options dialog box (choose Tools, Internet Options) and then choose the Content tab (Figure 21.4).

FIGURE 21.4

Step 1: Open Internet Options and then choose the Content tab.

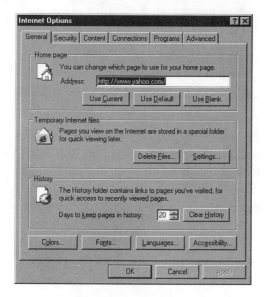

21

▼   2. Click the Enable button (Figure 21.5).

FIGURE 21.5

*Step 2: Click the
Enable button under
Content Advisor.*

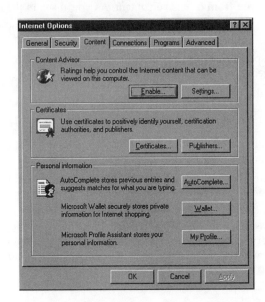

3. The Supervisor password prevents others from disabling Content Advisor or
   changing the settings. Type a password (it becomes the official Supervisor password from now on, so choose carefully). Then press Enter (Figure 21.6).

FIGURE 21.6

*Step 3: Choose a
supervisor password.*

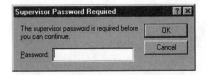

4. Click the Settings button and type the Supervisor password, if prompted for it
   (Figure 21.7).
5. The Rating scale appears, showing the current setting for Language.

   Point to the slider control, click and hold, and drag the slider along the scale
   (Figure 21.8). As the slider reaches each marker on the scale, a description appears
   below the scale with the type of language that setting permits. The farther to the
   right you pull the slider, the more lenient the setting. (Think of 0 as a G rating, 1 as
▼   PG, 2 as PG-13, 3 as R, and 4 as X.)

▼ **FIGURE 21.7**

Step 4: *Click the Settings button.*

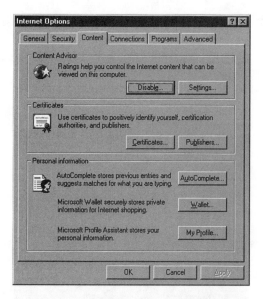

FIGURE 21.8

Step 5: *Adjust the slider.*

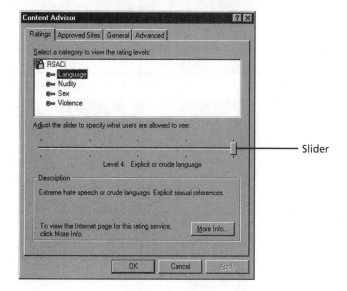

Slider

▼

21

▼   6. Release the slider at your preferred setting for Language (Figure 21.9).

FIGURE 21.9

Step 6: Leave the slider where you want the level to be set.

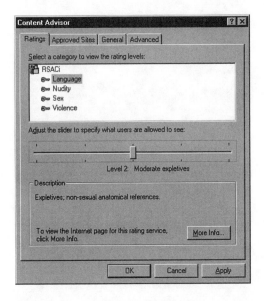

7. Click on Nudity and choose your rating for that category. Do Sex and Violence, too (Figure 21.10).

FIGURE 21.10

Step 7: Do the same for Nudity, Sex, and Violence.

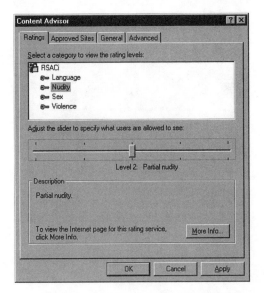

▼

▼   8. When you have finished choosing ratings, click the General tab and check either
         (or neither, or both) of the following options (Figure 21.11):

         Users Can See Sites That Have No Rating. Check this check box to allow the dis-
         play of unrated pages. Content Advisor will continue to block rated pages that
         exceed your settings, but will permit unrated pages regardless of their content.

         Supervisor Can Type a Password to Allow Users to View Restricted Content. When
         this check box is checked, a dialog box pops up prompting for the Supervisor pass-
         word whenever someone tries to open a page that Content Advisor would block. If
         the password is typed, the page appears. With this useful option, your kids can
         appeal to you for a temporary censorship waiver for a particular Web site.

Figure 21.11

*Step 8: Click the
General tab and then
select User options.*

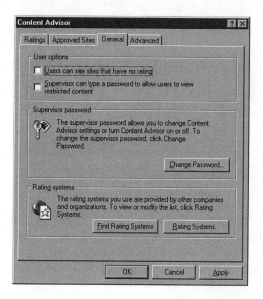

     9. Click the Approved Sites tab. Type the address of any Web site you want to be han-
         dled in a special way, and then click Always (to make this site always accessible,
         regardless of any other Content Advisor settings) or Never (to make this site inac-
         cessible). Continue typing addresses and clicking Always or Never until the list
▼   shows all the sites for which you want special handling (Figure 21.12).

21

▼ 10. Click OK on any tab, and then click OK on the Internet Options dialog. Your settings are now in effect, and they will stay in effect until you change them or click the Disable button on the Content tab. (The Supervisor password is required for disabling Content Advisor or changing the settings.)

FIGURE 21.12

Step 9: At the Approved Sites tab, enter lists of approved and disapproved Web sites.

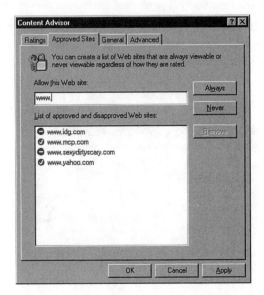

▲

Summary

As you can see, there's no sure-fire way to protect unsupervised kids online. But there's no reason to worry, either. A few smart choices, along with your supervision and guidance, will enable your family to enjoy the Internet's benefits while steering clear of its troubles.

I know I mentioned a lot of scary stuff here, but I do want you to relax and enjoy the Net. Look at it this way: People get hit by cars every day. Now, does that mean you should never leave the house, or lay awake worrying? No. It just means that you should look both ways and hold your kid's hand when crossing.

Q&A

Q **I thought I heard they passed a law against online porn. If they did, why is it still there?**

A The highly controversial Communications Decency Act (CDA) sought to impose penalties against anyone who made available online anything that was "harmful" to minors.

As everyone expected, the U.S. Supreme Court ruled the CDA unconstitutional in June of 1997, declaring that protecting freedom of speech includes protecting unpopular forms of expression.

So for the time being, the Internet is a protected free-speech zone, which is probably best. But new censorship initiatives continue to erupt, as do campaigns to counter them. To learn more about the controversy, check out the Electronic Frontier Foundation (a free speech online advocacy group) at www.eff.org.

21

HOUR 22

Buying and Selling on the Net

Only a few years ago, there was a huge hullabaloo about doing business online and the exploding interest in what we now call *e-commerce* (electronic commerce). But it was all talk—despite noises to the contrary, little real business was happening on the Web. Most business Web pages were mere e-advertising, not points of sale.

But today, you can buy or sell just about anything online. Companies are beginning to approach the Web not just as an intriguing place to experiment, but as a market they mustn't miss.

In this hour, you'll get a taste of e-commerce from both sides of the e-counter. First, we'll expand upon what you picked up in Hour 8, "Protecting Your Privacy (and Other Security Stuff)," by learning how to shop and invest online safely. Next, you'll learn the ways you can do business online, and learn how to get started.

At the end of the hour, you'll be able to answer the following questions:

- How do I find and purchase products online?
- Can I buy stocks and other financial stuff on the Web?
- What are my options for doing business on the Web, and how do I get started?
- How do I buy or sell stuff through an online auction?

Shopping 'til You Drop

Whattaya wanna buy? Whatever it is, you can probably buy it from a Web page that sells products, also known as a *virtual storefront* (see Figure 22.1).

NEW TERM   **Virtual storefront.** This is just a fancy, highfalutin' buzzword for a Web page from which you can buy stuff. In coming years, you'll see the word "virtual" tacked onto all sorts of online activities to make them sound cooler: virtual jobs, virtual travel, virtual dentistry…

FIGURE 22.1

Virtual storefronts are the hip way to buy online, 24 hours a day, with no snotty clerks standing over you to make sure you're not shoplifting.

Using only the Web-surfing skills you already possess, you can enjoy the benefits of online shopping:

- **24-hour, 365-day shopping.** Except for rare moments when the server is down for maintenance and repair, online stores are always open.

- **Access to product photos and specifications.** While you're browsing an online catalog, you often can click links to display product photos, lists of options, and even detailed measurements or other specifications. Such stuff can help you make an informed buying decision.

- **Search tools.** Pages with extensive product listings often include a search tool for finding any product available from the merchant.

- **Web specials.** Some merchants offer discounts or other deals that are available only to those ordering online and not to phone, mail order, or in-person customers.

- **Custom ordering.** Some stores feature forms that let you specify exactly what you want (see Figure 22.2). For example, PC sellers that are online, such as Dell or Gateway, let you choose your PC's specifications—processor, hard disk size, CD-ROM speed, and so on—from lists in a form. When you finish, the price for your system appears, along with a link for placing the order. At an online clothing shop, you can specify exact measurements, color, monogramming, and other custom specifications.

- **Mailing lists.** Many online merchants offer a form for subscribing to a mailing list with updates about new products and specials.

You know this already, but it bears repeating: Making an online purchase usually requires typing your credit card number and other sensitive information in a form. That's something you should never do on a site that's not secure (see Hour 8).

Explore virtual storefronts to your heart's content, comparing prices and other terms to make the best buy. But when you arrive at the actual page where you fill in your order form or open an account with the merchant, confirm that the page is secure. In most browsers, a secure site is indicated by either a locked golden padlock or a solid (unbroken) gold key near the bottom of the window. If you see a broken key, an unlocked padlock, or no icon at all, buy elsewhere.

FIGURE 22.2

Forms on virtual store-fronts can help you configure a custom order or get a price quote on one.

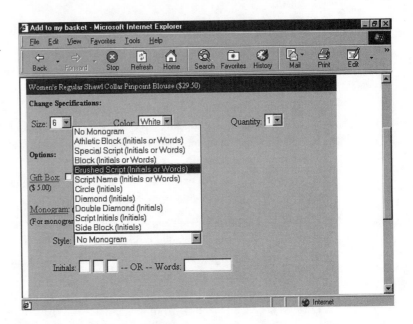

Caveat emptor—buyer beware—online as anywhere else. As an online consumer, it behooves you to be an informed one. You can find reviews of products and merchants all over the Web. One good way to find reviews is to use the product name along with the word "review" as a search term.

You may also want to check out the Web pages of consumer advocates who alert us to schemes, scams, and duds:

Consumer's Union (publishers of *Consumer Reports* magazine): www.ConsumerReports.org

Consumer World: www.consumerworld.org

Using Accounts and Shopping Baskets

You already know how to fill out a form, and usually that's all there is to shopping. But many merchants equip their storefronts with either or both of the following to make shopping there more convenient:

- **Accounts.** When you set up an account with an online merchant, you give that merchant a record of your name and shipping address, and often your credit card information too. After entering this information once, you can shop and buy there anytime without having to enter it again. All you have to do is enter an account username and password, and the site knows who you are, how you pay, and where to ship your stuff.

- **Shopping baskets** (aka **shopping carts**). A shopping basket lets you conveniently choose multiple products and then place the order for all of it, instead of having to order each item as you select it. Shopping baskets also provide you with a chance to look over your list of selections and the total price so you can change or delete items before committing to the order.

> Often, accounts and shopping baskets require the use of *cookies* on your computer (see Hour 8). If you have configured your browser to reject cookies and you try to set up an account or make a purchase, you may get a message from the site informing you that you must accept cookies in order to shop there.

In the following To Do, you can get a feel for accounts, shopping baskets, and virtual storefronts by finding and ordering music CDs from CD Universe, a popular source for CDs, tapes, and videos. Note that you don't actually have to make a purchase; I'll show you how to cancel before committing.

To Do: Find Some CDs and Put Them in a Basket

1. Go to CD Universe at `www.cduniverse.com` (Figure 22.3).
2. In the Quick Search form at the top of the page, type the name of a recording artist in the box to the right of the Artist box, and then click the Go button (Figure 22.4).

FIGURE 22.3

Step 1: Go to CD Universe.

FIGURE 22.4

Step 2: Enter the name of a recording artist and click Go.

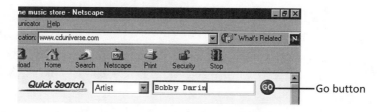

▼ 3. After a few moments, a list appears with titles available from that artist (Figure 22.5). If CD Universe isn't sure which artist you want, a list of artists matching your search term appears first. Choose one to display the list of titles.

FIGURE 22.5

Step 3: Review the list of albums.

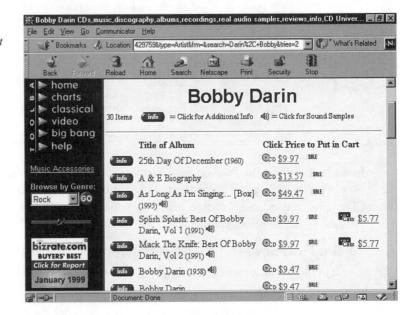

4. Choose a CD or tape by clicking its price (Figure 22.6).

FIGURE 22.6

Step 4: Choose a CD or tape by clicking on its price.

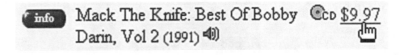

5. Review the info on the Shopping Cart screen, and then click Continue Shopping (Figure 22.7).

6. Choose another title by clicking its price. You now have two CDs in your cart (Figure 22.8). Click Secure Mode Purchase to start the purchasing process.

FIGURE 22.7

Step 5: Review your selection and then click Continue Shopping.

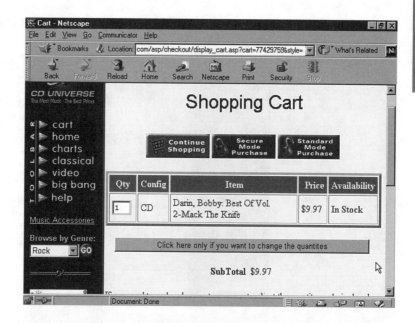

FIGURE 22.8

Step 6: Choose another CD and click Secure Mode Purchase.

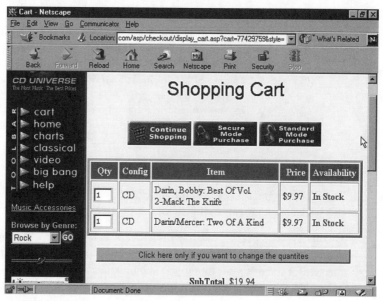

7. To quit without purchasing anything, just leave the site now. To order your selections, click New Account, complete the form that appears, and follow any prompts (Figure 22.9).

▼
FIGURE 22.9

Step 7: Either cancel your order now or fill out the New Account form to order your selections.

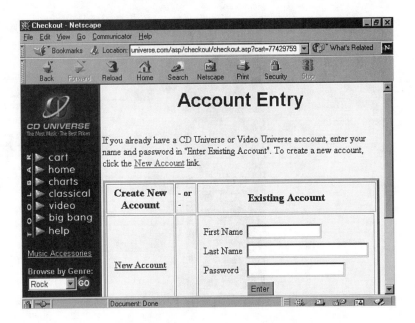

▲

Immediately after you place an order from an online store, some sort of confirmation of your order should appear in your Web browser. Many stores also email you a confirmation of your order.

Make a note of any information that appears in the confirmation—especially anything called an *order number*—and save any email message you receive. You'll need this information to query the merchant if your merchandise doesn't arrive within the time promised, or if it isn't what you ordered.

Buying Stocks and Such

The Web is a great place to sell intangible goods, such as stocks or securities. After all, if the product is intangible, why shouldn't the transaction be?

Obviously, such purchases carry the greatest risk of all online shopping activities. They generally involve moving around large amounts of money and putting it at risk in investments. But if that's your thing, you should know that trading online can be substantially cheaper than using a traditional broker, and in many cases your transactions are executed much more quickly—usually within minutes.

The steps for online investing are roughly the same as those for buying anything else online. Typically, you set up an account with an online brokerage, after which you may buy and sell at will.

However, note that opening an account with an online broker typically requires disclosing detailed information about yourself. You'll have to disclose your bank account numbers, Social Security number, and other private, sensitive information you don't have to reveal when making other kinds of purchases online.

Investment Starting Points

To learn more about investing online, or to take the plunge and buy those 1,000 shares of PepsiCo, consult the following sites.

For Financial Information and Advice

To learn more about online investing, read company profiles, and explore other money matters, check out the following sites:

- Stockpoint: www.stockpoint.com
- CNN's Financial News Network: cnnfn.com
- Wall Street Journal: www.wsj.com
- Dow Jones Business Information Services: bis.dowjones.com
- MoneyAdvisor: www.moneyadvisor.com
- *Success* Magazine: www.successmagazine.com
- Yahoo! Finance: quote.yahoo.com
- Finance Online: www.finance-online.com
- NASDAQ: www.nasdaq.com

For Making Investments

If you're ready to go ahead and put your money on the line (online!), visit these online brokers:

- Mr. Stock: www.mrstock.com
- American Express Financial Services Direct: www.americanexpress.com/direct
- E*Trade: www.etrade.com
- Charles Schwab: www.eschwab.com
- Wall Street Electronica: www.wallstreete.com

Selling on the Net

If you're thinking about taking your own business into cyberspace, or if you've been put in charge of exploring that option for your employer, you already know that your research must consist of more than half a chapter in this book. But this is a good place for you to start considering what your company's Web presence should be like.

NEW TERM **Web presence.** Also referred to as *online presence*, this term describes a company's online identity and means of accessibility. A company with a Web page and an email address has a Web presence.

Other than learning about your options for establishing a Web presence, you must also consider the laws and other issues related to expanding the scope of your business—online or off.

Your business Web page will make you an interstate (even international) business, one that must follow regulations pertaining to collection of sales tax, currency conversions, truth in advertising, and other laws of interstate and international commerce. Today, most of these laws are the same as those you'd follow if you did interstate/international business by mail order or telephone, although in coming years a distinct set of rules governing online commerce will evolve.

> Why establish a Web presence? Well, you probably already know the answer, but I'll offer the simplest, most compelling one: When a customer does a Web search of companies carrying a particular product or service, do you want the hit list to include your competitors but not you?

To learn more about doing business online, check out the following sites:

- The *Web Commerce Today* newsletter: `www.wilsonweb.com/wct/`
- BizWeb: `www.bizweb.com`
- AT&T's Business page: `www.att.com/business`
- U.S. Small Business Administration: `www.sbaonline.sba.gov`

Choosing a Degree of Presence

An important first step in taking your business online is choosing your initial degree of presence, the extent to which your company does business online. Many companies choose merely to promote themselves online, but don't actually sell there. Others are committed to offering online every product and service they have.

Each level of Web presence requires a different level of commitment and resources from the company in the form of time, money, and personnel.

Take care to choose a degree of online presence that you or your company can keep up with. Many companies overreach in their early forays online, deploying elaborate Web sites that they fail to update regularly and keep working smoothly. To establish a good online reputation, it's generally better to field a modest—but well-maintained—Web presence than to put up a state-of-the-art site and let it crumble.

Virtual Storefront

The virtual storefront is the Holy Grail of Web presence, and for companies offering products that can be shipped easily or services that can be delivered over a wide geographic range, it's a great way to expand.

But a real virtual storefront—including a catalog and ordering system—also requires the greatest commitment from the company. Above and beyond the demands of creating a Web page, which anyone can do (see Hour 23, "Creating Web Pages and Multimedia Messages"), an online ordering system requires the following:

- **Programming.** An ordering system requires scripts to process orders from what customers type into online forms. Writing those scripts demands programming experience and knowledge of a language such as Java, JavaScript, or CGI. Programmers with such skills are in high demand today, so they rarely come cheap (if they're good).

- **Security.** Processing orders demands creating and maintaining a secure Web site, which takes the skills of a dedicated, full-time administrator. To ensure maximum security for transactions, most companies own and operate their own Web servers—which dramatically increases the cost of a Web presence.

- **Customer service.** A script can process orders, but dealing with customer questions and complaints requires experienced customer service personnel who customers can contact via email or phone. Too often, companies expect existing personnel to also service Web customers, forcing those customers to wait days or weeks for responses to queries. That's bad e-business.

- **Professional design.** Sure, you can send some entry-level employee off to a corner with a computer and a Web authoring book, and he or she will manage to produce a Web page. But if you take a look at what your competition is doing, you may notice that companies that are seeking a professional-looking online identity hire highly skilled professional Web designers.

There are services that enable you to set up a storefront without dealing with any of the tricky security or programming that comes with creating your own storefront.

Sites like GeoCities (www.geocities.com) let you set up a store on their site for a fee or a cut of your sales. You supply your online catalog and other pages, but when a visitor to your site makes a purchase, the processing of that sale is handled securely by GeoCities. A growing number of local and national ISPs offer similar services.

Although this approach entails many compromises when compared to having a real storefront, it may serve as a safe and economical way to get started for some smaller online sellers.

Informational/Advertising Page

For companies that are just starting out online, a full ordering system is prohibitive and unnecessary. Even today, most companies use the Web not to sell directly, but to promote themselves and to provide customers (or investors) with company and product information. On such pages, you'll often find a toll-free number for placing orders. This approach is a great first step for a company that has an organization in place for telephone sales or mail order sales, but that is not yet ready to create and maintain an effective online ordering system.

A promotional page has another benefit: By offering Web discounts that a customer can use when calling, the company can easily track the amount of business generated by the Web. This information is critical to evaluating whether and when the company should move up to a full virtual storefront.

Any Web programmer or ISP can add a *hit counter* to a Web page to record the number of visitors. A hit counter is a valuable tool, but it can be misleading. On most sites, a very small proportion of the hits represent potential customers; the rest are just window-shoppers who happened to stroll by.

Selling Online but Off-Web

Finally, it's worth noting that the Web is not the only medium for selling online.

22

A mailing list (see Hour 14, "Joining a Mailing List") can make an excellent sales tool. Many Internet programmers can set up and maintain an automated mailing list for you, which you can promote to customers through a simple Web page or through your print and mail advertising. And because customers have the power to subscribe to and unsubscribe from the list, you know that those on the list at any given time are interested, well-qualified sales leads.

As an alternative to a mailing list, you can broadcast email promotions to thousands of customers. But as I hope you learned from the discussion of spam in Hour 16, "Emailing Through the Web, Stopping Junk Mail, and Other Tips," sending unsolicited commercial email may win you more enemies than buyers. Limit your bulk emailing to customers who have explicitly expressed the desire to receive it. (Using a mailing list can help you ensure this.)

In general, do not attempt to advertise or sell in newsgroups. There's little to prevent you from doing so (although the moderators of some newsgroups do delete commercial messages). But the newsgroup culture harkens back to a time when much of the Internet operated under policies that barred commercial activity. Though the policies are gone, many newsgroup folks flame advertisers who invade their space. When you advertise in a newsgroup, you may antagonize the very customers to whom you want to sell.

Some newsgroups are tolerant of advertisers, though. Carefully watch the groups in which you want to sell. If you see no negative response to ads that others post there, you may be able to post an occasional, brief, non-pushy pitch without eliciting a backlash.

Publicizing Your Storefront

After you've established a Web presence, you have to get the word out to let everybody know that cyberspace is your space, too.

Within a month or so after you put your company online, most of the search tools based on crawlers (see Hour 9, "Getting Started with Searching") will have found your page and added it to their databases. But to ensure that customers find you, you should also visit such sites as Yahoo! and Excite and manually add your page to their databases (see Figure 22.10).

FIGURE 22.10

Through links offered on search sites like Yahoo! and Excite (pictured here), you can fill in forms to add your Web page and description to the sites' databases.

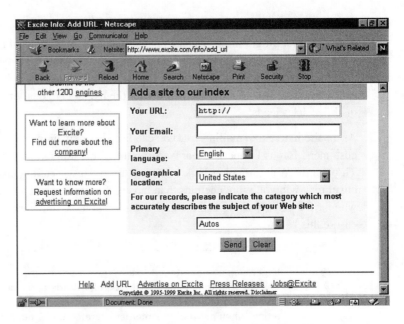

For example, to add your site to Yahoo! (www.yahoo.com), browse to the category in which you want your site to be listed, and then click the Add URL button at the top of the page. Follow the prompts and you'll soon arrive at a form in which you can type your site's URL and descriptive information. Be sure to phrase descriptive information carefully; the better you describe your site, the better the chances that your page will show up on the hit lists of customers looking for your kind of company.

An increasingly important part of having a Web presence is having one's own *domain*, a unique Internet server address that identifies a company (or person) online. Sites such as www.toyota.com or www.kodak.com have domains that identify—and thus promote—their owners.

For example, I can set up a Web page on an ISP's server (see Hour 23) without getting my own domain. But my page's URL would be something like www.isp.com/users/ned.htm. If I buy a domain, I can be found at www.ned-snell.com, which is much better for establishing my online identity.

If you set up and maintain your own Web server, you get your own domain along with it. If you use space on someone else's server but want your own domain, you must apply for the domain and pay a fee (usually $70 to create the domain and $35 a year thereafter to maintain it). The owner of the server will help you apply for the domain and pay the fee, which goes to InterNIC, the organization that controls Internet domains.

Besides adding your site to search tool databases, you can promote it through the following:

- **Print/broadcast advertising.** Make sure your domain name, Web site address, and/or email address appears prominently in all of your ads. A growing number of companies even incorporate their site addresses in store signs and company logos.

- **Company stationery.** Next time you print business cards or letterhead, add your URL. Put the Web site URL on all employee business cards, along with the employee's email address.

- **Email.** Most email programs let you create a *signature*, which is a boilerplate block of text that's added automatically to the bottom of every message you send. If you use a signature, you can include your Web site address in it.

Buying and Selling Through Online Auctions

Lately, auction houses have joined the ranks of the hottest places to pick up bargains or unusual items on the Net. Not only are online auction houses great places to pick up new and used merchandise—and especially hard-to-find collectibles—but the bidding process can be a lot of fun, too. eBay, at www.ebay.com (see Figure 22.11), may be the most popular online auction house now, but there are others, including the following:

- Yahoo! Auctions: auctions.yahoo.com
- Amazon.com Auctions: auctions.amazon.com
- Butterfield & Butterfield: www.butterfields.com
- AuctionNation: www.auctionnation.com
- Cyber Auctions: www.cyber-auctions.com

How Online Auction Houses Work

Although you can usually view the items up for auction without registering, you typically must register with the auction house—a quick process of filling in an online form—to bid on items or to sell an item. Once registered, you can use the search tools or categories on the auction house's page to browse for items to bid on. Note that most auctions go on for several days, and some go on for a week, so it's not necessary to sit in front of your computer for hours to join in the fun.

FIGURE 22.11

eBay, a popular online auction house.

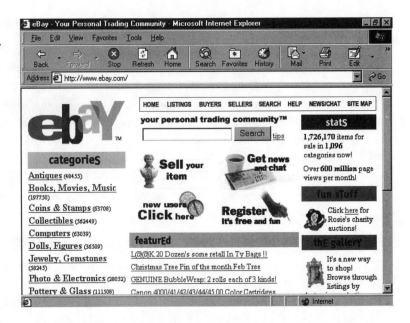

The auction house usually has no role in the actual financial transaction between seller and buyer, so a secure page is not really necessary. Typically, if you win an auction, the auction house emails both you and the seller to notify you about the win and to give you each other's contact info. After that, you and the seller have a set period of time in which to contact each other to arrange payment and shipping. Many sellers who use these auction houses are commercial merchants who can accept payment by credit card via email or telephone. Some individual sellers may require that you pay by money order or personal check.

eBay features a Feedback Forum (see Figure 22.12) where buyers and sellers can post positive and negative comments about their experiences with each other. Before buying, you can always check out the comments others have made about the seller to determine whether that seller is a safe person to do business with.

To minimize the risk on bigger-ticket items, auction houses offer links to *escrow services* that make purchasing a little safer for buyer and seller (for a fee, of course).

The buyer pays the escrow service, not the seller. The seller does not ship anything until he knows that the escrow service has the buyer's money. When the buyer informs the escrow service that the item has arrived, the escrow service pays the seller.

FIGURE 22.12

Some auction houses have feedback forums so you can see what others have to say about a person before you do business with that person.

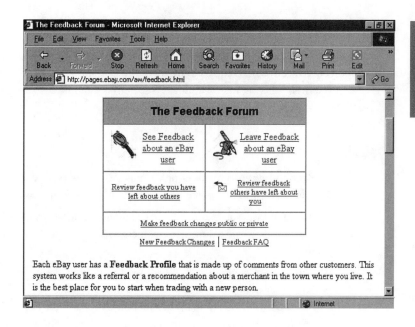

Bidding Tips

If you want to try online auctions, here are a few important tips:

- Always check out the feedback about a seller before bidding to make sure the seller is reliable.

- Before you bid on an item, always search the Web or other sources to see if the same item is for sale elsewhere and for how much. That way you can be sure not to bid more than you would pay for the same item elsewhere.

- Check out any payment terms in the listing. If no terms are listed, use the links provided to email the seller and ask what forms of payment the seller accepts (check, money order, and so on). You may want to think twice (or use an escrow service) before dealing with a seller who accepts only money orders, which is the second riskiest way to pay by mail after cash.

- Don't get carried away. In the heat of the auction, it's easy to get caught in a bidding war and wind up paying way too much for that Elvis candleholder you think you simply *must* have. Decide the most you're willing to pay and stick to it. If you lose, there will be other auctions.

Summary

By now you're ready to begin spending money online, making money online, or both. I hope you've seen that actually buying or selling on the Web is pretty easy, but doing either one *well*—taking into account all of the risks and issues surrounding these activities—takes preparation, care, and practice.

Q&A

Q **You say to buy only from shops I trust. I'm not sure who I can trust in my** *family*. **How am I supposed to know who to trust online?**

A Well, you aren't. You can't trust *any* company until you've had some experience with it. But there are a few steps you can take to decrease your chances of getting stung.

When possible, deal with online companies you've already dealt with offline, such as mail order companies whose print catalogs you've used or retailers whose stores you've visited. If the company was reliable on the phone or at the store, it probably will be okay online. If an online company is new to you, see whether it offers a toll-free number for phone orders. Try placing a phone order first. If that works out well, order online next time. If you can't test the company that way, make your first order small and cheap and place a second order only if the first one goes well.

Finally, always make purchases with credit cards. I know that sounds funny, given my warnings about sending credit card numbers to insecure sites. But when the site is secure, using a credit card is safest. If a merchant lets you down, you can call the credit card company and dispute the charge.

When you're using an online auction, always check out the seller's feedback, if available. And when you're purchasing a big-ticket item you've won at auction, consider using one of the escrow services the auction houses offer.

Hour **23**

Creating Web Pages and Multimedia Messages

Got something to say, or to sell? Want to offer your experiences or expertise to the world? There's no better way to do that today than by creating and publishing your own Web page.

Building a Web page is easier than you might think—if you know how to surf the Web and to use any word processing program, you already possess the prerequisite skills for Web authoring. This hour takes you the rest of the way, showing you several ways to create attractive Web pages. The basic skills you'll learn here will form a foundation upon which you can build later, on your own, to add scripts, multimedia, and other advanced techniques to your skill set. You'll also learn how to create fancy, formatted email and newsgroup messages in this hour.

At the end of the hour, you'll be able to answer the following questions:

- What exactly is a Web page, and what does it take to create one?
- How can I use a wizard or template to produce a simple page very quickly?

- How can I compose and edit Web pages in a Web page editing program?
- How do I publish my pages on a Web server?
- How can I apply my Web authoring skills to create email and newsgroup messages adorned with fonts and pictures?

Understanding Web Authoring

Before you can dive into creating a Web page, you need to pick up a more intimate understanding of how a Web page works than you'll get simply by surfing the Web.

What's in a Web Page?

A Web page is actually a file in a format called HTML, which stands for Hypertext Markup Language. An HTML file contains nothing but text: the actual text you'll see online, and instructions for how that text is to appear (see Figure 23.1).

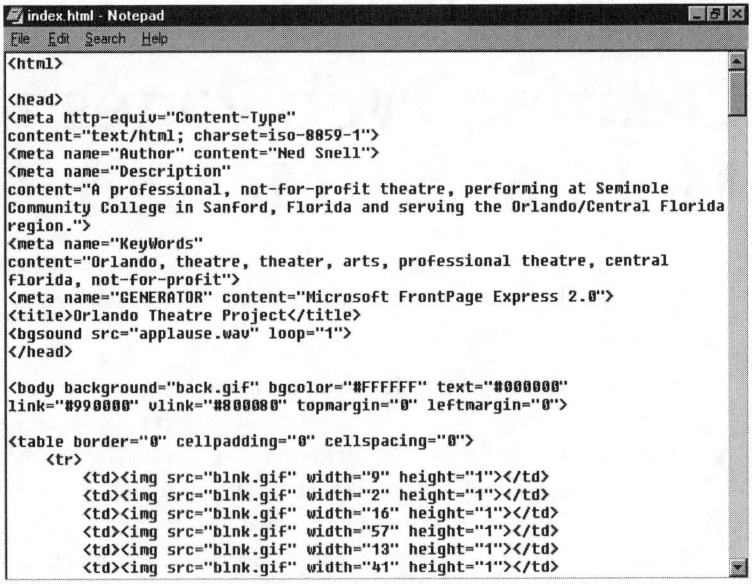


```
<html>

<head>
<meta http-equiv="Content-Type"
content="text/html; charset=iso-8859-1">
<meta name="Author" content="Ned Snell">
<meta name="Description"
content="A professional, not-for-profit theatre, performing at Seminole
Community College in Sanford, Florida and serving the Orlando/Central Florida
region.">
<meta name="KeyWords"
content="Orlando, theatre, theater, arts, professional theatre, central
florida, not-for-profit">
<meta name="GENERATOR" content="Microsoft FrontPage Express 2.0">
<title>Orlando Theatre Project</title>
<bgsound src="applause.wav" loop="1">
</head>

<body background="back.gif" bgcolor="#FFFFFF" text="#000000"
link="#990000" vlink="#800080" topmargin="0" leftmargin="0">

<table border="0" cellpadding="0" cellspacing="0">
    <tr>
        <td><img src="blnk.gif" width="9" height="1"></td>
        <td><img src="blnk.gif" width="2" height="1"></td>
        <td><img src="blnk.gif" width="16" height="1"></td>
        <td><img src="blnk.gif" width="57" height="1"></td>
        <td><img src="blnk.gif" width="13" height="1"></td>
        <td><img src="blnk.gif" width="41" height="1"></td>
```

FIGURE 23.1

The actual text of an HTML file.

The text in an HTML file also includes the URLs of any links on the page, as well as the filenames, locations, and page positions of any pictures or other multimedia files, which are stored in their own separate files.

When an HTML file is viewed through a browser, the browser formats the text onscreen as ordered, locates the picture files, and displays them in their specified positions. The browser also reads and remembers the URLs that the links point to, so it knows where to take a visitor who clicks a link. Figure 23.2 shows the very same file as Figure 23.1, but now interpreted by a Web browser.

FIGURE 23.2

The same file as Figure 23.1, now interpreted by a browser.

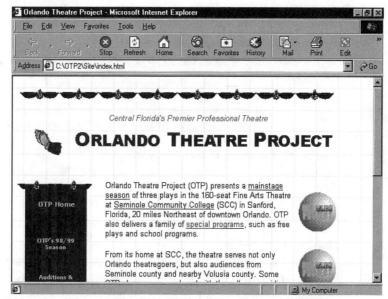

23

In general, the formatting instructions contained in an HTML file do not precisely control how the page will appear. Rather, the file provides a general idea of how the page is to appear, and each browser realizes those instructions slightly differently. That's why the very same Web page often looks different in two different browsers.

For example, the HTML file may specify that a particular line of text is to be displayed as a heading. One browser may follow that instruction by making the text big and bold, while another may follow it by underlining the text. This idea is often difficult to get used to for new authors accustomed to word processors that enable precise formatting control.

There are new, advanced Web authoring techniques that give you greater control, but the formatting applied by those techniques is not visible through all browsers. So it's still generally true that formatting a Web page is not about controlling *exactly* how the page will look, but rather about designating the role each element plays in the page: a heading, a normal paragraph, and so on.

A Web page can be made up of many different parts, but most Web pages contain most or all of the following core elements:

- A *title*, which browsers typically display in the title bar of the window in which the page appears. Note that the actual title does not appear within the layout of the page, although many authors repeat the title in a big heading near the top of the page layout.

- *Headings*, which browsers typically display in large, bold, or otherwise emphasized type. A Web page can have many headings, and headings can be *nested* up to six levels deep. That is, there can be subheadings, sub-subheadings, and so on.

> In HTML, there are six levels of headings, beginning with Heading 1 (the biggest and boldest, usually reserved for creating an on-page title) and going down to Heading 6 (a very small, minor heading, indistinguishable from normal text in many browsers).

- *Normal text*, which makes up the basic, general-purpose text of the page.

- *Horizontal lines* (sometimes called *rules*), which dress up the page and separate it into logical sections.

- *Hyperlinks* (or simply *links*) to many different things—other Web pages, multimedia files (external images, animation, sound, video), document files, email addresses, and files or programs on other types of servers (such as Telnet, FTP, and Gopher). Links may also lead to specific spots within the current page.

- *Lists*, bulleted (like this one) or numbered.

- *Inline images*, pictures that are incorporated into the layout of the page to jazz it up or make it more informative.

- A *background*, an inline image that, unlike a regular image, covers the entire background of the page so that text and other images can be seen on top of it. Instead of an image, you can use a solid background color.

- *Tables*, text and inline images organized in neat rows and columns.

What Tools Can I Use to Write a Page?

If you were skilled in HTML code, you could write a Web page simply by typing the correct code in a text file, using any word processor or text editing program (such as Windows Notepad). Some folks do it that way, but doing so makes it hard to see what you're creating; you have to jump from the editor to a browser every time you want to see how the page will look online.

A better choice is a WYSIWYG Web authoring program (see Figure 23.3). This shows you the page as it will look online, while you're working on it.

FIGURE 23.3

A WYSIWYG Web authoring program such as Netscape Composer, shown here, lets you use familiar word processing techniques to create a Web page.

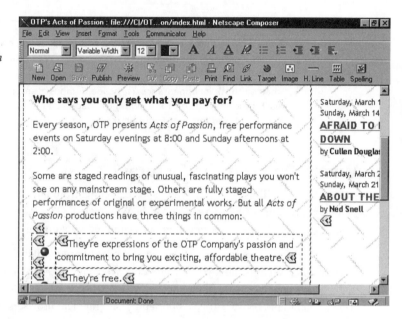

23

WYSIWYG (What You See Is What You Get). This term describes a program that shows you, as you create something, exactly how it will look in its finished form, on paper or onscreen. For Windows and the Mac, most word processors, presentation programs, desktop publishers, and Web authoring programs are WYSIWYG.

If you're careful to select and install the complete suite, you get a WYSIWYG editor with either of the Big Two:

- The full Netscape Communicator suite includes Composer, which you open from within Netscape Navigator by choosing Communicator, Composer.

- The full Microsoft Internet Explorer suite includes FrontPage Express (not to be confused with the more sophisticated program FrontPage; see below), which you open from the same menu where you can open the browser. In Windows 95/98, choose Programs, Internet Explorer, FrontPage Express.

Other commercial (not free) Web authoring packages include Microsoft's FrontPage (included in some editions of the Office program suite) and Adobe's PageMill. These more sophisticated programs are worth looking into if you're ambitious about authoring. But most beginners will find that the free programs included in the browser suites more than meet their needs.

You can learn about and download other Web authoring programs from the Tucows Internet software directory at www.tucows.com.

> Even when you're using a WYSIWYG editor, pages you create may look different when seen through different browsers. WYS is not always WYG.
>
> And it's always a good idea to display the document in a browser now and then to check its appearance. Netscape Composer and FrontPage Express each include a button for viewing the page you're editing in Netscape Navigator and Internet Explorer, respectively.

Where Do I Get the Pictures?

The pictures you'll use on your Web pages can come from anywhere. You can draw them in a paint program such as CorelDRAW or Windows 95/98's Paint accessory, scan them from your own photos, or even use images captured by a digital camera.

What matters isn't the source of the pictures, but rather the image file format in which they're stored. The pictures you include on a Web page, either as inline images or as background images, must be in either the GIF (.GIF) or JPEG (.JPG) file format. (GIF is usually preferable because it is supported by all graphical browsers, although JPEG is also supported by most browsers and often produces better-looking results with photographs.) If the program you use to create images won't save in GIF or JPEG format, many paint programs (and some Web authoring programs) can convert your files to GIF or JPEG.

If you want to use pictures but don't want to create them, you can find libraries of commercial, shareware, and free clip art files in GIF and JPEG format both online and at your local software store.

> See Appendix A, "Fun Web Sites to Visit," for the URLs of great places to pick up clip art, animations, and other cool content for your Web pages.

Making Quick Pages with a Wizard

The quickest way to build a page is by running a *page wizard*. Both Netscape Composer and FrontPage Express have one of these wizards, which leads you through a few quick dialogs where you fill in blanks and choose some options. When you finish, the wizard spits out a finished Web page, ready for publishing.

A wizard doesn't give you as much control as composing the page in a Web authoring program does, but it is faster. And if the results aren't exactly what you want, you can always open your wizard-built page in your Web authoring program and change it.

The following To Do shows how to use Netscape Composer's wizard, which is unusual because you must use it while online. If you'd rather try out FrontPage Express's wizard, which works offline, open FrontPage Express, then choose File, New to open a list of options for starting a new page and then choose Personal Home Page from the list.

23

To Do: Create a Page Fast with Netscape Composer's Wizard

1. Open Netscape Navigator (not Composer) and connect to the Internet (Figure 23.4).
2. In Navigator, choose File, New, Page From Wizard (Figure 23.5).
3. In the active frame on the upper-right side of the screen, scroll down past Netscape's cheery introductory copy to display the START button (Figure 23.6).

To Do

FIGURE 23.4

Step 1: Open Netscape Navigator.

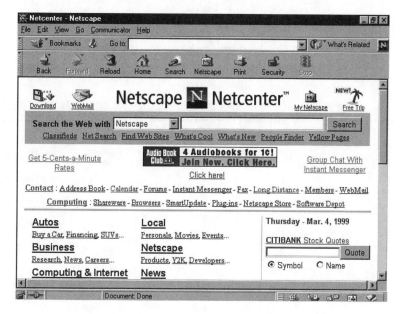

▼

FIGURE 23.5

Step 2: *Choose File, New, Page From Wizard.*

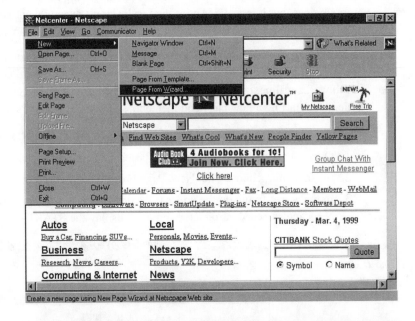

FIGURE 23.6

Step 3: *In the upper-right frame, scroll down to the START button.*

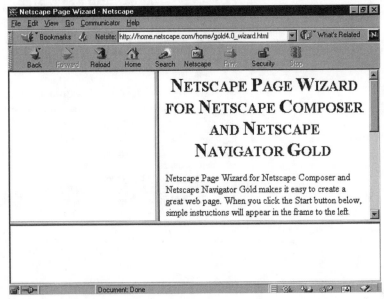

▼   4. Click the START button (Figure 23.7).

FIGURE 23.7

Step 4: Click the
START button.

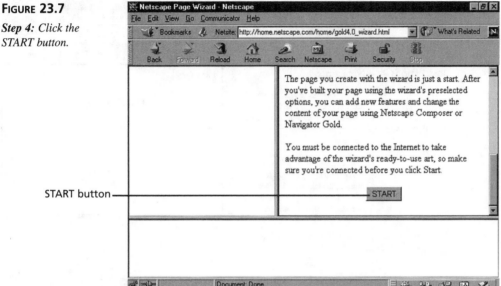

START button

5. Observe that the wizard page is split into three frames (see Figure 23.8):

   The upper-left frame, Instructions, describes each element you will create. Within each description are links that, when clicked, display a form or list of choices in the bottom frame.

   The bottom frame, Choices, is where you will type text in forms (to create page content) or choose aspects of your page's appearance from lists of choices.

   The upper-right frame, Preview, shows a preview of your page as you develop it.

6. Scroll down the Instructions frame until you see the give your page a title link, and click that link (Figure 23.9).

7. Delete the descriptive text that appears in the form in the Choices frame and type a title for your page. Then click the Apply button (Figure 23.10).

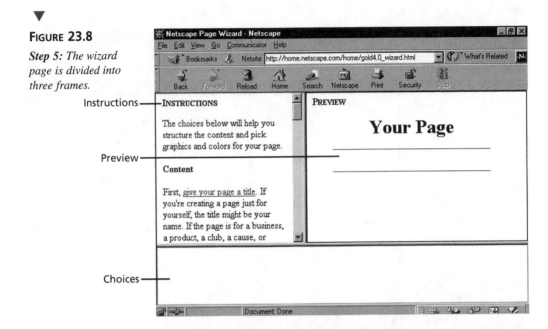

FIGURE 23.8

Step 5: The wizard page is divided into three frames.

Instructions

Preview

Choices

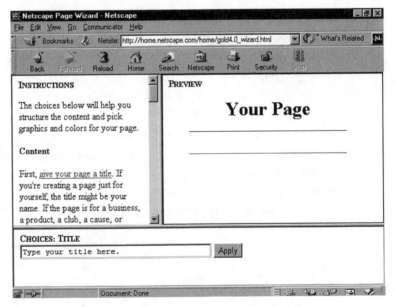

FIGURE 23.9

Step 6: Click the give your page a title link.

FIGURE 23.10

Step 7: Type a title into the Choices box in the bottom frame and then click Apply.

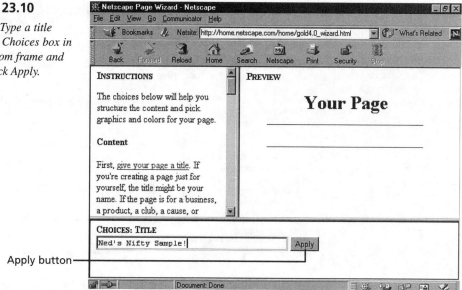

Apply button

8. Scroll down the instructions until you see another link to a page element you can create. Click it and then follow the instructions to complete the form in the Choices frame (Figure 23.11).

9. Continue defining page elements until the Preview frame shows a page to your liking. (Note that you can scroll the Instructions frame up at any time to make changes.)

10. When done, scroll to the bottom of the Instructions frame and click the Build button (Figure 23.12).

11. Here's your new page in Netscape Navigator. From the menu bar, choose File, Edit Page (Figure 23.13).

12. The page now appears in Netscape Composer. Choose File, Save As to save your new page on your computer.

▼

FIGURE 23.11

Step 8: Click on another link in the Instructions frame and then add another element in the box in the Choices frame.

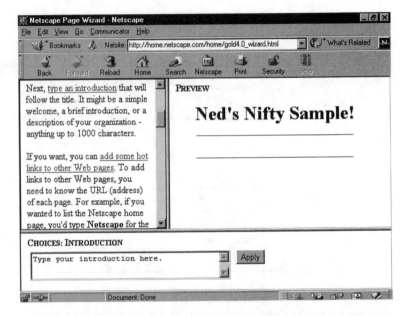

FIGURE 23.12

Step 10: When you're done, click the Build button at the bottom of the Instructions frame.

Build button ——

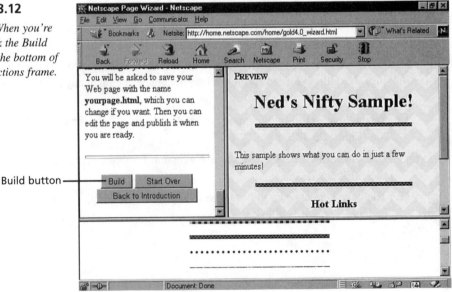

▼

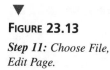

FIGURE 23.13

Step 11: Choose File, Edit Page.

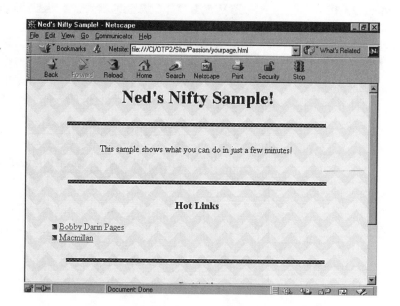

23

Composing a Page in a WYSIWYG Editor

Composing a Web page in a WYSIWYG editor is very much like composing and formatting a document in any word processor. You type your text and then format it by selecting it with your mouse and applying formatting—such as bold, fonts, and so on—from toolbar buttons or menu items. If you look at the toolbars in FrontPage Express (see Figure 23.14) or Composer, you'll probably recognize many of the tools, such as a dropdown list for choosing a font or a big "B" for applying boldface.

Although the Web authoring programs present you with lots of formatting tools, it bears repeating here that precise formatting you apply—such as font selections—may not be supported by all browsers. The formatting that matters most is the application of *styles*, which you choose from a drop-down list on the toolbar in both Composer or FrontPage Express. It's the style that really tells browsers how to handle a block of text.

Besides using a Web authoring program or a wizard, there's one more way to create a page: your word processor. The latest versions of both Microsoft Word and WordPerfect can save files in HTML format.

A word processor is not as a good for authoring as a real authoring program, but it will do in a pinch. More importantly, these programs make it easy to convert existing documents into Web page files. For example, you can open your resume in Word and then save it as an HTML file. Now it's ready for the Web.

FIGURE **23.14**

Using a WYSIWYG Web authoring program is very much like using any Windows or Mac word processor.

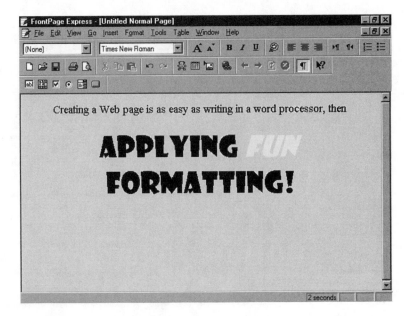

Publishing Your Web Page

After your Web page is finished, you must upload it to a Web server so that others on the Internet can see it. So first you need space on somebody's Web server—enough to hold all the files that make up your page (the HTML file plus picture files). A typical Web page with a picture or two usually requires less than 100KB of space on a server. The larger and more picture-laden your page, the more server space you'll need.

Preparing to Publish

If your page is related to your job, you may be able to get permission to publish it on your company's server. Talk to your company's network administrator or Webmaster. Most colleges and universities also have Web servers and often allow students and faculty to publish on them.

If you don't have permission to publish your Web page on your company's or school's server and don't plan to create your own server (which is prohibitively expensive and technical for beginners), you need to acquire space on somebody else's Web server, usually your ISP's.

After you know whose server will hold your Web page files, you must upload the files from your PC to the server. The exact procedures for doing this differ from one ISP to the next. You must get complete uploading instructions directly from the company whose server you will use. In particular, you need to know the following:

- The server's address, such as http://www.server.com or ftp.server.com.
- The *uploading protocol* used by the server (either HTTP or FTP).
- Any username and password that you need to use to gain access to the server. (If you're using your ISP's server, these may be the same username and password you use to connect to the Internet.)
- The particular directory in which your files will be stored, such as http://www.server.com/ned/.

Using a Publishing Utility

Once your ISP provides you with instructions for uploading your files, you can make uploading easy by supplying those instructions to a Web publishing program like those built into FrontPage Express and Netscape Composer.

> Most servers allow you to upload Web page files through an FTP client program. Although the publishing programs included in some authoring programs may make publishing simpler, they're not always any easier than simply doing a good old-fashioned FTP upload. See Hour 19, "Tools for the Serious User: FTP and Telnet," to learn more about FTP.

To use either of these utilities, first open your Web editor and open the page you wish to publish. Then do the following:

- **In Netscape Composer,** click the Publish button and follow the prompts.
- **In FrontPage Express,** choose File, Save As to open the Save dialog. In Page Location, type the complete URL the page will have on the Web. Click OK and follow the prompts.

> The first time you use one of these publishing utilities, you need to spend a few minutes supplying information about the Web server you'll use. After you've done that, your uploads from then on will be very quick and easy. These utilities remember all your server information, so after you enter the information once, you don't need to fiddle with it again. Just start the publishing procedure as before, and most of the steps happen automatically.

23

Creating Formatted Email and Newsgroup Messages

In Hour 13, "Sending and Receiving Email," you created email messages—wonderful, simple email messages containing nothing but text. What you may not know is that email can contain the same kinds of content and formatting you use in a Web page (see Figure 23.15). You can send messages containing all kinds of fonts, colors, pictures, and links. If it can be put in a Web page, it can go in a message.

FIGURE 23.15

In HTML-supporting messaging programs, you can create and display email and newsgroup messages with all the pizzazz of Web pages.

There's one hitch to sending fancy messages like this: Your recipient may not be able to display them. Like a Web page, a fancy message must be created in HTML format. To read the message, your recipient must use an email program that's capable of displaying HTML-based messages in addition to regular email messages, such as Netscape Messenger or Outlook Express.

> In general, it is not necessary to send an HTML message just to send links. Anytime you type a URL or email address in the body of a message, the recipient's email program will detect it and format it as a link (that is, if the recipient has an up-to-date email program, such as Outlook Express or Netscape Messenger). The recipient can click the link to go where it leads, and you can click the links in messages received from others.

The majority of people using Internet email today cannot receive HTML messages. So unless you happen to know that your intended recipient has an email program that can show HTML messages, it's best to stick with plain text messages.

When you're composing an HTML message in either program, you'll notice that the toolbar and menu bar show most of the tools and options available in the suite's Web authoring program. You compose and format an HTML message in Outlook Express exactly as you do a Web page in FrontPage Express, and you compose and format an HTML message in Netscape Messenger exactly as you do a Web page in Netscape Composer.

Starting a New HTML Message

To create an HTML message, do the following:

- **In Outlook Express,** open a new message window as you usually would. From the message window's menu bar, choose Format, Rich Text (HTML).

- **In Netscape Messenger,** you may need to change the Preferences to send HTML messages. Choose Edit, Preferences, and then choose the Formatting subcategory under the Mail & Newsgroups category. Choose the option near the top called Use the HTML editor to compose messages. When you compose messages, you'll see a toolbar for applying fancy formatting.

> By default, most programs that can send HTML messages automatically send replies in the same format in which the message was received. In other words, if someone sends you an HTML message (which means the sender's email program can display HTML) and you click Reply to respond to it, the message you create is automatically in HTML format.

Using Stationery (Yes, Stationery!)

In Outlook Express, you have a fast and easy way to create really cool-looking HTML messages: Stationery, or predefined HTML message templates into which you can plug your message.

To use stationery, just choose Message, New Message Using from Outlook Express's menu bar. You'll see a selection of different stationery styles you can use (see Figure 23.16).

Figure 23.16

Choose a stationery to start a cool HTML message in Outlook Express.

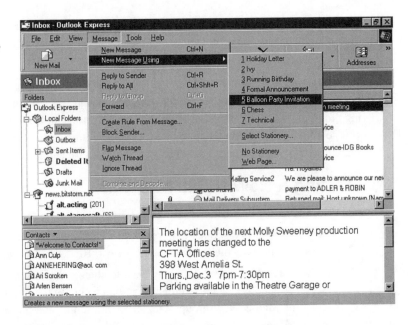

When the stationery appears (see Figure 23.17), you can then compose your message and edit its appearance in any way you want. Have fun!

Figure 23.17

Stationery gives you an attractively designed template into which you can plug your own messages.

Summary

You don't have to create your own Web page—it's not like there's a shortage. But if you really do have something to say, you'll find creating and publishing a page pretty easy, especially if you rely on the tools in an Internet suite.

Q&A

23

Q What about Java? What about video clips, and sound, and forms, and frames? I want to be a Web *auteur*!

A Well, Web authoring is a very big topic. You've learned a huge part of it in just one hour, but there are thousand-page books devoted to the subject, and even 1,000 pages doesn't cover everything about authoring.

Besides practicing and sharpening the skills you've already learned, your next step (other than learning frames, perhaps) should be to learn more about online multimedia, specifically how to do more with pictures and how to add sound, video, and animation to your pages. There are many good books about this. Also, carefully study the design and layout of pages that impress you. Learn from what others are doing.

After multimedia, the next hurdle is writing Java applets and JavaScript or CGI scripts, all of which can be used to enable special interactive capabilities that aren't part of plain HTML. There are many good books about these too, but many folks, upon learning about these topics, suddenly decide that they already know enough about Web authoring. Just about anybody can learn to create Web pages and add multimedia to them. But learning Java, JavaScript, or CGI takes thinking like a programmer, and that's a specialized talent.

HOUR 24

24 Ways the Internet Can Change Your Life

I'm sure there are more than 24 of these, but you and I are almost out of time…

In this final hour, you won't learn any new skills. You already possess all the basic Internet skills you require to take advantage of just about anything online. Instead, you'll discover here some surprising, possibly life-altering ways you can apply those skills—ways you may not have thought of on your own.

For each of the 24, I tell you what you can do, and how to get started. The rest is up to you. Note that the Web sites I direct you to are not necessarily the only place to begin the activity described; you may find other pages that do the same thing. But these are all places I've been, places I find useful and easy to use. Sometimes it's easier to have one good starting place than a dozen confusing options.

At the end of the hour, you'll be able to answer the following questions:

- What are 24 cool things you can do online that not everybody already knows about?
- For each of the 24, where's a good place to begin?

1. Find a New Job or Career

More and more companies and government organizations are finding their new employees online. They post their want ads on the Internet, use Internet-based recruiting agencies, read resumes posted online, and more.

If you know of a particular company you'd like to work for, the best place to start is on that company's Web site; many companies feature a Job Openings page. (To find a company's Web site, go to any search site and use the company's name as a search term.)

If you're not sure where you want to work, check out one of the general-purpose careers pages, such as Excite's Careers page (see Figure 24.1). To get there, go to Excite at www.excite.com, and click the link to Careers.

FIGURE 24.1

Excite's Careers page offers one-stop job shopping.

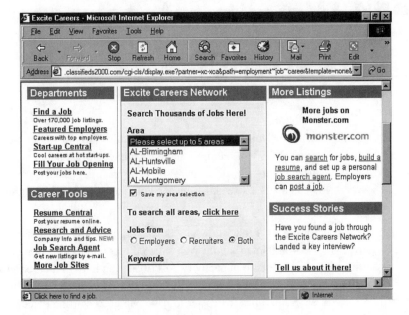

Note that big job sites like Excite Careers or Monster.com not only list job openings, but also can help you with your resume, choosing a career that matches your skills, and much more (see Figure 24.2).

FIGURE 24.2

Career sites offer not only job listings, but also help with resumes and other job-hunting-related services.

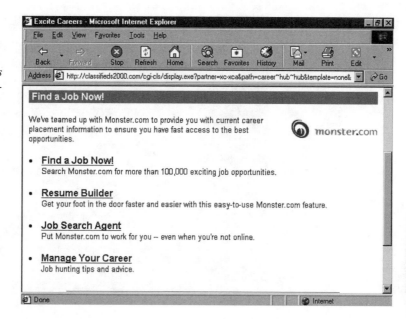

2. Get a Degree or Professional Training

Yes, you can get a fully accredited college degree online—in many cases, from the same major colleges and universities that offer the regular kind of degree. In addition to degrees, you can get many other kinds of training online, such as training for various kinds of non-degree certificates. Figure 24.3 shows Barrington University, a school in Canada that offers a wide range of fully accredited degree programs online.

NEW TERM   **Distance learning.** The name for a range of different methods for educating people dispersed across distances instead of grouped together in a classroom. The term includes training delivered by television, but also two kinds of Internet-delivered training: *asynchronous* and *synchronous*. In asynchronous distance learning (the most common type), you study online whenever it's convenient for you—even at 3:00 a.m., if that's when you have the time. In synchronous distance learning, you must be online at scheduled class times, and can interact "live" with your instructor and other classmates.

FIGURE 24.3

FIGURE 24.3

Barrington University is one of a growing list of colleges, universities, and other schools offering education online.

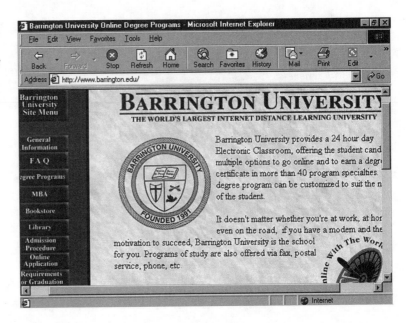

Some programs are entirely online, but in most cases, you'll be required to visit a nearby test center a time or two to take tests in person; this approach still enables you to do most of your studying online, whenever it's convenient for you, but also ensures the validity of the degree by making it impossible for cheaters to pay someone to complete a degree in their name.

The best way to start looking for training is to check out the Web sites of schools near you, to see if they offer any courses or programs online. Doing so ensures that getting to the test locations will be convenient for you.

If you can't find the program you want offered online by a nearby school, search on term "distance learning" followed by what you want to study.

3. Order Your College Transcript

Applying for a new job, and need a copy of your college transcript in a hurry? Find the Web site of your alma mater (just use the school's name as a search term), then explore the site to find out how to order transcripts. For those of you who happened to graduate from Indiana University Northwest (anyone...? anyone...?), Figure 24.4 shows the page on that school's Web site where you learn all the ways to get your transcript.

FIGURE 24.4

If you need your college transcript, you may be able to order it straight from your alma mater's Web site.

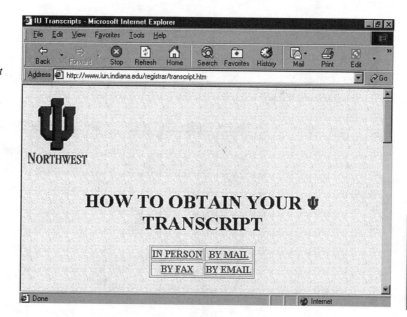

The Web sites of some colleges and universities are sometimes huge and very difficult to find your way around in. However, most have built-in search tools. If you can get to the site and then locate a link to the search tools, you can simply enter "transcripts" as a search term to locate the page where transcripts are covered.

A few schools have online order forms on which you can fill in your name, address, payment info (credit card number—make sure the site is secure!), and other information so that the school can mail your transcript to you right away. (You have to get it in the mail, on paper—schools do not yet issue "official" transcripts in electronic form, although they will one day.) On other sites, you can open and print a fax form you fill in and fax to the school to place your order.

4. Find a New Place to Live

Every few years, I get antsy and move. I dunno why. But if you're at all like me, you're always on the lookout for a new city or town to call home.

Using search techniques you already know, you can learn a lot about any community you're considering. But another way is to visit a site like Moving Center (www.moving-center.com). Moving Center is a thorough directory of links that lead to information and services that not only help you plan a move, but also help you decide *where* to move (see Figure 24.5).

FIGURE 24.5

Moving Center is a great first stop when you're trying to decide where to live.

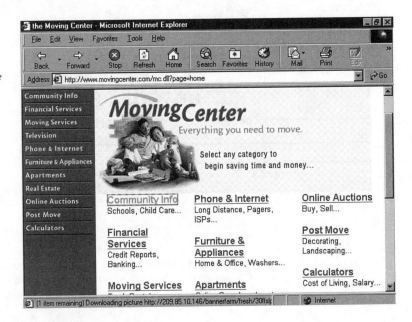

For example, you can click the link to Community Info to look up all sorts of useful information about hundreds of cities and towns: schools, cost of living, jobs, and much more. After you choose a city, Moving Center's links can help you find Realtors and rentals, calculate mortgage payments or moving costs, find a local Internet provider, and so on.

5. Buy (or Rent) Your Dream Home

Speaking of moving, you'll need somewhere with a roof. You'll find hundreds of Realtors and rental agencies online; one good way to start is to search the name of the city, followed by "real estate," rentals or apartments.

Another good starting place is Yahoo!'s real estate page, at realestate.yahoo.com (see Figure 24.6). There you'll find links leading to Realtors, rentals, and real estate classifieds, as well as other, related links to mortgage brokers, financial calculators (to figure out what you can afford), and much more.

Another way to find real estate to buy or rent is to check out the classified ads in the newspapers of the city or town you want to live in. See "Read Your Local Newspaper" later in this hour.

FIGURE 24.6

Yahoo!'s Real Estate page is a great place to start when you're looking for a new home to buy or rent.

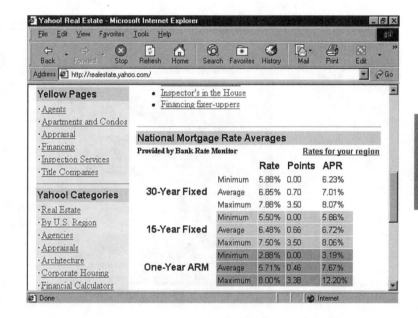

24

Yes, you can apply for a mortgage online (and all other sorts of loans, too, like car loans), so it's worth checking out the mortgage companies you can reach through links on Yahoo!'s Real Estate page.

But keep in mind that there are many aspects to a mortgage that are inherently local: appraisals, closings, codes, and so on. Unless you can get a substantially better deal online (and today, that's not likely), it's probably smarter to deal with a local company or broker—someone you can deal with face-to-face.

6. Get Medical Advice

Where does it hurt? Really? Well, here's what you should do: Get off the silly Internet and go see the doctor!

Still, as long as you're not using it as an excuse to avoid the doctor when you really need one, the Internet is a great place to learn more about what ails you and/or those you love. One great starting point is DrKoop.com (yes, *that* Dr. Koop, the former U.S. Surgeon General), a one-stop shop for authoritative medical info (see Figure 24.7). You'll find it at `www.drkoop.com`.

FIGURE 24.7

DrKoop.com is a great starting point for medical questions and advice. (But you STILL need to see your doctor!)

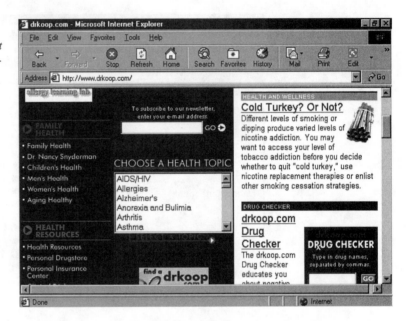

7. Track UPS or FedEx Packages

Sent a package by UPS or FedEx? Or are you waiting for a package from someone else? Did you know that you can track those packages online, finding out exactly where they are en route and when they will arrive at their destination?

All you need is the tracking number of each package. You get that on your slips and receipts when you send; if you're the receiver, you can ask the sender to tell you the tracking number. (Many online stores automatically send you the tracking number in an email message when confirming your order.)

Go to the Web site of the carrier: UPS is at `www.ups.com`; FedEx is at `www.fedex.com` (see Figure 24.8). Find a link for Tracking, click it, and then type the tracking number in the form provided and click the button near the form that submits the form.

FIGURE 24.8

Federal Express (shown here) and UPS both let you track packages online, if you know the tracking number.

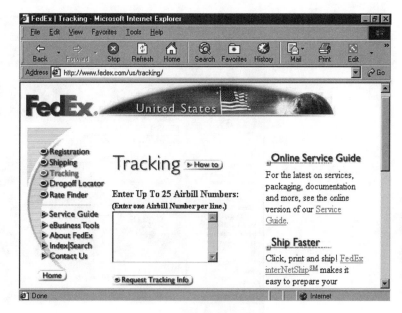

A summary report may appear at first, giving only a little information. But on the UPS site, a tiny button appears next to each package in the report. Click it, and you'll see a report of where the package has been, and when it will arrive.

8. Consult *TV Guide*

TV Guide is online, and free (see Figure 24.9). Just go to www.tvguide.com, and click the link for TV listings. (You may be prompted for you ZIP code, so that the guide can show your local programming and list times for your time zone.) Programs appear in an onscreen grid; you can click on a show's name in the grid to learn more about it.

If you have one of those pizza-size satellite dishes, you can also see a complete program guide on the Web sites of the companies that provide your programming. Check out www.directv.com. (That site's programming grid shows both DirecTV and USSB programs.)

FIGURE 24.9

What's on tonight? TV Guide *online can tell you.*

9. Learn the Next Time Your Favorite Star Will Be on TV

You a big fan of Van Johnson? William Shatner? Sidney Poitier? Lucille Ball? With all the different broadcast and cable channels showing reruns and old movies, you can easily miss a show or movie with your favorite star in it.

But not if you visit TV Now, at www.tv-now.com. There you can click a link to Star's TV Schedules, and type your favorite star's (or director's) name in the form that appears. A complete list appears, showing everything that star appears in for the next month on every broadcast, cable, and satellite channel—TV shows, guest appearances, reruns, old and new movies, everything. Figure 24.10 shows a part of the list for actor Denzel Washington, telling me that Washington's film *Cry Freedom* will air on the TNT cable network on April 29, at 2:00 a.m. Now I can set my VCR.

If you visit TV Now every month, and print the report for your star, you can keep it taped to the wall, and never miss another Lucille Ball film.

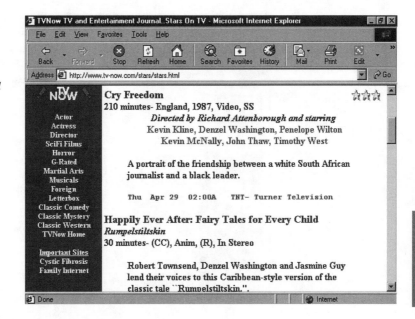

FIGURE 24.10

TV Now can tell you the time and channel of every appearance your favorite star will make on TV for the next month.

10. Read Your Local Newspaper

Yes, you can pay to have the daily paper delivered, or—in a growing number of cities— you can read the same paper online, for free, and reduce the size of your recycling pile. Me, I prefer to hold a paper paper, but to each his own. (My job is to tell you what you *can* do, and let you make up your own mind.)

Figure 24.11 shows the online version of the *Orlando Sentinel*, the major daily newspaper for the Orlando, Florida metro area. The online version includes the complete text of the day's paper, including such handy items as classified ads and job listings.

You can usually find any paper's Web site address listed somewhere within the printed version. You can also try to guess its address by simply sticking "www" in front of the paper's name, and ".com" on the end (as in www.orlandosentinel.com), and you may hit it right. Failing that, use the paper's name as a search term.

> How come the paper's free online but costs 50 cents a day in print? A newspaper makes most of its money from ads, not the cover price. The cover price really only pays for the cost of the printing and distribution. Because ads appear on the online version, and there are no printing costs, the ads alone pay for the online paper.

FIGURE **24.11**

*More and more major
daily newspapers offer
an online version that
features the complete
text of the printed ver-
sion.*

 You usually cannot read today's online newspaper tomorrow, as you can
with a printed paper. Each day, the current day's online newspaper displaces
yesterday's.

11. Find Out What's Playing at Your Local Movie House

Wanna know what's playing at nearby movie houses, and at what time? Just stop by one
of the online movie-time sites, such as Movie.Guide.Com (at `movie.guide.com`). As
Figure 24.12 shows, you can type your ZIP code on the top page, and the guide will display a listing of what's playing at all theatres near you, and when.

FIGURE 24.12

Visit Movie.Guide.Com to learn what's playing at your local movie houses, at what times.

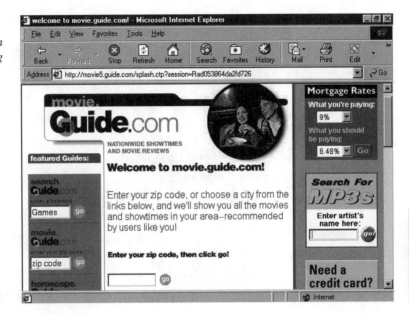

24

12. Learn to Play the Piano

Well, OK, you can't exactly learn how to play the piano online. It's just that, when we think of the Internet, we tend to think of it for purposes that are mired in either technology or money (or both). It can also be a window to art, to personal expression.

The Piano Education Page at www.unm.edu/~loritaf/pnoedmn.html contains all sorts of useful info about learning piano, including reviews of software for learning piano, and links for downloading that software (see Figure 24.13). So if you learn the piano from software that you downloaded from the Internet, that's pretty close to "learning piano online," yes?

FIGURE 24.13

You can't really learn piano online, but the Piano Education Page gets you close.

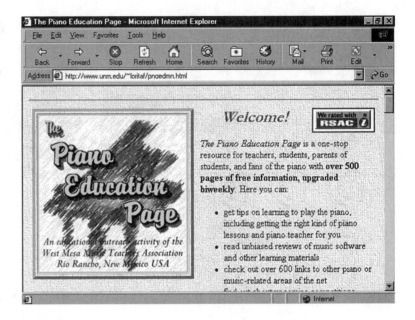

13. Buy a Car

You can, in fact, really buy a car online. You can research features, prices, and reviews; calculate loan payments; find out the fair trade-in value of your old car; apply for a car loan; get prices for the car you want from actual dealers; find out what rebates are currently in effect; negotiate a final price; and finally *buy*—all online. All you have to do offline is sign some papers when you take delivery.

But as I'm sure you know, nothing online substitutes for a real, in-person test-drive. And most of the so-called "online" buying services do little more than forward your name, contact information, and desired model to one of your local dealers, who then contacts you with a price—that's hardly a huge advantage over going to see the dealer yourself. And in a recent report, *Consumer Reports* determined that there are advantages to car shopping online, but that you should not expect to wind up with a better price than you'd get offline.

What you can get online is *information*. For example, once you've decided which car you want to buy (both from reading online information and from taking test-drives), you can easily learn online the exact invoice price for the car you want (or retail value, for a used car), and the amount of the dealer's "holdback" (the phantom payback dealers get above invoice). This information enables you to walk into a dealer knowing what the dealer paid, and what a reasonable profit might be. That's powerful negotiating information.

There are plenty of good starting points for car shopping, including the sites of the car-makers themselves (www.ford.com, www.honda.com, and so on). But a better place to start is CarPrices.com (www.carprices.com; see Figure 24.14), which features links to reviews, invoice and sticker prices, manufacturer's Web sites, payment calculators, online buying services, and much more.

FIGURE 24.14

CarPrices.com is a great first stop when you're thinking about new wheels.

24

14. Rent a Car

Yep, you can visit the Web sites of all of the major auto rental companies to learn their rates and locations, and to reserve a car where and when you need it (see Figure 24.15). From some rental sites, you can even get other useful stuff, like maps and directions for the place you're going.

To visit a rental company's site, just make an address out of the company's name (www.avis.com, www.hertz.com, and so on). If that doesn't do the trick, use the company's name as a search term.

FIGURE **24.15**

Major auto rental companies like Avis let you rent through their Web sites.

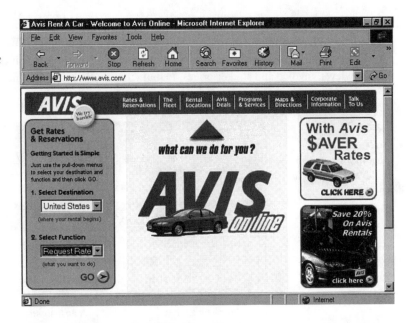

15. Sample CDs Before You Buy

The Web is awash with sound clips presented as samples of CDs. When considering purchasing a CD, you can listen to the samples online, to try before you buy.

If you use any of the major online CD-buying sources (www.cdnow.com, www.cduniverse.com, www.amazon.com) and display a description of a particular CD's contents, you'll often find links on that same page that download or play sound clips from the CD. You'll find similar links on the Web sites of all of the major record companies; in Figure 26.16, I'm playing a RealAudio clip of Ricky Martin's hit "Livin' La Vida Loca," which opened when I clicked a link on the Columbia Records Web site (www.columbiarecords.com).

Exactly how you play the clips depends upon what file format they're presented in, and what kind of player programs you have on your computer.

Most clips are provided in .WAV or .MP3 formats, which you download and then play in a player program, online or off. Some clips are provided in RealAudio format, for which you must have the RealPlayer, and which must be played online.

To review the ins and out of playing audio, see Hour 7, "Playing Online Video, Music, and Broadcasts."

FIGURE 24.16

Online CD stores and record companies (like Columbia Records, shown here) often offer online sound clips, to give you a taste of a CD before you buy it.

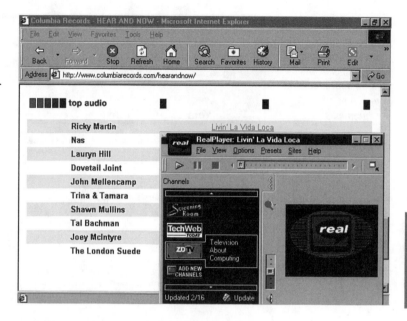

24

16. Write Your Congressperson

I cannot tell you that your congressperson cares what you have to say—that's between you and your representative. All I can tell you is that you can easily learn online exactly *who* your congressperson is (admit it—you don't know, do you?), and you can write to him or her.

An easy way to start is to go to the House of Representatives Web site, at www.house.gov (see Figure 24.17). Click the link to <u>Write Your Representative</u>, and a form appears on which you can enter your mailing address to learn the name, email address, and even Web site address of your representative.

Some people have suggested that some congresspeople may pay more attention to email than to letters or phone calls, on the theory that they assume emailers have more money (computers and Internet accounts require disposable income) and are motivated and therefore likely to vote.

I don't know if that's true, but if it is true, it's good news and bad. It's good news for you, because you can now make your voice heard in Washington. It's bad news for our society, because it's evidence that we may be fragmenting into a new class structure wherein the Internet "haves" have more political clout than the "have nots."

I'm all for using the Internet to communicate with government. But I want a government that listens equally to email, phone calls, letters, and the guy on the street corner. That's called democracy.

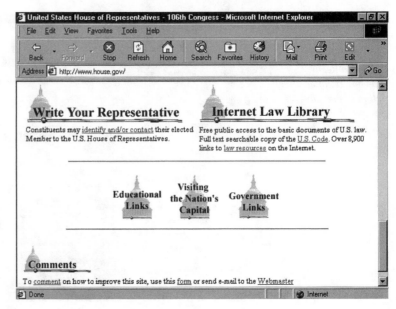

FIGURE 24.17

Visit the House of Representatives site to learn the name and contact information for your rep in Washington.

17. Order Your Credit Report

You may not know this, but by law you are entitled to one free copy per year of your credit report from each of the major credit reporting bureaus. So don't go spending money when you can call up the bureaus and get a free report mailed to you.

That said, you can also get your credit reports online for just a few bucks. A good starting place is CreditReport-Net.com, which you'll find at (do I really need to say?) `www.creditreport-net.com`. As Figure 24.18 shows, you can get your report from all three major credit bureaus, online, in 30 seconds, for eight bucks.

18. Order Federal and State Tax Forms

I dunno about you, but whenever I need a particular IRS publication, it's never available from the stacks at my library or bank. You can get nearly any federal tax form, instructions booklet, or other publication straight from the Internal Revenue Web site (see Figure 24.19). In most cases, you can download the publication and print it right from your computer.

To reach the IRS Web site, start at `www.irs.gov`, and follow the links you see.

FIGURE 24.18

CreditReport-Net.com offers easy access to your credit history.

FIGURE 24.19

You can download federal tax forms and instructions from the IRS Web site.

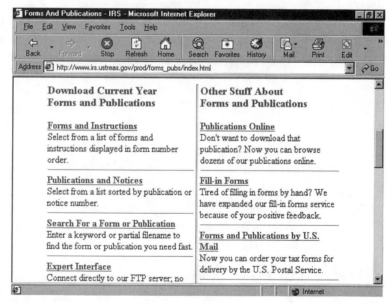

Where you get state tax forms and information depends, of course, on your state. But there is a one-stop place to get state tax publications for any state in the U.S. Go to the Federation of Tax Administrators (FTA) site at www.taxadmin.org, and click the link for <u>Links to State Tax Forms</u> (see Figure 24.20).

FIGURE 24.20

The FTA Web site has a one-stop link to tax forms and instructions for all states in the United States.

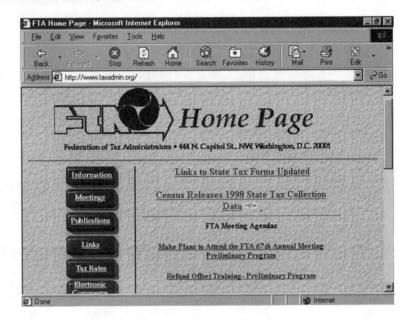

19. Form a Corporation

Yep, you can fill in a form on a Web site to create a real corporation. I'm not saying you should do that. I'm saying you can. Corporate law is a tricky thing, and personally, I'd want to form my corporation face-to-face. But to each his own.

Start at the home page of America Incorporators Ltd. (www.ailcorp.com), which is authorized to form legal corporations in 48 states. Follow the links to the form where you fill in all the info required to form your Inc (see Figure 24.21).

20. Write Your Will

You will die. (Sorry to break the news.) Got a will? I don't, but that's just 'cause I don't have anything anyone would want to inherit. There are several sites online where you can draft legal wills (which you should probably still file through an attorney, after drafting). Try WillDrafter at www.willdrafter.com (see Figure 24.22).

FIGURE 24.21

From the American Incorporators Ltd. Web site, you can form a corporation online.

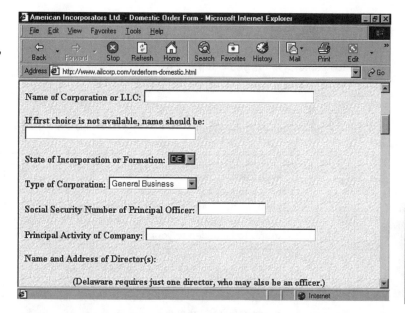

24

FIGURE 24.22

WillDrafter helps you create a last will and testament online.

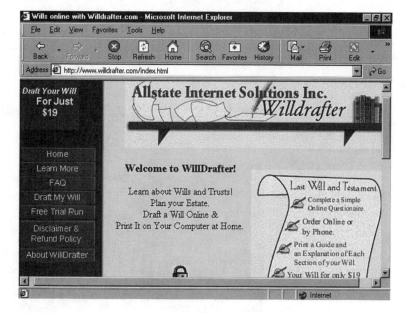

21. Play Games

There are tons of interactive games on the Web. Some you play against a computer, like video games. Others you can play "live" against other players that are online at the same time as you.

A good starting point for linking to online games is the Games You Can Play on the WWW directory at `www.grouper.com/play.html` (see Figure 24.23).

Web-based games are made possible through a wide variety of different technologies. Some games are very simple, and can be played through any browser. But many of the newer, cooler games require browsers capable of processing Java programs, and others require special plug-ins or player programs to be added to your browser. (See Hour 7 to learn more about Java and plug-ins/player programs.)

When you click a link in the Games You Can Play on the WWW directory, the page you go to tells you about any special technical requirements for playing the game, and will probably also offer links for downloading any programs required for play.

Because interactive games may have these special requirements, if you intend to play a lot of games, it's important that you keep up with the latest release of your browser, and use a well-equipped, fast computer and fast (56K) Internet connection.

FIGURE 24.23

The Games You Can Play on the WWW page provides links to dozens of interactive games.

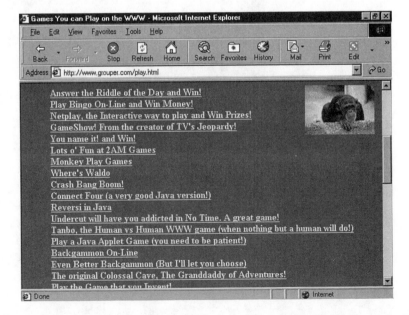

22. See What's Fun to Do Where You Live— Or Where You're Going!

Folks tend to think of the Internet as a tool for finding out what's happening far away. But it's also handy for finding out what's going on in your community: special events, theater, community meetings and local politics, school lunch menus, and much more.

Most cities and towns have one or more community Web sites with links to such information. If you don't have the addresses of those sites, another way to go is to check out the Yahoo! page for your community.

Begin by going to Yahoo! at www.yahoo.com. Scroll to the bottom of that page, where you'll see a link labeled Yahoo! Get Local (see Figure 24.24). Enter your ZIP code in the box provided, and Yahoo! will offer you links to one or more pages of communities near that ZIP code. Choose one, and you'll see a "Local Web Directory" (see Figure 24.25) of links leading to community information: local news, shopping, schools, weather—and, yes, the community's local Web site, if it has one.

24

FIGURE 24.24

Enter your ZIP code at the bottom of the Yahoo! home page to reach a local page for your community.

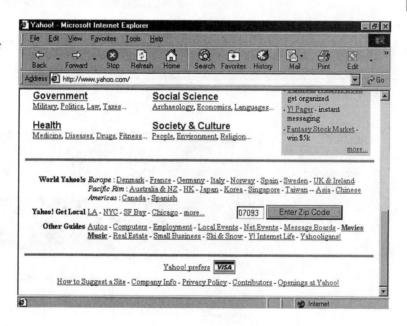

FIGURE 24.25

Yahoo!'s local Web pages include information for just one community, such as this page for the town of West New York, New Jersey (a suburb of NYC).

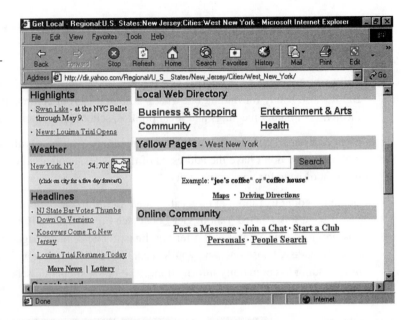

23. Avoid Highway Construction Snaggles

Taking a driving trip, and want to know which route to take in order to avoid construction delays? Check out Rand McNally's road construction Web site at www.randmcnally.com/construction (see Figure 24.26).

FIGURE 24.26

On Rand McNally's construction site, you can learn where the roadwork is—so you can plan another route.

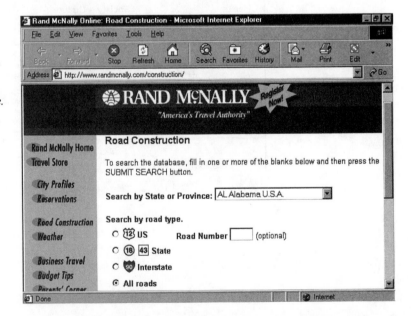

24. Find Out About the Next-Generation Internet: *Internet2*

Most of the technology that makes the Internet work is over 20 years old. That's not bad—that's part of why it works so well. But the online research community has already recognized that soon we'll need a whole new Internet—one that's faster and more versatile. Leading technology companies and universities are now hard at work defining what will become the next-generation Internet, now called Internet2 until they can think of something catchier.

Internet2 probably won't affect everyday users like you and me for five years or so. But if you want to keep up with Internet2's development, stop by www.internet2.edu (see Figure 24.27).

24

FIGURE 24.27

Internet2 is what the Internet will be, a few years down the road.

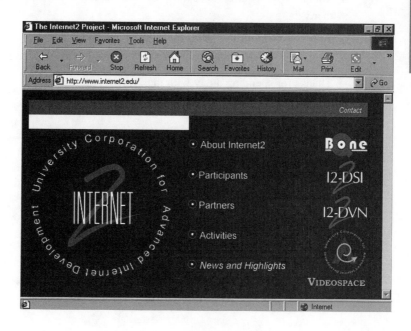

Summary

Have you already thought of number 25 on your own? Bet you have. The more you get into the Internet, the more useful it becomes to you.

When you come across a Web site or other Internet resource that changes *your* life—something that's just so unique and fantastic, or something that wasn't even possible before the Internet came along—let us, and your fellow readers of this book, know about it.

Visit us at www.tyinternet.com and add your favorite site to the list—it might even show up in a future edition of this book!

Q&A

Q Well, I finished your book, and I just wanted to point out that it only took me 21.25 hours to teach myself the Internet. What do you plan to do about that?

A You are now required to spend 2.75 hours in free study, exploring the Internet. So there.

Q That's pretty lame. I demand a better answer.

A Well, then, I would have to say… *Ooops*—so sorry, our time is up.

Thanks for spending a day with me. See you online.

Appendix

APPENDIX **A**

Fun Web Sites to Visit

Browsers and Other Client Programs

Addresses for the two most popular Internet client software suites—Internet Explorer and Netscape Communicator—are included in the following list.

Note that in your Web travels, however, on all sorts of pages, you will encounter little buttons with the Netscape or Internet Explorer logo on them, usually accompanied by the words "Download Now." Clicking one of these buttons takes you directly to the download page for the product.

- Tucows Directory of Internet Clients
  www.tucows.com

- Client Software Directory
  www.w3.org/hypertext/WWW/Clients.html

- Microsoft Internet Explorer
  www.microsoft.com/ie

- NeoPlanet
  www.neoplanet.com

- Netscape Communicator (Navigator)
  www.netscape.com or home.netscape.com

Plug-Ins, Helpers, and Other Browser Accessories

- Adobe Acrobat Reader
  www.adobe.com

- Macromedia Shockwave/Flash Players
  www.macromedia.com

- Microsoft Free Downloads
  www.microsoft.com/msdownload

- Netscape Plug-ins Directory
  home.netscape.com/comprod/products/navigator/version_2.0/plugins

- Plug-In Plaza
  browserwatch.internet.com/plug-in.html

- RealAudio/RealVideo
  www.real.com

General-Purpose Software Download Sites

- Download.com
  download.com

- Kitty-Kat Software (Mac Stuff)
  www.newc.com/kks

- Shareware.com
  shareware.com

- Shareware Junkies
  www.sharewarejunkies.com

- Softword Technology
  users.aol.com/shareware/index.htm

Search Engines

- Alta Vista
  www.altavista.com

- Excite
  www.excite.com

- HotBot
  www.hotbot.com

- Infoseek
  www.infoseek.com

- Lycos
  www.lycos.com

- Open Text
  www.opentext.com

- Snap
  www.snap.com

- WebCrawler
  www.webcrawler.com

- Yahoo!
  www.yahoo.com

A

Web Authoring Resources

Clip Art and Templates

- Free Graphics
  www.jgpublish.com/free.htm

- WWW Homepage Starter Kit
  www.isisnet.com/mlindsay/kitrex3.html

- Cyberspace Portal
  www.infomediacom.com/preview.htm

- Clip Art Universe
  www.nzwwa.com/mirror/clipart/

- Yahoo's Clip Art Directory
  www.yahoo.com/Computers_and_Internet/Multimedia/Pictures/Clip_Art/

- Index to Multimedia Information Sources
  `viswiz.gmd.de/MultimediaInfo/`

- MPEG Archive
  `www.powerweb.de/mpeg`

- Multimedia/Clip Art Directory
  `www.clipart.com/`

General Web Authoring

- Netscape Developer's Edge
  `developer.netscape.com/library/documentation/jsframe.html`

- Off-the-Net Insider Newsletter
  `home.netscape.com/assist/net_sites/off_the_net.html`

- Yahoo's WWW Listings
  `www.yahoo.com/Computers/World_Wide_Web/`

- The Virtual Library
  `WWW.Stars.com/`

- The Web Toolbox
  `www.rtis.com/nat/user/toolbox/`

- The Developer's JumpStation
  `oneworld.wa.com/htmldev/devpage/dev-page.html`

- The HTML Reference Guide
  `developer.netscape.com/library/documentation/htmlguid/index.htm`

- The HTTP Specification
  `www.w3.org/pub/WWW/Protocols/`

Arts, Culture, and Society

- Actors Interactive
  `actors-interactive.com`

- African American Museums Association
  `www.artnoir.com/aama.html`

- American Council for the Arts
  `www.artsusa.org`

- ArtsNet
  `artsnet.heinz.cmu.edu`

- ArtSource
  www.uky.edu/Artsource

- BooksOnline
  www.cs.cmu.edu/booktitles.html

- Classical Music Online
  www.onworld.com/CMO

- Florida Museum of Hispanic and Latin American Art
  www.latinoweb.com/museo

- Internet Underground Music Archive
  www.iuma.com

- Jazz Online
  www.jazzonln.com

- The Louvre
  www.paris.org/Musees/Louvre

- Museum of Modern Art (MOMA)
  www.sva.edu/moma

- Virgin Records
  www.virginrecords.com

- Ultimate Band List
  www.ubl.com

A

Business

- BizWeb
  www.bizweb.com

- CD Rate Scanner
  bankcd.com

- CNNfn (Cable News Network Financial Network)
  www.cnnfn.com

- CommerceNet
  www.commerce.net

- Dow Jones Interactive Publishing
  bis.dowjones.com

- The Economist
  www.economist.com

- Financial Services Directory
  `www.orcc.com/banking.html`

- Inc. Online
  `www.inc.com`

- Microsoft Investor
  `investor.msn.com`

- smallbizNet
  `www.lowe.org/smbiznet`

- Wall Street Directory
  `www.wsdinc.com`

Government

- FedWorld
  `www.fedworld.gov`

- Library of Congress
  `lcweb.loc.gov`

- The U.S. Senate
  `www.senate.gov`

- The U.S. House of Representatives
  `www.house.gov`

- The White House
  `www.whitehouse.gov`

Education

- 100 Most Popular College & University Sites
  `www.100hot.com/college`

- College Board Online
  `www.collegeboard.org`

- Homeschooling Zone
  `www.caro.net/~joespa`

- Online Educational Resources
  `quest.arc.nasa.gov/OER`

- United Negro College Fund
  www.uncf.org

- U.S. Department of Education
  www.ed.gov

Entertainment/Media

- Best Video Guide
  www.tbvg.com

- DirecTV (Digital Satellite)
  www.directv.com

- Roger Ebert
  www.suntimes.com/ebert/ebert.html

- Film.com
  www.film.com

- MovieReviews.com
  moviereviews.com

- Mr. Showbiz
  www.mrshowbiz.com

- *TV Guide*
  www.tvguide.com

TV Networks

- ABC
  www.abc.com

- American Movie Classics
  www.amctv.com

- CBS
  www.cbs.com

- NBC
  www.nbc.com

- PBS
  www.pbs.org

- Fox
  www.foxworld.com

A

- Cinemax
  www.cinemax.com

- HBO
  www.hbo.com

- MTV
  www.mtv.com

- The Disney Channel
  www.disney.com/DisneyChannel

- ESPN
  www.espn.com

Movie Studios

- MCA/Universal
  www.mca.com

- Metro Goldwyn Mayer
  www.mgmua.com

- Paramount Pictures
  www.paramount.com

- Sony Pictures
  www.spe.sony.com/Pictures/SonyMovies/index.html

- 20th Century Fox
  www.tcfhe.com

- Walt Disney Studios
  www.disney.com/DisneyPictures

- Warner Brothers
  www.movies.warnerbros.com

Health

- Alcoholics Anonymous
  www.alcoholics-anonymous.org

- Deaf World Web
  deafworldweb.org/dww

- Good Health Web
  www.social.com/health

- Health World Online
  www.healthy.net

- HIV InfoWeb
  www.jri.org/infoweb

- National Breast Cancer Coalition
  www.natibcc.org

- World Health Organization
  www.who.ch

Kid Stuff

- Children's Literature Home Page
  www.parentsplace.com/readroom/childnew/index.html

- Children's Storybooks Online
  www.magickeys.com/books/links.html

- Clubs for Boys
  www.worldkids.net/clubs/boys.htm

- Crayola
  www.crayola.com

- Cyberkids' Club
  mack.rt66.com/kidsclub/home.htm

- DC Comics Online
  www.dccomics.com

- Girlsworld Online Clubhouse
  www.agirlsworld.com

- Indianapolis Children's Museum
  www.a1.com/children/home.html

- Kid's Corner
  kids.ot.com

- Kid's Town
  www.cybertown.com/cybertown/kidtwn.html

- News for Kids
  www.newsforkids.com

A

- The Ultimate Children's Internet Site
  www.vividus.com/ucis.html

- Web Guide to Children's Literature
  www.ucalgary.ca/~dkbrown

Shopping Malls

- Awesome Mall
  malls.com/awesome

- Cybermall
  cybermall.com

- Internet Shopping Outlet
  www.shoplet.com

- Magic Market
  magicmarket.com

- Shopping Utopia
  shop-utopia.com

- 21st Century Plaza
  www.21stcenturyplaza.com

Sports

- AudioNet Sports Guide
  www.audionet.com/sports

- CNNsi (Sports Illustrated)
  cnnsi.com

- Golf.com
  www.golf.com

- Major League Baseball
  www.majorleaguebaseball.com

- National Basketball Association
  www.nba.com

- National Football League
  www.nfl.com

- New York Yankees
  www.yankees.com

Travel

- American Automobile Association
  www.aaa.com

- American Express Travel
  www.americanexpress.com/travel

- Fodor's Travel Guides
  www.fodors.com

- Frugal Travel News
  www.ftns.com

- Internet Travel Network
  www.itn.com

- TravelNow Worldwide Hotel Reservations
  www.travelnow.com

- World Travel Guide
  www.wtg-online.com

Computer-Related Sites

Computer Systems

- Apple Computer
  www.apple.com

- Compaq
  www.compaq.com

- Dell
  www.dell.com

- Digital Equipment Corporation (DEC)
  www.dec.com

- Gateway 2000
  www.gateway2000.com

- IBM
  www.ibm.com

A

- Sun Microsystems, Inc
  www.sun.com

- Toshiba
  www.toshiba.com

Printers

- Brother
  www.brother.com

- Canon
  www.canon.com

- Epson
  www.epson.com

- Hewlett-Packard
  www.hp.com

Modems

- Hayes
  www.hayes.com

- Microcom
  www.microcom.com

- Practical Peripherals
  www.practinet.com

- US Robotics
  www.usr.com

- Zoom
  www.zoom.com

Major Commercial Software Companies

- Adobe Systems Incorporated
  www.adobe.com

- Apple Computer
  www.apple.com

- Borland
  www.borland.com

- Broderbund
  www.broderbund.com

- Claris
  www.claris.com

- Corel Corp.
  www.corel.com

- Electronic Arts
  www.ea.com

- FTP Software
  www.ftp.com

- IBM
  www.ibm.com

- Intuit
  www.intuit.com

- Microsoft
  www.microsoft.com or home.microsoft.com

- Netscape Communications
  www.netscape.com or home.netscape.com

- Novell
  www.novell.com

- Quarterdeck
  www.quarterdeck.com

A

GLOSSARY

ActiveX. Files that include the program code necessary to teach an ActiveX-capable **browser** how to display them. See Hours 7 and 11.

address book. A feature in some **email** programs that stores your contacts' **email addresses** and other information for reference and to make addressing an email message easier.

attachment. A computer file (graphics, text, program, or any other type) sent with an email message. See Hour 13.

authoring. The process of writing a **Web page**. See Hour 23.

BCC (blind carbon copy). When emailing, it is a way to send a copy of an email message without letting the other recipients know you are sending a copy. See Hour 13.

Bookmark. Netscape Navigator's method for letting a user create a short-cut back to a Web page the user will want to revisit. See also **Favorite**.

Boolean operators. These operators are designed to put conditions on a search. The most common Boolean operators are AND, OR, and NOT. See Hour 10.

browse. To wander around a portion of the Internet, screen by screen, looking for items of interest. Also known as *surfing* or *cruising*.

browser. An Internet program used to explore the **World Wide Web**; two examples are **Internet Explorer** and **Netscape Navigator**.

cable Internet. A new way to get very fast Internet service (in limited areas) through the same cable through which you get cable television.

CC (carbon copy). A copy of an email message, sent to someone other than the message's principal recipient. See Hour 13.

cellular modem. Used most often in portable computers, a **modem** that communicates without connection to a phone line, just as a cellular phone does. Can be used to access the Internet from places where no phone line is available. See also **wireless modem**.

certificate. A file used in secure connections to authenticate the server to a client. See Hour 8.

Chat. An Internet resource, sometimes also known as Internet Relay Chat (IRC), that allows two or more Internet users to participate in a live conversation through typing messages. See Hour 18.

chat client. The program required for participating in a **chat**.

client. A software tool for using a particular type of Internet resource. A client interacts with a **server** on which the resource is located. See Hour 1.

Communicator. Also known as Netscape 4, it is a suite of Internet tools from Netscape Communications Corp. It includes a Web browser (**Navigator**), email and newsreader (Messenger), and Web authoring (**Composer**).

Composer. The Web authoring component of Netscape Communicator. See Hour 23.

compression. The process of making a computer file smaller so that it can be copied more quickly between computers. Compressed files, sometimes called Zip files, must be decompressed on the receiving computer before they can be used. See Hour 11.

cookie. A collection of information that a Web server can leave on your computer for later access. See Hour 8.

cross-posting. A method by which you can post a single article to multiple **newsgroups**. See Hour 15.

cyberspace. A broad expression used to describe the activity, communication, and culture happening on the Internet and other computer networks.

dial-up IP account. An Internet account, accessed through a modem and telephone line, that offers complete access to the Internet through TCP/IP communications.

direct connection. A permanent, 24-hour link between a computer and the Internet. A computer with a direct connection can use the Internet at any time.

DNS (Domain Name System). A method of translating Internet **IP addresses** into word-based addresses, *domain names*, that are easier to remember and work with. See Hour 4.

domain name. See **DNS**.

download. Transferring a file from a host computer to your computer. See Hour 11.

email. Short for *electronic mail*. A system that enables a person to compose a message on a computer and transmit that message through a computer network, such as the Internet, to another computer user.

email address. The word-based Internet address of a user, typically made up of a username, an @ sign, and a domain name (`user@domain`).

emoticons. Short for *emotional icons*, these character combinations are a way to express emotion in typed messages, such as email and newsgroup messages. For example, `:)` is a smile. See Hour 14.

Explorer. See **Internet Explorer**.

FAQ file. Short for *Frequently Asked Questions file*. A computer file containing the answers to frequently asked questions about a particular topic. See Hour 15.

Favorite. Internet Explorer's method for letting a user create a shortcut back to a Web page the user will want to revisit. See also **Bookmark**.

filter. A system for automatically organizing and deleting selected email messages. See Hour 16.

flame. Hostile messages, often sent through email or posted in newsgroups, from Internet users in reaction to breaches of **netiquette**. See Hour 15.

form. A part of a Web page in which users can type entries or make selections. See Hour 8.

frame. A discrete part, or "pane," in a Web page in which the screen area has been divided up into multiple, independent panes, each of which contains a separate document. See Hour 5.

freeware. Software available to anyone, free of charge (unlike shareware, which requires payment). See Hour 11.

FrontPage Express. The WYSIWYG (What-You-See-Is-What-You-Get) HTML (Web page) editor built in to Internet Explorer.

FTP. Short for *File Transfer Protocol.* The basic method for copying a file from one computer to another through the Internet. See Hour 19.

GIF. A form of image file, using the file extension .GIF, commonly used for inline images in Web pages. See Hour 23.

Gopher. A system of menus layered on top of existing resources that makes locating information and using services easier. See Hour 19.

helper program. Programs that run or show files that aren't part of a Web page and don't appear as part of the Web browser. See Hour 7.

home page. Frequently, this term refers to the cover of a particular Web site. The home page is the main, or first, page displayed for an organization's or person's World Wide Web site. "Home page" also describes the page a Web browser is configured to access first when you go online, or anytime you click the browser's Home button. See Hours 5 and 6.

HTML (Hypertext Markup Language). The document formatting language used to create pages on the World Wide Web. See Hour 23.

hyperlink. See **link**.

imagemap. In a Web page, a single picture that contains multiple **links**, each leading somewhere different. See Hour 5.

inline image. An image that appears within the layout of a Web page.

instant message. A message that appears to its recipient the instant you send it, if the recipient happens to be online at the time.

Internet. A large, loosely organized internetwork connecting public and private computer systems all over the world so that they can exchange messages and share information.

Internet Explorer. A **browser** for the World Wide Web, created by Microsoft and available for free download from the Web and in a variety of software packages. Can be confused with Windows Explorer, which is the basic file/folder management system in Windows 95.

Internet Relay Chat. See **Chat**.

Internet service provider. A company from which you can obtain access to the Internet. This term, or its abbreviation, ISP, is often used to distinguish the many companies that offer Internet access from **online services**, another kind of Internet provider.

intranet. An internal corporate network, usually a local area network, that is based on Internet technologies, such as the use of Web **browsers** to display information.

IP address. The number-based Internet address of a user or computer, made up of four sets of numbers separated by periods; for example, `192.480.77.69`. In practice, Internet users more often encounter word-based addresses (`nsnell@kooky.com`), which are translated from the numerical IP addresses by the domain name system (**DNS**).

IRC. See **Chat**.

ISP. See **Internet service provider**.

Java/JavaScript. Two of the programming languages used for enabling some advanced capabilities in Web pages.

link. In a **Web page**, block of text, an image, or part of an image that the user can activate (usually by clicking) to make something happen. Clicking on links can jump the user to another Web page, start a program, or **download** a file.

listserv. A program that automatically manages a mailing list. See Hour 14.

log on. The act of accessing a computer system by typing a required username (or user ID) and password. Also described by other terms, including sign on/in, or log in. See Hour 4.

lurking. Reading a newsgroup without posting to it, to study its culture.

mailing list. An online discussion group in which members share news and information through broadcasted email messages. See Hour 14.

MIME (Multipurpose Internet Mail Extensions). A standard for designating how various types of files are to be treated online.

modem. A device that allows your computer to talk to other computers using your phone line. See Hour 2.

MP3. A type of computer file, available for **download** from the Internet, that contains CD-quality music you can play offline. See Hour 7.

multimedia. A description for systems capable of displaying or playing text, pictures, sound, video, and animation, or a way of describing that material.

Navigator. The name of the popular browser from Netscape Communications Corp., available by itself, or within the **Communicator** suite. Navigator is often referred to casually as "Netscape," after its creator. Like Internet Explorer, it may be **download**ed free from the Internet.

netiquette. The code of proper conduct (etiquette) on the Internet. See Hour 15.

NetMeeting. A voice/video conferencing client included in the Internet Explorer suite. See Hour 17.

Netscape. See **Navigator**.

network. A set of computers interconnected so that they can communicate and share information. Connected networks together form an internetwork.

newsgroup. An Internet resource through which people post and read messages related to a specific topic. See Hour 15.

newsreader. A **client** program for reading and posting messages on **newsgroups**. See Hour 15.

offline. The state of being disconnected from a network.

online. The state of being connected to a network.

online service. A company such as America Online or CompuServe that offers its subscribers both Internet access and unique content available only on the service.

outbox. A term used in some **email** programs to describe a folder where outgoing messages are stored temporarily until the user is ready to send them. See Hours 13 and 20.

pane. See **frame**.

password. A secret code, known only to the user, that allows the user to access a computer that is protected by a security system.

plug-in. A program that increases the capabilities of a Web browser. See Hour 7.

portal. A Web page that is designed to serve as a popular starting point for Web-surfing sessions. Portals typically include tools for searching the Web; links to news, weather, and sports scores; and other popular links. See Hours 6 and 9.

PPP. (Point-to-Point Protocol) One kind of communications protocol that enables a **dial-up IP** connection.

search tool. A Web page that provides tools for finding specific information on the Internet. See Hour 9.

server. A networked computer that serves a particular type of information to users or performs a particular function.

shareware. Software programs that users are permitted to acquire and evaluate for free. Shareware is different from freeware in that, if a person likes the shareware program and plans to use it on a regular basis, he or she is expected to send a fee to the programmer. See Hour 11.

shortcut. See **Favorite** and **Bookmark**.

shorthand. A system of letter abbreviations used to efficiently express certain ideas in email messages, newsgroup postings, and Internet Relay Chat sessions. Examples are IMO (in my opinion) and BTW (by the way). See Hour 15.

spam. Mass emailed material meant for promotion, advertisement, or annoyance. See Hour 16.

spider. A program that searches methodically through a portion of the Internet to build a database that can be searched by a search tool. See Hour 9.

streaming audio/video. The capability of multimedia to begin playback as the file is being downloaded; makes live audio/video broadcasts through the Internet possible. See Hour 7.

TCP/IP (Transmission Control Protocol/Internet Protocol). The fundamental internet-working protocol that makes the Internet work.

Telnet. A facility for accessing other computers on the Internet and for using the resources that are there. See Hour 19.

thread. A series of newsgroup articles all dealing with the same topic. Someone replies to an article, and then someone else replies to the reply, and so on. See Hour 15.

upload. Transferring a file to a host computer from your computer. See Hours 19 and 23.

URL. Short for *Uniform Resource Locator*. A method of standardizing the addresses of different types of Internet resources so that they can all be accessed easily from within a Web browser. See Hour 5.

username. Used with a password to gain access to a computer. A dial-up IP user typically has a username and password for dialing the access provider's Internet server. See Hour 4.

Web. See **World Wide Web**.

Web email. A method of sending and receiving email that is used through a browser rather than an email client program. See Hour 16.

Web page. A document stored on a Web server, typically in the file format HTML (.htm or .html). Web pages are retrieved from **servers** and displayed by Web **browsers**.

Web site. A collection of World Wide Web documents, usually consisting of a home, or top, page and several related pages.

wireless modem. Used most often in portable computers, a **modem** that communicates without connection to a phone line, using radio communications or another medium. A wireless modem is used the same way as a **cellular modem**, but does not use the cellular telephone networks for its communications.

World Wide Web (WWW or Web). A set of Internet computers and services that provides an easy-to-use system for finding information and moving among resources.

Zip file. See **compression**.

INDEX